Florida's Paved Bike Trails

Florida A&M University, Tallahassee
Florida Atlantic University, Boca Raton
Florida Gulf Coast University, Ft. Myers
Florida International University, Miami
Florida State University, Tallahassee
University of Central Florida, Orlando
University of Florida, Gainesville
University of North Florida, Jacksonville
University of South Florida, Tampa
University of West Florida, Pensacola

Florida's Paved Bike Trails

An Eco-Tour Guide

Jeff Kunerth and Gretchen Kunerth

University Press of Florida
Gainesville · Tallahassee · Tampa · Boca Raton
Pensacola · Orlando · Miami · Jacksonville · Ft. Myers

06 05 04 03 02   6 5 4 3 2

Library of Congress Cataloging-in-Publication Data
Kunerth, Jeff.
Florida's paved bike trails: an eco-tour guide / Jeff Kunerth and Gretchen Kunerth.
p. cm.
Includes index.
ISBN 0-8130-1851-X (pbk.: alk. paper)
1 Bicycle touring—Florida—Guidebooks. 2. Florida—Guidebooks. I. Kunerth,
Gretchen. II. Title.
GV1045.5.F6 K86 2001
917.5904'64—dc21   00-064883

The University Press of Florida is the scholarly publishing agency for the State
University System of Florida, comprising Florida A&M University, Florida Atlantic
University, Florida Gulf Coast University, Florida International University, Florida
State University, University of Central Florida, University of Florida, University of
North Florida, University of South Florida, and University of West Florida.

University Press of Florida
15 Northwest 15th Street
Gainesville, FL 32611–2079
http://www.upf.com

To Team Primal Scream

Contents

List of Illustrations   ix
Acknowledgments   xi
Introduction   xiii
How to Use This Book   xv
Safety Tips   xvii

North Florida

Blackwater Heritage State Trail   1
Pensacola Beach Trail   5
Highway 30A Parallel Bike Path   10
Tallahassee–St. Marks Historic Railroad State Trail   16
Suwannee River Greenway at Branford   21
Jacksonville-Baldwin Rail Trail   25
Blackcreek Trail   30
Gainesville-Hawthorne State Trail   34
Depot Avenue/Waldo Road Greenway   39

Central Florida

Withlacoochee State Trail   44
General James A. Van Fleet State Trail in the Green Swamp   53
Lake Minneola Scenic Trail   59
West Orange Trail   63
Cady Way Trail   70
Cross Seminole Trail   74
Little Econ Greenway Trail   79
Kissimmee–Neptune Road Bike Path   83
Pleasant Hill Road Recreational Pathway   88

East Coast

Flagler County Trail   92
Brevard/A1A Bike Path   98

West Coast

Pinellas Trail   105
Fort De Soto Park Trail   114
Friendship TrailBridge   117
Bayshore Trail   120
Flatwoods Loop   124
Jay B. Starkey Wilderness Trail   128
Boca Grande/Gasparilla Island Rail Trail   131
Sanibel Island Bike Paths   137

South Florida

Pompano Beach Air Park Bike Path   144
Palm Beach Lake Trail   148
John Prince Park Paths   154
Okeeheelee Park Paths   158
Dyer Park Paths   162
Key Biscayne/Old Cutler Road Trail   166
M-Path Bike Trail   176
South Dade Bus-Way Bike Trail   181
Shark Valley Loop   184
Florida Keys Bike Paths   189
Key Largo–Plantation Key   190
Islamorada/Lower Matecumbe Key   194
Marathon   199
Key West   203

On the Way: Future Bike Paths   209
Contacts   211
Index of Place Names   213

Illustrations

Fig. 1.   White sand dunes on Pensacola Beach Trail   7

Fig. 2.   Wooden bridge on Blackcreek Trail   33

Fig. 3.   Depot Trail bike memorial   41

Fig. 4.   Whistle marker on Withlacoochee Trail   47

Fig. 5.   Van Fleet Trail, heading north   57

Fig. 6.   Tree canopy on West Orange Trail   67

Fig. 7.   Multiuse recreation on Cady Way Trail   73

Fig. 8.   Cross Seminole Trail trestle bridge   76

Fig. 9.   Pinellas Trail: Dunedin depot   111

Fig. 10.   Boca Grande/Gasparilla Island Trail range light   134

Fig. 11.   Palms and hedges on Palm Beach Lake Trail   151

Fig. 12.   Judges' stands on Okeeheelee Park bike path   161

Fig. 13.   Key Biscayne/Old Cutler Trail: mangrove tunnel in Matheson Hammock Park   173

Fig. 14.   Gator encounter on Shark Valley Loop   187

Fig. 15.   Marine mural on Key Largo bike path   193

Fig. 16.   Sea and asphalt on Lower Matecumbe Key   197

Acknowledgments

Many thanks to Jean Booker in Miami, Larry Kahn in Marathon, Kathy Kiely and Jim Robison in Orlando, the Department of Transportation's bike/ped coordinators, the Department of Environmental Protection's Office of Greenways and Trails, and the Rails-to-Trails Conservancy. Special thanks to David Wersinger.

Introduction

Florida is a great place to ride a bicycle. The climate offers year-round cycling. The land is flat (most of it). The scenery is as varied as you can get: beaches, woods, hills, swamps. Best of all, many of the most beautiful places in Florida are accessible by paved bike paths. Just about wherever you live, wherever you visit, in Florida, there is a paved bike path within a short drive. These paths take you through woods, fields, towns, subdivisions, past beaches, museums, attractions, and landmarks.

This book will help you to find those paths, and to know what to expect when you get there and what you might find along the way. Each chapter will tell you what is there now, what came before, and what's up ahead.

"Multiuse" paved paths are popping up all over the state as governments realize the recreational and ecotourism value of safe "linear recreational facilities" for bicyclists, joggers, walkers, and strollers. We refer to these facilities as bike paths because this guidebook is aimed at cyclists, but they truly are shared-use paths that attract people who like to get out and enjoy the scenery whether on bike, foot, rollerblade, or horse.

The bike paths' popularity is proven. In 1995, an estimated 2.6 million cyclists used Florida's paved bike paths. The Pinellas Trail alone attracts 1.2 million users, ranking it as the third most popular trail in the nation.

Within the first decade of the twenty-first century, more than 250 miles of paved bike paths are scheduled for completion, including a 120-mile loop around Lake Okeechobee and the 41-mile Suncoast Trail between Tampa and Orlando.

The paved multiuse paths being built across the state offer a safe alternative to riding in the road, especially for families with young children and for inexperienced bicyclists. This book is intended as a guide for those who prefer not to ride in the road, but it is not limited to children and novices. There are plenty of great paved bike paths that offer a good ride for experienced cyclists who like to get out and ride hard without having to worry about getting clipped by the side mirror of a pickup, jarred by the slipstream of passing trucks, or taunted by irate drivers who believe the road belongs only to motor traffic.

This is not to encourage reckless cycling or racing on the bike paths—remember there are other people using these shared-use facilities—but to identify those places where a good hard ride is one of the rewards of paved bike trails with isolated stretches of asphalt.

Although aimed at cyclists, the book also offers a guide to rollerbladers and skateboarders who are often chased off city sidewalks, streets, and parking lots. We also note which bike trails are wheelchair accessible. All the paths in this book are three miles or longer. We have excluded bike-path networks within subdivisions. Although they may be available to the public, they were intended for the use of residents and often lack the amenities of parking, rest rooms, and water. We have included some bike paths that might resemble sidewalks alongside roadways, but only when they are wide enough to accommodate bikes and offer something worth seeing along the way.

Aside from exercise and recreation, the bike paths also provide access to parks, museums, attractions, restaurants, cafes, and shops. Some of Florida's favorite vacation spots have bike paths that offer sightseeing and exercise as parallel pleasures. For cyclists who prefer the open road, the bike paths are a great starting point, with trailheads that provide a place to park, fill up the water bottles, and empty the bladder.

We believe the paved bike paths of Florida are an excellent way to enjoy what the state has to offer bicyclists. So wherever you live, or wherever you go, take a bike—and this book.

How to Use This Book

This guide will give you a description of what to expect along the bike path. You don't need a cyclometer to use this book, but it helps. Some paved bike paths have mile markers along the way, some don't. Use the description of the bike path to determine where you are and how far you have gone.

The "something you should know" section at the end of each narrative will give you an idea of future plans for the bike path and a historical perspective of the area through which the bike path crosses.

The list of future bike paths at the end of the book includes trails that are under construction or well into the planning stage. The length is given for the whole trail, but some paths are built in segments that may be in use before the entire project is completed. For the status of future bike paths, contact the agencies listed in the back of the book, and the county or city recreation and public works departments.

Safety Tips

Although paved bike paths are safer for cyclists than the streets, roads, and highways, they are not free of hazards. When riding on bike paths, keep these tips in mind:

1. Be alert for cars at cross streets and driveways. When approaching a car at an intersection or driveway, make eye contact with the driver to make sure the person sees you. A wave of the hand, a simple friendly gesture, will tell you whether the driver sees you or not.

2. Watch out for loose sand and dirt, sticks, broken glass, holes, and debris on the path. Most paths are kept clean and well maintained. Some are not.

3. Don't ride at night. The rural, rails-to-trails bike paths are not lighted, and most close at sunset. The urban trails are also not lighted and may cross through neighborhoods where you are safe during the day but put yourself at risk at night.

4. If you do ride at night, Florida law requires a headlight, taillight, red rear reflector, white front reflector, pedal reflectors, and wheel reflectors.

5. Use your brain and protect your noggin. Wear a helmet. Florida law requires children under the age of sixteen to wear a bike helmet. So should you. These are paved bike paths, and when skull meets pavement, bones crack easier than asphalt and concrete. Most bicycle fatalities are the result of head injuries.

6. Ride on the right side of the bike path. When approaching others from behind, alert them to your presence and then pass on the left. No need to shout. Just say loud enough to be heard: "I'm right behind you. Passing on the left."

7. Don't make an obstacle of yourself. If you stop, pull off the pavement.

8. Ride with water. This is Florida. It gets hot. On a bicycle, it's easy to get dehydrated without knowing you are sweating. Some paved paths have water stops along the way. Many do not.

9. Wear sunblock and insect repellent, especially during the summer and on the bike paths along swamps, rivers, and lakes.

10. It's all right to ride side by side. It's one of the benefits of using a paved bike path. But move to single file when you encounter someone headed the other way or coming up from behind.

11. Be courteous. Some of the multiuse paths are heavily used by rollerbladers, runners, dog walkers, and baby strollers. On the paths, bicyclists and bladers should yield to pedestrians and joggers. The only way for multiuse paths to work is if the multiusers give each other space and respect. Leave your road rage in the car.

12. Bring a bike lock on the ride. It's a long walk back to the car if someone steals your bike.

13. Lock valuables in the car trunk. Don't make your car a tempting target to thieves while you're off riding your bicycle.

14. Obey traffic signs and signals. Even on a bike path, bicycles are considered vehicles and must stop at stop signs and traffic lights.

15. Florida law prohibits wearing a headset or headphones while riding a bicycle.

Blackwater Heritage State Trail

The Countryside Ride

Length: 9.6 miles.
Location: Milton. From Interstate 10, take exit 7. Turn north on Avalon Road. Turn right on Highway 90. Turn left on Highway 87. Trailhead is on the right.
Amenities: parking, rest rooms, water, picnic facilities, ice cream shop, maps, ATMs, equestrian trail, wheelchair access.
Surface: 12-foot-wide asphalt with mile markers written in white paint.

From a town once known as Scratch Ankle to a military base that once held German POWS, the Blackwater Heritage State Trail takes cyclists on a bucolic tour of back-roads rural Florida. Among the swamps, pine tree farms, and pastureland, cyclists might find alligators, ospreys, redheaded woodpeckers, otters, bobcats, whitetail deer, raccoons, opossums, pine snakes, and wild pigs. They will also pass the fragile pink and white blooms of mimosa trees, the white flowers and waxy leaves of giant magnolia trees, endangered whitetop pitcher plants, and the dainty yellow flowers that poke above the rust-colored swamp water that flows around seven wood-rail bridges.

Opened in October 1998, the Blackwater Heritage State Trail follows the route of a railroad track that was built in the early 1900s and supported the timber operations of the Bagdad Lumber and Land Company until the 1930s.

The Milton trailhead includes rest rooms, water, maps, and covered picnic tables—and a Tastee-Freez next door. Be sure to bring water and food along, as there are no stores or rest rooms on the trail once you leave Milton.

Starting from the trailhead and heading north, here's what to look for on the Blackwater Heritage State Trail:

- Within the first mile watch out for traffic where the trail crosses Berryhill Road and Munson Highway as it winds through Milton's residential neighborhoods.

- Approaching mile 1, the trail passes Milton's city hall and the Santa Rosa Public Library. Between the city hall and the library, the brick building on

Blackwater Heritage State Trail

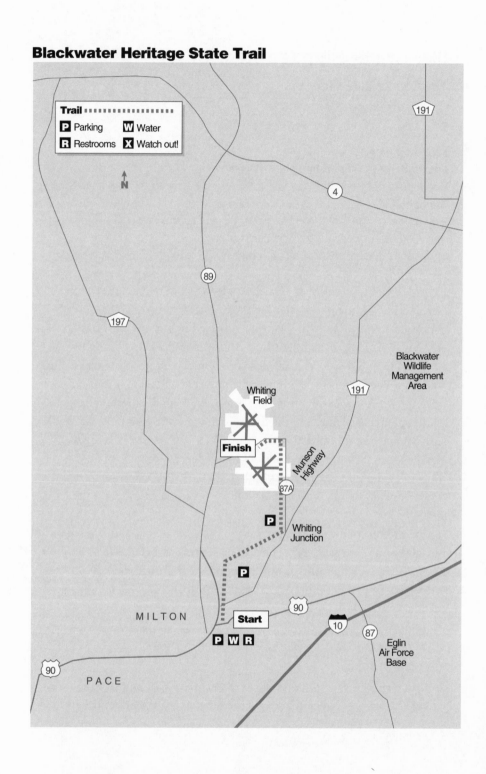

the left that looks like a warehouse is the back side of the West Florida Community Care Center, a state-run psychiatric hospital.

- A second parking lot with room for horse trailers is located 2.5 miles along the trail at Munson Highway.

- Around 3 miles, look for alligators and waterfowl as the path crosses beneath the power lines and over a series of small bridges.

- At 6.5 miles, the trail runs past a row of mimosa trees and towering magnolias on the left and the orderly rows of a pine tree farm on the right.

- At 7 miles, the Blackwater Trail reaches the Whiting Junction parking lot with an information board telling the story of the Whiting Field Naval Air Station, where helicopter pilots have been trained since 1943. Originally intended as a World War II prisoner of war camp, the four-thousand-acre Whiting Field now trains twenty thousand naval aviators a year. Just beyond the parking lot, the trail wiggles through a scenic little patch of trees.

- At 8.5 miles, the trail reaches the gates to Whiting Field. The path continues for another mile inside the military base, passing the base administration center, gymnasium, and chapel built by German POWs during World War II. The trail ends at the west gate of the base where the Clear Creek nature trail takes hikers on a 1.5-mile trip through woods and along a boardwalk through a swamp. Cyclists entering the base are required to wear helmets, and to leave before the gates close at sunset.

- For experienced cyclists, the path crosses two-lane roads that will take you on the back roads of rural Santa Rosa County for longer rides. Watch for Okaloosa Street at 1 mile, Pat Brown Road at 4 miles, and Parker Road around mile 5.

With few major cross streets, the Blackwater Heritage State Trail is a good ride for children and inexperienced bicyclists. And on days when there aren't too many joggers, bladers, and baby strollers, the trail is also a good ride for experienced cyclists who like to ride hard and fast.

Something you should know: Plans for the Blackwater Heritage State Trail include a 1.5-mile extension of the trail south from its present trailhead. An equestrian trail sprouting from the parking lot on Munson Highway is also in the works. There is also talk of joining the trail with the five-mile remnant of the old Spanish Trail—a one-lane brick road on the east side of Milton. The highway once linked Pensacola to St. Augustine.

Down the road are visionary dreams of some 120 miles of Panhandle bike paths, mostly through state-owned land, linking Milton with Pensacola, the beach communities of Santa Rosa County, and the 184,000-acre Blackwater River State Forest—the largest state forest in Florida.

The first six miles of the trail follow the old railroad tracks used by the Bagdad Lumber and Land Company to transport logs to the mill town of Bagdad south of Milton on County Road 191. From the 1820s until the 1930s, Bagdad boasted dozens of sawmills. The railroad was abandoned after the last mill closed in 1939, and the town all but disappeared. Parts of the original railroad tracks are on display at the West Florida Railroad Museum in Milton. In the 1980s the Santa Rosa Historical Society restored many of Bagdad's remaining Victorian homes to create a historical village. The society was also responsible for restoring Milton's 1913 opera house, the Imogene. The Exchange Hotel, originally built in 1912 as a telephone exchange, has been restored as a bed-and-breakfast. In its days as a hotel, the Exchange was home to baseball great Ted Williams during his stint as a World War II flight instructor at Whiting Field.

Established in 1825 as a trading post, Milton was originally known as Scratch Ankle and Hard Scrabble—two names that spoke to hard times in the Panhandle. The name was changed to Milton before it became the county seat of Santa Rosa, but the origin of the name is the subject of dispute. Some contend it's a corruption of Milltown. Others say it honors the patriarch of a pioneer family, Milton Amos. And there are those who attribute the name to John Milton, a Civil War governor of Florida. Nobody claims the name has anything to do with dead English poets.

Today Milton is a community of 7,200 residents, numerous antiques stores, and the West Florida Railroad Museum, and is a jumping-off spot for canoeists and kayakers who take the same Blackwater River route to Pensacola Bay and the Blackwater River State Forest once used by mercantile schooners. Designated the "canoe capital of Florida," Milton celebrates its humble origins every March with the Scratch Ankle Spring Festival.

For more information, call the Blackwater Heritage State Trail park ranger, (850) 983-5363, and the Santa Rosa Chamber of Commerce, (850) 623-2339.

Pensacola Beach Trail
The Rubbernecker Ride

Length: 6 miles.
Location: Pensacola Beach. From Interstate 10, take exit 4. Take Interstate 110 south to Highway 98. Follow the signs to Pensacola beaches, taking Highway 98 over the Pensacola Bay Bridge. Take County Road 399 over the Bob Sykes Bridge to Pensacola Beach. Toll is $1 per car.
Amenities: parking, rest rooms, water, picnic facilities on the beach, ATMs, convenience stores, restaurants.
Surface: 8-foot-wide asphalt without mile markers.

There is plenty of scenic beauty for cyclists on Pensacola Beach. And we don't just mean the sugary white sand. The old Redneck Riviera now rivals Daytona Beach in its attraction of college students. Preservation of the dunes along this slice of Florida's Gulf Coast has created majestic mounds of sand you won't find anywhere else in the state. Lovers of architecture will enjoy the classy new homes going up, obviously influenced by the colors and styles of the resort communities of Seaside and Destin. And for those who appreciate the unusual, there's even a house shaped like a UFO—and it's for rent!

The best place to start on the Pensacola Beach Trail is the Information Center parking lot after the tollbooths at the intersection of County Road 399 and Fort Pickens Road. This puts you not only at the apex of the bike trail but right in the middle of the island's shopping district of restaurants, bars, convenience stores, gift shops, ATMs, and hotels. Free maps at the Information Center show the locations of businesses along the trail and in the vicinity.

There is also beachside parking available at both ends of the six-mile-long bike path. The parking on the west end includes rest rooms, water, and picnic facilities. Parking on the east end is without facilities.

Heading west from the Information Center parking lot, here's what to look for on the Pensacola Beach Trail:

· The white sand dunes are what make Pensacola Beach so unique and scenic. Dune restoration along the first 2.5 miles of the bike path allows

5

Pensacola Beach Trail

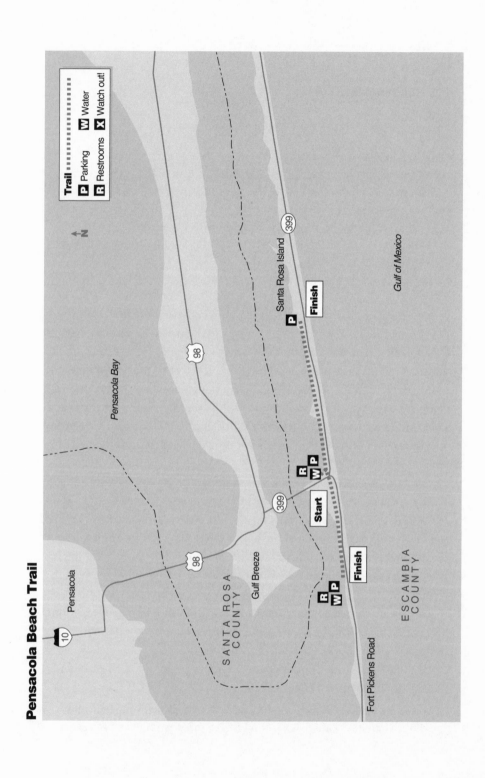

Fig. 1. White sand dunes on Pensacola Beach Trail

sand to flow and drift against snow fences, creating hills of sand, sea oats, sea grape, and scrub oak. There are times when the path cuts between the dunes, and there are spots where you need to watch out for loose sand that drifts across the pavement and makes the surface slick to thin-tired road bikes.

· A boardwalk at mile 1 gives beachgoers—and bicyclists—access to the beach and Gulf waters. There are several such walkways scattered along the trail, admitting people to the beach while saving the sand dunes. Dune restoration prohibits people from walking or climbing over the sand mounds. On the right just beyond the 1-mile mark, at the peak of one of the restored dunes, is a cross commemorating the first religious service in the Pensacola area, performed by Dominican friars accompanying Spanish explorer Tristán de Luna in 1559.

· Beyond the cross-on-the-sand dune, on the right, is a row of those eye-catching developments sprouting along the Gulf beaches with three-story nouveau Victorian homes painted Popsicle colors.

· At 2 miles, a beachside parking lot with a boardwalk over the dunes marks the beginning of a stretch without commercial development that extends into the Gulf Islands National Seashore. The path ends at 2.5

miles in a parking lot that serves another beach area with picnic tables, rest rooms, and water. Cyclists can cross the road to take a rest break and a dip in the Gulf, or turn around and head back to the beach community's commercial district and the other half of the Pensacola Beach Trail.

Just beyond the west end of the bike path is the entrance to Fort Pickens National Park and a two-lane road leading to the nineteenth-century brick fort where the first shots of the Civil War in Florida were fired. The road to the park has only light traffic. Admission to the park is $3 for bicyclists, $6 for cars. Park hours are 7 A.M.–10 P.M.

Heading east from the Information Center parking lot, cross County Road 399 and Fort Pickens Road at the traffic light. On the eastern leg these are things to look for:

- A trail marker outside the Santa Rosa Island Authority designates this section of the Pensacola Beach Trail the Michael Keenan Memorial Bike Paths—named for a local cyclist who was killed in an accident.

- The path temporarily disappears in a strip center parking lot at .5 mile. Watch out here for cars pulling in and backing out of parking spaces.

- The bike path here is narrow, bumpy, and in need of repair in several places. Battered aluminum posts have been planted in the asphalt to keep motorized vehicles off and create two lanes of traffic for bicyclists and pedestrians. Where some of those posts have been lost or removed, watch out for the stumps that remain planted in the bike path.

- Around 2 miles, the bike path starts getting funky. There are folk-art-style benches, colorful hand-painted mailboxes, a double-decker deck with a spiral staircase leading to the circular upper deck, and a house with a rental spaceship perched on top. Described as a "local Pensacola Beach landmark" by its owner, the Space Ship contains one bedroom, one bath, and two little green men looking out the window. Available for "anniversary, honeymoon, romantic or adventurous getaways," the pod-shaped Space Ship rents for $100 a night.

- About 2.5 miles, look for the mermaid carving to the right, across Via DeLuna Road, just before the path reaches the Pensacola Beach fire station. On the other side of the fire department is a unique elementary school built on stilts. Next to the elementary school are tennis courts with parking and rest rooms.

• After a stretch of sand-turning-into-high-rent-housing, the trail ends abruptly at 3.5 miles. Across the road is a beachside parking lot.

Whichever way you go, there is plenty to see on the Pensacola Beach Trail—some of it pretty, some of it odd, all of it interesting.

Something you should know: Plans, but no funding yet, call for extending the Pensacola Beach Trail five miles into Fort Pickens National Park. Already under way is a seven-mile bike path on the east end of the barrier island at Navarre Beach. The Panhandle's bike path visionaries would like to see the beach trails become part of a forty-mile loop of interconnecting paths.

Big dreamers go way back in the history of Pensacola Beach. Before the founding of St. Augustine, there was explorer Don Tristán de Luna whose plan to create a colony of 1,400 Spaniards on the Gulf barrier beaches in 1559 ended after a hurricane destroyed their ships and killed their livestock. Although de Luna abandoned Pensacola Beach more than 440 years ago, his name remains on streets, high rises, and real estate offices. Same goes for the Native Americans who met de Luna when he landed. The tribe is extinct, but its name—Panzacola—remains affixed to the land.

For more information, call the Santa Rosa Island Authority, (850) 932-2257; the Western Panhandle Bike/Pedestrian Coordinator, (850) 595-8910; and the Pensacola Beach Chamber of Commerce, 1-800-635-4803 or (850) 932-1500.

Highway 30A Parallel Bike Path

The Seaside Ride

Length: 10 miles.
Location: Walton County. From Interstate 10, take exit 14. Turn south on
U.S. 331. Turn right on County Road 30. Turn right on County Road 30A.
Amenities: parking, rest rooms, water, picnic areas, ATMs, bike shops,
restaurants, convenience stores, shops.
Surface: 8-foot-wide asphalt without mile markers.

Walton's Highway 30A Parallel Bike Path is just like it sounds: It runs parallel
to County Road 30A along the barrier islands just west of Panama City. The
path is actually two segments of bike trail separated by about two miles. But
right in the middle of the missing link, acting as the fulcrum, is the movie-set
resort town of Seaside.

A planned community invented in 1981, Seaside is an upscale beachside
community of class and whimsical architecture. Anyone who has seen the
Jim Carrey movie *The Truman Show* will recognize the town as the real-life
setting for fictional Seahaven. The town's designers combined traditional
small-town designs with flourishes of architectural eccentricity and humor.
The combination of down-home familiarity and whimsy extends to the residents themselves. The houses are each identified by family members' names,
hometowns, and nicknames: Frumious Bandersnatch, It's A Wonderful Life,
Plum Lazy, and (an oddball in every crowd) The House with No Name.

The town of "1,029 residents, including cats and dogs" features art galleries, fine restaurants, beachwear shops, jewelry and gift boutiques, ice cream
parlors, beachside bars, banks with money machines, and, of course, real
estate agencies. Except for the '50s-style cabins of the Seaside Motor Court,
there are no motels in Seaside, but the town does have a bed-and-breakfast,
rental cottages, and a row of identical beachside honeymoon cottages.

There is a bike rental and repair shop in Seaside at the Swim and Tennis
Club. Butterfly Bike and Beach Rental sells, repairs, and rents bikes in the
neighboring community of Seagrove Beach. You can also rent bikes and have
them delivered for free from Bikes Are Us Rentals in nearby Sandestin.

Walton 30A Parallel Bike Path

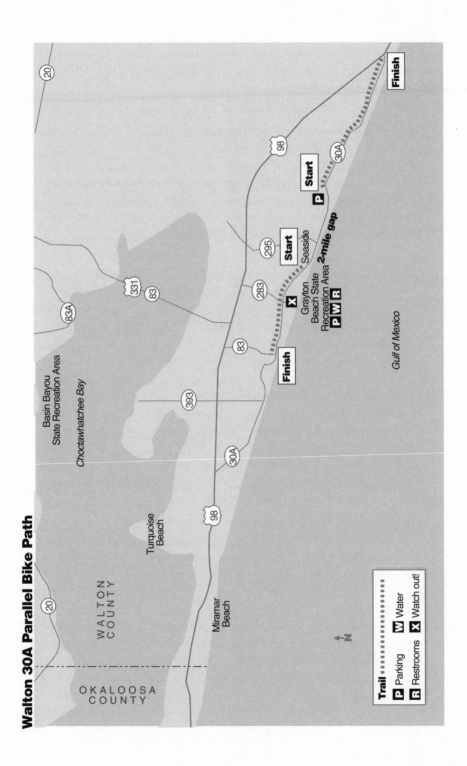

The bike path extends westward nearly four miles from Seaside. To the east, there is a bike lane on County Road 30A that extends through Seagrove Beach to another bike path that runs for six miles.

Heading west from Seaside, here's what to look for:

- The path merges with two-lane Highway 30A at several points. Although cyclists are separated from the traffic only by a white line, there is enough room on the eight-foot-wide bike lane to provide a good margin of safety for cyclists. Nonetheless, you want to stay alert and remember you are no longer on a bike path separated from the traffic. The first of these mergers comes along at .5 mile when the bike path crosses the bridge over Western Lake.

- At 1 mile is the entrance to Grayton Beach State Recreation Area. A two-lane road with little traffic leads into the 1,133-acre seaside park opened in 1968. The park's white sand dunes rise like cliffs above the roadway. Shaped by the wind and salty ocean spray, the dunes sprout tufts of vegetation that look like shrubs but, in some cases, are the treetops of slash pines and Southern magnolias buried up to their necks in sand. On the other side of the dunes, the Gulf of Mexico spreads out to the horizon in stripes of blue and green water. It doesn't take long to understand why this was designated one of the best beaches in the world by Beaches Rated expert Stephen Leatherman in 1994.

  Since parking is at a premium at Seaside, this is a good place to start your bike ride. The park's entrance fee is $3.25 per car and $1 for bicyclists. Inside the park grounds there are rest rooms, showers, water, soda machines, picnic facilities, fishing, a boat ramp, and thirty-seven campsites. For more information, call (850) 231-4210.

- At 1.5 miles is historic Grayton Beach, founded in 1890. The town, with its entrenched artists colony, competes with Seaside with an assortment of classy restaurants, boutiques, and watering holes. There is an ATM at the First American Bank, and a bike rack behind a sign that says "Grayton Trail," staking a claim on the western segment of Walton's bike paths for the community.

  Next to the bank is Monet Monet, a garden shop and art gallery based on Impressionist painter Claude Monet's home and gardens in Giverny, France. The store's owner, Jonathan Quinn, photographed and measured and sketched Monet's gardens in France to replicate a water lily pond and Japanese footbridge. The store is closed on Tuesdays.

• Take care crossing County Road 283 as you leave the Grayton Beach business district. Experienced riders might want to note the bike lanes on County Road 283, which tempt cyclists to try the blacktop roads of Walton County.

• After the path passes Little Red Fish Lake around 2.5 miles, watch out for cars coming out of blind drives that lead to homes tucked behind walls of trees.

• Around 3.5 miles, the path takes a dip just before merging with the road and crossing over Big Red Fish Lake. For a moment, when the path descends and starts up a little hill, the air is scented with the smell of pines instead of the sea.

• Just before the bike path ends at 3.8 miles, there is some loose gravel you need to watch out for as the trail dead-ends at Sand Dunes Road, just a short way from County Road 83. A nice surprise awaits the cyclist at the west end of the trail—Uniques, an interesting little art and fashion boutique sitting all by itself at the side of the road.

The eastern segment of the 30A Parallel Bike Path is a little less accessible from Seaside but can be reached via the bike lane that goes through Seagrove Beach. If you ride that bike lane, look for the white mannequin "male box" on the right side of the road.

The six-mile eastern segment of the bike path starts at the intersection of County Road 30A and Eastern Lake Road. Look for Abbot and Andrews Realty. Parking is available on Eastern Lake Road.

This part of the bike path also has stretches that merge with the road to form a bike lane. Same advice applies: There's plenty of room to ride on the bike lane, but stay alert.

Heading west from Eastern Lake Road, here's what to look for:

• Next to the real estate office, on the right, the path passes an unusual plant nursery—the Gourd Garden and Curiosity Shop—where you will find the oddest assortment of gourds anywhere. The store also sells container plants and vegetation suited to the salt-sun-and-sand climate of Gulf Coast Florida.

• At 1.5 miles, the path crosses a bridge with a scenic outlook alcove that gives a preview of the Deer Lake State Park up ahead. Created in 1996, the 1,900-acre park encompasses a freshwater coastal lake nestled among majestic sand dunes. Although the park lacks facilities, it provides a view of cypress dome wetlands, salt marsh, open-canopy wire grass, longleaf pine, spring azaleas, and golden asters. There is no admission charge, but get out before sundown when they lock the gates. For more information, call (850) 231-4214.

· At 3 miles, look to the right for a row of lakefront cabins with stairs leading down to docks as the bike path merges with the road to cross Damp Creek Lake.

· Beyond the 3-mile mark, the path curves and climbs a small hill and enters the seaside town of Seacrest. New homes painted lollipop colors and houses with white rooftop widow's walks nudge side by side. Mailboxes carved to look like pelicans, whales, flamingos, and fish flank driveways to beachside homes given names like Cloud Nine and the Lazy Snail.

· Around 5 miles, the asphalt bike path surrenders to a six-foot-wide concrete sidewalk that passes by a parade of new housing developments and seaside high-rises. The most notable is the community of Rosemary Beach, a nostalgic-styled place that didn't exist before 1995.

· At 6 miles, the sidewalk ends. A gravel roadway separates the end of the sidewalk and the resumption of the asphalt bike path that ends .2 mile down the road in the parking lot of an E-Z Serve convenience store and gas station at Highway 98. Across County Road 30A from the convenience store is the Tiki Hut, one of those once-common roadside tourist attractions of bamboo and thatch roofs selling everything from pottery, tropical art, gifts, and sterling silver to other "unique stuff."

Grab some refreshments at the convenience store, turn the bike around, and head back for a six-mile return trip through time, from untouched dunes and mangroves to lemon-colored high-rises and homes echoing another era.

Something you should know: Seaside was designed for pedestrians and bicycles but was not, unfortunately, built to include a bike path or bike lanes. When County Road 30A passes through Seaside it narrows to two lanes without room for a bike lane or sidewalks. The road shoulder is loose sand and crushed oyster shells. That should change. Walton County has plans to fill in the 3.5-mile gap through Seaside and Seagrove Beach and extend the west end of the path to Highway 98. When completed, the 30A Parallel Bike

Path will extend twenty-three miles from one end of Highway 98 to the other.

The Panhandle has always had to do more with less. Beyond the affluence of the beachside communities, this is one of the poorest regions in the state. Money for amenities like paved bike paths has been hard to come by. Walton County overcame its money constraints by using the asphalt scrapings from the repaving of Highway 30A to form the base for the bike path that parallels the road.

The architectural jewel in that asphalt necklace will always be Seaside, a town of affluence and style that has been called everything from the reinvention of the village for the twenty-first century to the most important new piece of architecture in the country. The town sits on eighty acres of land originally intended as a summer camp for the employees of Robert Davis's grandfather, who purchased the land in 1946. The summer camp never materialized. Instead Davis, a Miami developer, commissioned architects Andres Duany and Elizabeth Plater-Zyberk to design a beach community that incorporated some of the architectural traditions of Florida—porches, balconies, deep roof overhangs, cross-ventilation—with small-town layouts. Urban designer Leon Krier came up with a floor plan for the city that made everything accessible within a quarter-mile walking distance. The original downtown, which now includes a wine shop, chocolate shop, smoke shop, and flower shop, began as tables beneath canvas tents where folks sold fruits and vegetables, crafts, and flea market items.

Designed for bike and pedestrian travel, Seaside has become so popular with visitors that its main problem has been parking and the stream of cars passing through on Highway 30A.

For more information, call the Walton County Commission, (850) 231-6266; the Western Panhandle Bike/Pedestrian Coordinator, (850) 595-8910; and the Seaside Visitors Center, 1-800-277-8696.

Tallahassee–St. Marks Historic Railroad State Trail
The Granddaddy of Rails-to-Trails Rides

Length: 20 miles.
Location: Tallahassee. From Interstate 10, take exit 29. Turn south onto Monroe Street (Highway 27) through downtown Tallahassee. Veer left on Woodville Highway (County Road 363). Trailhead is on the right.
Amenities: parking, rest rooms, water, maps, benches, picnic tables, bike and in-line skate rental shop, wheelchair access.
Surface: 8- and 12-foot-wide asphalt with mile markers painted on the pavement.

The Tallahassee–St. Marks Historic Railroad State Trail has a split personality. One is the skinny, eight-foot-wide rural trail that runs sixteen miles south from the trailhead to the St. Marks River. The other is the three-mile, twelve-foot-wide urban extension northward through Tallahassee's industrial neighborhoods to Florida A&M University. The first is the granddaddy of Florida's rail trails, opened in 1988. The other was conceived in the late 1990s and is still growing.

Both begin on Woodville Highway, just south of Capital Circle (State Road 263). A bike and in-line skate concession stand is adorned with a carved wooden "Trail Head" of a cyclist wearing a helmet and goggles. A large paved parking lot, rest rooms, water fountains, benches, picnic tables, and trail maps are available at the trailhead. A twelve-foot stretch of the original railroad track has been saved as a reminder of the rail line that began with mule-drawn carts linking the seat of Florida government with the Gulf.

There are signs along the bike path that caution cyclists, joggers, and bladers not to use the trail alone or after dark—which doesn't mean the St. Marks trail is any more threatening than any other of the state's paved paths that are unlighted at night and cut through isolated, wooded sections. The signs are just a reminder not to lock your personal safety awareness inside your car when you go out on the trails.

Tallahassee-St. Marks Historic Railroad State Trail

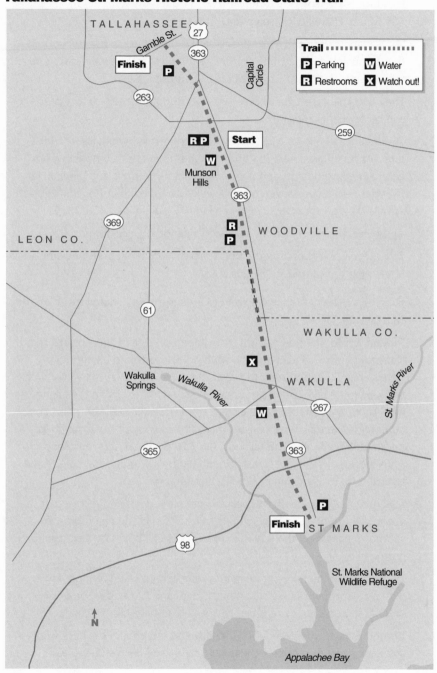

Heading north from the trailhead, here's what to look for on the Tallahassee–St. Marks Historic Railroad State Trail:

- The Seminole Pick-and-Pull salvage yard promises big-buck savings and free admission if you want to scavenge for alternators, carburetors, and five-dollar tires from the rows of wrecked automobiles.

- The Olde Things antique shop offers used furniture, dusty bric-a-brac, and secondhand appliances.

- The American Folk Art Museum and Gallery across Woodville Road features art masquerading as bathtubs, lawn ornaments, scripture and angels painted on boards, and a mountain of bicycle parts and pinwheels. The museum is open seven days a week "by appointment or chance." Admission is $3 for adults, $1 for children. Phone: (850) 656-2879.

- At 2 miles, the trail reaches a park-and-ride lot at Gaile Street.

- The last mile includes a pretty, tree-shaded stretch that ends at Gamble Street near the campus of Florida A&M.

For a more scenic ride, here's what to look for when headed south on the St. Marks Trail:

- Around 1 mile, the trail reaches the wilderness edge of the Apalachicola National Forest trailhead and the Munson Hills off-road biking trails. Here's an early opportunity to get off the bike, refresh at the water fountain, chain the bike to the bike rack, and stretch the legs on the hiking trail. There is a rest room at the start of the 7.5-mile Munson Hills Loop mountain-bike trail, which passes through a canopy of trees, sandhills, ponds, and wetlands. The Tall Pine Shortcut creates a 4.25-mile loop from the larger trail. The forest is inhabited by a woodpecker colony, fox squirrels, foxes, porcupines, skunks, and turkeys.

- Around 2 miles, the path reaches another parking lot and rest stop at the Woodville County Complex with its baseball fields and rest rooms. A short distance down the trail is an emergency call box. The next call box is at 3 miles.

- During the summer, look for Linda J's refreshment stand around 4 miles with an assortment of ice cream bars, soda, and Gatorade. For a rest break, she also provides a table, chairs, and an umbrella for shade.

- Around 5 miles, the Woodville United Methodist church sits back from the road, separated from the bike path by a wide lawn studded with shade trees. The church is near the junction of Woodville Highway and Natural Bridge Road, which leads six miles to the Battle of Natural Bridge Historic Memorial—site of a skirmish in 1865 between Union forces trying to capture Florida's capital and a ragtag regiment of Confederate boys and old men left to defend the city.

- At about the 7-mile mark, just before the bike path crosses the Leon County line into Wakulla County, cyclists pass the tree-shaded Aces High Stables where horses loiter amid jumping fences and other obstacles.
- Watch out for two sandy intersections around the 9-mile mark after the bike path passes the Wakulla Methodist Church.
- At 11 miles, the curtain of pine trees, foliage, and vines parts on the right for a little roadside respite of benches and a rustic water fountain made of stone.
- Beginning around mile 13, the arrow-straight Tallahassee–St. Marks Trail goes though curvy gyrations for a mile or so, weaving left and right with a dividing line drawn down the middle to minimize head-on collisions with cyclists, in-line skaters, and joggers headed in the opposite direction.
- The trail finishes up with a tunnel of trees that is one of the prettiest, most scenic stretches of the ride.

A decision awaits cyclists at the end of the Tallahassee–St. Marks Historic Railroad State Trail. You can either turn around and go back, head right for a trip back in history, or take a left for the kind of rest and refreshment that only a fresh batch of Apalachicola oysters and a cold beer can provide.

To the left is the quintessence of life on the Gulf Coast of Florida—beer and oysters at Posey's Oyster Bar, a rustic structure on the water with worn wood floors that bills itself as Home of the Topless Oyster. Hundreds of satisfied patrons of seafood and shellfish have decorated the interior with business cards stapled to the beams and rafters of the restaurant.

To the right, about half a mile down Old Fort Road, is the San Marcos de Apalache State Historic Site with its remnants of Spanish, British, American, and Confederate occupation dating back to 1528. The execution of two British men accused by Andrew Jackson of inciting Indian raids in the 1800s sparked an international crisis between the United States and Great Britain.

The San Marcos de Apalache Historic Site is open 9 A.M.–5 P.M., Thursday–Monday; closed Tuesday and Wednesday. Museum admission is $1, free under age six. Phone: (850) 925-6216 or (850) 922-6007.

Museum or oysters? History or beer? It gives you something to think about while riding the oldest multiuse trail in the state.

Something you should know: Plans are to continue extending the Tallahassee–St. Marks Trail north into Tallahassee, linking it with Florida State University and the two-mile Stadium Drive bike path. There are also plans for a trailhead on the south end with parking, rest rooms, and water.

The Tallahassee–St. Marks Trail occupies the roadbed of the Tallahassee/St. Marks Railroad, the state's longest-operating rail line, dating back to 1837. Abandoned by the Seaboard Railroad in 1983, the rail right-of-way was purchased by the Florida Department of Transportation and paved with $660,000 from the state legislature.

The St. Marks National Wildlife Refuge at the southern end of the trail is a 67,000-acre preserve that stretches twenty miles across three Florida panhandle counties. The area around St. Marks includes a wildlife drive, seventy-five miles of trails, and many of the refuge's more than 270 species of birds. The refuge is a favorite place for bird and butterfly watchers. In the fall, swarms of Monarch butterflies stop in St. Marks on their migration to Mexico.

The St. Marks Lighthouse, built in 1829 and rebuilt in 1842 as the result of erosion, is a favorite observation point for birders. Automated in 1960, the lighthouse stands eighty feet tall and contains a covered observation deck overlooking the marsh.

For more information, call the Tallahassee–St. Marks Trail park office, (850) 922-6007; the Tallahassee–Leon County Bike/Pedestrian Coordinator, (850) 891-8090; or the St. Marks National Wildlife Refuge, (850) 925-6121.

Suwannee River Greenway at Branford

The Bike and Dive Ride

ڶ

Length: 4.5 miles.
Location: Branford. From Interstate 10, take exit 40. Go south 28 miles on U.S. 129. In Branford, turn left on Owens Avenue to reach trailhead.
Amenities: parking, water, rest rooms, picnic facilities, convenience stores, restaurants, bike rentals, ATM.
Surface: 10-foot-wide asphalt without mile markers.

Behind the old Branford trail depot converted into a clubhouse by the local Shriners, the wide tea-colored Suwannee River glitters through the tree branches in the afternoon sun. It's a slow-flowing river with the pace of a different time, an era of steamboats and coal-fired locomotives. All that remains of the steamboats is sunken ruins on the bottom of the river. All that remains of the trains is the old depot with a row of fold-up seats on the back porch facing the river. Branford was a town of size and substance when the Suwannee River was a highway for river commerce, the trafficking of cotton and lumber. It's now a town of seven hundred people and a 4.5-mile-long rails-to-trails bike path it hopes will help draw ecotourists interested in cycling, kayaking, canoeing, and diving.

Already known as the "spring diving capital of the world," Branford is the first leg of what proponents hope will someday be a sixty-mile network of paved bike paths called the Suwannee River Greenway that will link several North Central Florida spring towns and state parks. The town has restaurants, antiques, guns and ammo, and bike rentals at the Steamboat Dive Shop.

The Branford Trail begins with an unpaved parking lot opposite the Shriners' Branford depot. From the trailhead, the bike path stretches south for almost two miles toward Ichetucknee Springs State Park and three miles north toward Little River Springs Park.

Heading south from the trailhead, here's what to look for on the Suwannee River Greenway at Branford:

- Watch out crossing U.S. 27 at .2 mile. There is no crosswalk at this busy intersection. On the other side of U.S. 27 is the Ivey Memorial Park with

21

Suwannee River Greenway at Branford

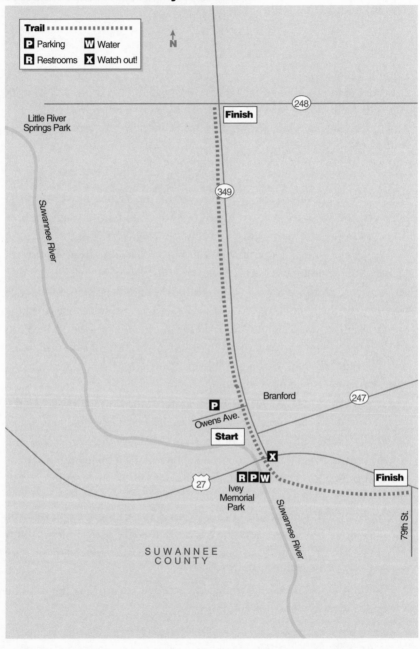

Trail ....
P Parking   W Water
R Restrooms X Watch out!

N

248

Finish

Little River
Springs Park

Suwannee River

349

P

Branford

247

Owens Ave.

Start

X

27

R P W

Finish

Ivey
Memorial
Park

Suwannee River

79th St.

SUWANNEE
COUNTY

paved parking, boat ramps to the Suwannee, water, food, rest rooms, and picnic tables. There's a dive shop and a bait and tackle store in a building that straddles a canoe-launching ramp. Off to the side is a little cul-de-sac spring with a semicircular wooden deck that cups the swimming hole in its hand. The shady park overlooking the Suwannee is the perfect place to spend a few minutes watching nature flow by.

· The first mile runs through shade and sun alongside a seldom-used two-lane road. Between stands of trees and brush, the trailside is splattered with wildflowers in the spring. Blue and purple phlox mingle with yellow daisies.

· At 1 mile, the path runs between a nursery on your left and a pine tree farm on your right—neat rows of trees in containers on one side and orderly rows of pine trees on the other.

· The path crosses 79th Street at 1.5 miles and then comes to an abrupt stop where the asphalt ends in a corridor of trees. Facing east at the unfinished trail, you are looking at the route the path will take for another six miles to Ichetucknee Springs State Park. If you're looking for a good place to eat or a quaint place to stay, take a right on 79th, then hang a right on River Road (a hard-packed limestone road) to the Suwannee River Cove Restaurant and campground. The restaurant, sitting on the Suwannee River, is open 4:40 P.M.–10 P.M., Thursday–Saturday, and noon–10 P.M. on Sunday. Cabins are $75 a night.

Heading north from the trailhead, here's what to look for:

· Running parallel to U.S. 129, the three-mile northern leg of the Branford trail is straight, flat, and smooth. Lacking busy cross streets and other interference, it's possible to reach some speed on the Branford trail. There are no speed limit signs on this rails-to-trails outpost, but stay alert for other users on this multipurpose path.

· Just beyond the 1-mile mark, look to the right for a remnant left by the railroad—a cement post marking mile 693.

· Around 2 miles, look to the right for the homemade rodeo ring on the other side of U.S. 129. The scenery on the Branford trail is a mixture of pastureland, fields, ferns, flowers, and prairie.

· At 3 miles, the path ends at County Road 248. Turning left, the two-lane road leads 1.5 miles to Little River Springs Park on the Suwannee River. The road has little traffic and dead-ends at the park, which has another beautiful spring.

Branford's motto is A Nice Place to Live. And it's a nice place to visit. The remoteness of the town is made up for by its beauty. This is a town left behind by the steamboats and trains, and bypassed by the interstates. But it has stayed in synch with its springs and rivers, and in close touch with nature, which makes it worth spending a day biking, swimming, diving, and canoeing.

Something you should know: Plans are under way to extend the Suwannee River Greenway at Branford twenty-four miles north to Live Oak. With this addition, and the six-mile extension to Ichetucknee Springs State Park, the Branford Trail will stretch nearly thirty-five miles.

Railroad magnate Henry B. Plant, whose train tracks stretched from Savannah to Tampa, personally named the town in 1882 after Branford, Connecticut, a place he once called home.

For more information, call the Branford Town Hall, (904) 935-1146.

Jacksonville-Baldwin Rail Trail

The Ride Through the Woods

Length: 14.5 miles.
Location: Duval County. From Interstate 295, take exit 9. Take Common-wealth Boulevard one mile west. Turn right on Imeson Road. Trailhead is on the left.
Amenities: parking, picnic area, equestrian trail, wheelchair access.
Surface: 12-foot-wide asphalt with miles marked by wooden posts.

Don't let the first three miles of the Jacksonville-Baldwin Rail Trail fool you into thinking this is another urban-industrial bike path running beneath power lines, past auto salvage yards, and behind blue-collar neighborhoods. Just as the power lines fall away, the true beauty of the Jacksonville-Baldwin trail begins—more than ten miles of pines, oaks, maples, and sumac trees that create an extensive canopy of shade unmatched by any other paved bike path in Florida. The tunnel of limbs and branches above and leaves and pine needles below is the closest thing to off-road cycling you'll find on a paved surface.

If the Jacksonville-Baldwin Trail has a fault, it's the lack of water and rest rooms at either end of the bike path. Efforts are under way to add trailheads at both ends, and a visitors center at 12.5 miles, but until then be sure to bring your own water on the ride. The trail, opened in late 1999, also lacks the benches and shelters of other rural trails like the Van Fleet and With-lacoochee.

The trail is straight, wide, flat, and clean, with only a few cross streets. It's a good trail for those who like to ride hard, but an even better trail for those who like to take their time to look for deer, bluebirds, wild turkeys, porcu-pines, and the occasional coyote. And don't be surprised if you find the trail blocked by a stray herd of dairy cows.

Along the way, bicyclists will pass the bushy green rows of pine tree farms, sepia-toned cattle grazing, and a smattering of farmhouses and homes be-fore reaching the small farming and railroad town of Baldwin.

Heading west from the Imeson Trailhead, here's what to look for on the Jacksonville-Baldwin Rail Trail:

Jacksonville-Baldwin Rail Trail

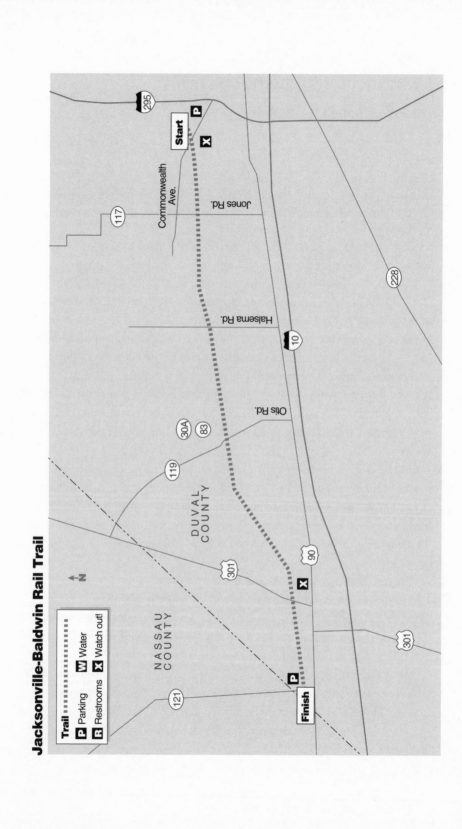

- Within the first .5 mile, watch out for cars when the trail crosses busy Commonwealth Avenue.
- Just before the 3-mile mark, look on the left for a triangular railroad mile-marker post left over from the days when the CSX railroad used to haul pulpwood, limerock, and cattle between Jacksonville and High Springs near Gainesville.
- Nearing 4 miles is the first of several pretty stretches where the trees arch over the trail. It's like riding inside a tube of trees.
- Another shady stretch around 6.5 miles arrives with a pop-pop-pop from a shooting range in the distance. Don't worry. The shooters fire small-caliber weapons away from the trail, so there is no danger to cyclists, joggers, and in-line skaters using the multipurpose trail.
- Near 8 miles, the path crosses Otis Road, which has a paved bike lane heading south one mile to Pope Duval Park.
- Beyond the 8-mile mark is another cathedral of trees where the path is padded with leaves. The carpet of leaves and pine needles continues for about two miles.
- Around 11 miles, on the left you can see the aluminum roofs of the sheds and milk barns of Mecklenburg Farms, an eight-hundred-acre dairy farm with more than a thousand cows. The farm's owner, Ingo Krieg, also once owned the Tea Men, a Jacksonville soccer team that moved down from Boston.
- Just beyond 12 miles, watch out for the railroad tracks that cross the trail.
- At 12.5 miles is the Baldwin Senior Center with its parking lot, pine grove picnic area, and a huge oak tree encircled by a wooden bench. Here is where the Jacksonville-Baldwin Visitors Center is planned, with water and rest rooms.
- Across from the senior center is a hazardous-waste site that was once the leading employer in Baldwin—a plant that produced creosote, a liquid used to coat telephone poles and railroad ties to prevent them from rotting. The plant closed in the early 1990s under orders from the federal Environmental Protection Agency, which is now in the thirty-year process of removing all the buildings and cleaning up the site.
- At 13 miles, that's the Mammie Agnes Elementary School on the left.
- The Jacksonville-Baldwin Rail Trail ends at 14.5 miles with a parking lot at Brandy Branch Road. There are trash cans, but no facilities.

There are paved bike paths in Florida that are more isolated than the Jacksonville-Baldwin Rail Trail, but none that provide as pleasant and tranquil a ride through the woods and pastureland of rural Florida. The shade along the way makes this a nice ride no matter what time of year, but especially enjoyable in the fall and winter when the leaves crackle and crunch beneath your wheels.

Something you should know: If North Florida's horse-and-buggy lobby gets its way, the Jacksonville-Baldwin Rail Trail will include alongside the asphalt path an equestrian trail wide enough for a horse and buggy, which would make Jax-Baldwin the first combination bike-and-buggy trail in the state. Buggies, usually built from kits, are popular in this part of Florida. There is even an organization of horse-and-buggy owners in Macclenny called The Whips.

Future plans also call for a connector trail from Pope Duval Park that will take cyclists under Interstate 10 to the abandoned Yellow Water Weapons Depot—a 2,200-acre slice of the navy's Cecil Field that is being redeveloped to include trails, ball fields, and an equestrian complex with "horse-and-buggy-friendly amenities." And another abandoned railroad corridor is being eyed for a spur trail that would take cyclists four miles north to Cary State Park.

Baldwin, the western terminus of the trail, began its existence in 1835 as a stagecoach stop called after a tavern owner named Thigpen. Tired of Thigpen jokes, residents changed the name to Baldwin in 1860 in honor of A. S. Baldwin, a former state legislator. Four years later, Union troops burned the city, which was used by the Confederates to store supplies and equipment, to the ground. Today Baldwin is a one-square-mile, no-traffic-lights town of 1,750 residents that proclaims itself Small But Proud. "We really consider ourselves a big family rather than a small town," says Baldwin mayor Marvin Godbold Jr., who has worked for the city for twenty-four years. A true train town sitting at the junction of railroad tracks heading in all four directions, Baldwin relies less on the railroad and farms for its existence these days than on retirees and Jacksonville commuters. The town is proud to maintain its autonomy with a police department and city council independent of the consolidated government of Jacksonville/Duval County. Residents recommend that cyclists looking for local color and home-style cooking try

Everybody's Restaurant, a family-owned institution in Baldwin for forty years.

For more information, call the Jacksonville Department of Parks and Recreation, (904) 630-3596; the Jacksonville/Duval Bike/Pedestrian Coordinator, (904) 630-1911; and Baldwin City Hall, (904) 266-4221.

Blackcreek Trail

The Trail-of-Bridges Ride

Length: 8 miles.
Location: Orange Park. From Interstate 295, take exit 3. Go south on U.S. 17 for ten miles. Trailhead entrance is on the right just before the Blackcreek bridge.
Amenities: parking, water, rest rooms, picnic facilities, convenience stores, ATMs, restaurants, wheelchair access.
Surface: 10-foot-wide asphalt with mile markers on the pavement.

Five miles from the trailhead, the bike path crosses the defining feature of the Blackcreek Trail—a wooden bridge nearly one mile long. The boards of the straight, flat bridge rattle and the wood railings click by as you ride over a wetland area spared from the advancing subdivisions. In the center of the bridge, protruding toward the road, is a deck where cyclists can ponder the traffic on Highway 17, or the trees and birds and palmettos of the untamed wetland.

At the northern end is another bridge. This one rises high over Doctors Lake, separated from the rush of traffic by a two-foot-high concrete barrier. Here the view is of the wide blue lake below and the docks of the waterfront homes poking out from the shoreline like paddle wheels.

There are two other wooden boardwalk bridges on the eight-mile trail that give cyclists a peekaboo ride through woods and past upscale subdivisions, always alongside the highway. Along the way, the path dips into the shade and returns to the sun while weaving in and out of wetlands and woods.

On the south end of the path, the Blackcreek Trailhead was dedicated in April 1999. It has paved parking, rest rooms, water, picnic tables, grills, and bike racks.

Starting from the southern trailhead, here's what to look for on the Blackcreek Trail:

- The first half mile of the ride, where the trail is totally immersed in trees and shade, is one of the prettiest stretches of paved bike path anywhere.

Blackcreek Trail

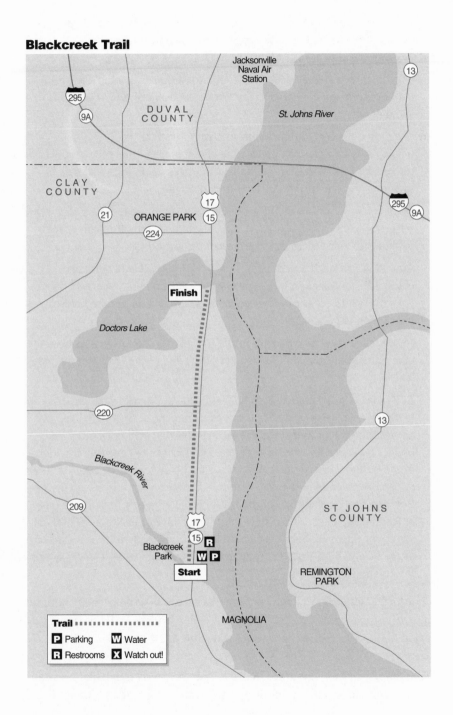

It's a cool tunnel of green and dark green through a hardwood hammock before the path hitches to the right and undiluted sunlight.

- Shortly after the trail passes the traditional white frame Fleming Island Baptist Church at the 1-mile mark, look for a nursery on the left with a park bench beneath a large shade tree—an unofficial rest stop on a hot summer day.

- The path emerges from a dip into the woods before the 3-mile mark, passing a Tyson "feeding you like family" hatchery where they grow future drumsticks. Then it ducks behind the trees again for a half mile before reaching one of the shorter wooden bridges.

- Nearing the 4-mile mark, the path reaches County Road 220, a major intersection with crosswalks. After the busy intersection, the path retreats behind the trees before crossing a second short bridge.

- Around 4.5 miles, the path passes Eagle Harbor Parkway before it reaches the entrance to the Eagle Harbor development, where it changes from asphalt to concrete. The asphalt picks up again after the landscaped subdivision entrance.

- At 5.5 miles, the trail dips back into a tunnel of trees before it reaches the long bridge that runs for .7 mile along the edge of the road and the wetlands.

- At 7 miles, the last stretch before Doctors Lake, the bike path passes next to a convenience store with rest rooms, water, air, and an ATM. The trail narrows to six feet as it starts the ascent over the arching Doctors Lake bridge. It widens to about eight feet as it reaches the concrete shoulder of the bridge and is separated from the traffic by the cement barrier. The bridge rises high over the water, above the trees and rooftops, a change from the sea-level altitude of the rest of the Blackcreek Trail. In this part of Florida, like much of the state, high-rise bridges substitute for hills. Enjoy the perspective, but take care on the downhill slide to the conclusion of the bike path at Holly Point Road West. The road leads left into a tree-shrouded neighborhood.

Running alongside a highway, the Blackcreek bike path could be little more than a glorified sidewalk, but the wooden bridges and dips into hardwood hammocks make this a scenic and enjoyable ride.

Something you should know: Orange Park looks pretty much like any other Jacksonville suburb today, but in the 1880s it was one of a string of resort

Fig. 2. Wooden bridge
on Blackcreek Trail

towns attracting wealthy tourists with soothing spring waters. Northerners arrived by the boatload via the St. Johns River to stay in majestic old hotels at Orange Park and Green Cove Springs—which at one time had twelve hotels. The sulfur springs were believed to be the youth-restoring waters sought by Ponce de Leon. The hotels closed or were converted into boarding houses when Henry Flagler's railroad bypassed Clay County on its way to Key West.

The bike path crosses an area that was once all orange groves—from which the town took its name in 1876—potato fields, flower-bulb farms, and plantations. At Hibernia the path passes one of the small "river churches" that once were strung along the St. Johns River like pearls on a necklace.

For more information, call the Clay County Recreation Department, (904) 284-6378.

Gainesville-Hawthorne State Trail

The Meadows, Woods, River, and Lake Ride

Length: 16 miles.
Location: Gainesville. From University Avenue (State Road 26) heading east, turn right on SE 15th Street for about one mile. The trailhead at Boulware Spring City Park is on the right.
Amenities: parking, water, rest rooms, picnic tables, maps, equestrian trail, wheelchair access.
Surface: 10-foot-wide asphalt with mile marker posts on the side of the trail.

Five miles down the Gainesville-Hawthorne State Trail, the bike path crosses one of the most scenic junctions of any trail in the state. Prairie Creek, passing beneath a wooden trail bridge, is a favorite for canoeists who glide along the river's tea-colored water beneath a canopy of oaks and cypress trees. It's a dark, cool, tranquil spot where recreation and nature intersect.

Few paved bike paths in Florida pack such variety of landscape, vistas, and topography in such a short distance as the Gainesville-Hawthorne trail. The asphalt strip curves and dips through woods, farmland, fields, and lakeshore as it skirts the Paynes Prairie State Preserve and the Lochloosa Wildlife Management Area.

Opened in 1992, the trail links Gainesville, home to the University of Florida, with Hawthorne, a small farming town dating back to 1850. The western terminus is located at Boulware Spring City Park, where Gainesville was born during a gathering in 1854. The park retains the majestic, gnarled, Spanish-moss-draped oak trees under which the town's organizers first picnicked. Parking, picnic tables, water, maps, and a portable toilet are available at the park.

One word of advice: Cyclists should not leave valuables in their cars at the Boulware trailhead. Lock valuables in the car trunk before you leave—good advice no matter where you're riding.

Heading west from the Boulware trailhead, here's what to look for on the Gainesville-Hawthorne State Trail:

Gainesville-Hawthorne State Trail

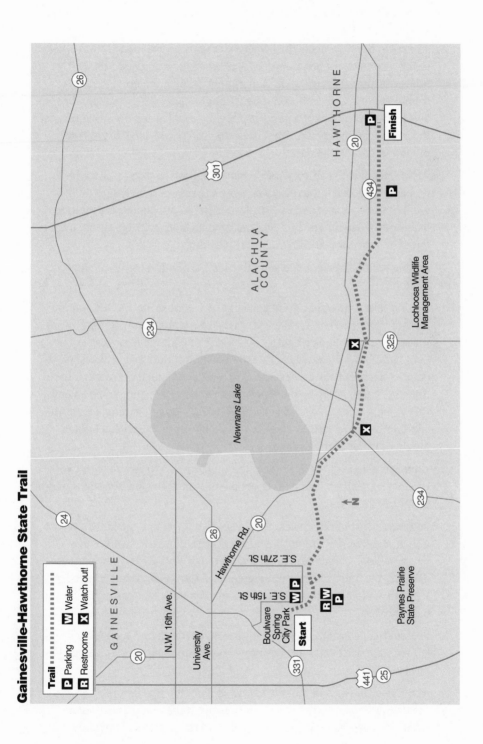

- At 1 mile, the trail meets the Sweetwater Branch Overlook, a short diversion that provides a panoramic view of wetlands being restored with funds collected by the Florida Department of Environmental Protection from polluters. Such a short distance from the Boulware trailhead, the Sweetwater Overlook is a popular place for couples and cyclists watching the sun set on the prairie. From here, you can witness the day end without riding back in the dark.

- At 1.5 miles is the La Chua Trail, which includes a walking trail to the remnants of a ranch that operated from the turn of the century until it was bought by the state in 1970. A small stone bunkhouse is all that remains of the ranch. The La Chua trailhead includes parking, water, picnic tables, a rest room, and an interpretive center.

- For the next half mile, the bike path curves around the Small Sinkhole Outlook.

- Around mile 2, the peaceful Alachua Lake Outlook offers a tree-framed view of light sparkling off the water while birds chirp and, around sunset, the low, guttural honk of gators is heard. The wide, shallow lake at one time served as a waterway for steamboats transporting agricultural products from a port near Gainesville. Commerce continued on Alachua Lake from 1871 until a sinkhole opened overnight in 1891 and drained away the water, leaving ships suddenly dry-docked. Today the remnants of that lake comprise the 15,000-acre Paynes Prairie State Preserve, a jigsaw puzzle of water and grassland.

- After the Alachua Lake Overlook, the trail passes a large oak with two benches beneath it just begging people to stop and enjoy the shade and beauty of the setting.

- Between 2 miles and 3 miles, the trail passes through a meadow and into a shady hardwood hammock where it curves, dips, and swerves in a downhill slope. Wood fences protect trees from bicyclists getting carried away by the roller-coaster topography, and signs warn riders to Keep Right to avoid head-on encounters with rollerbladers, joggers, hikers, and baby strollers.

- Beyond the 4-mile mark, watch for the Red Wolf Pond Overlook on the left where a deck with benches provides a panoramic view of a small tree-lined lake.

- At 5 miles, daisies and other wildflowers flank the trail before it reaches the Prairie Creek Bridge, one of those scenic Kodak moments. Watch, within the next half mile, for one of the whistle posts left behind by the railroad. The vertical concrete markers were painted white with black horizontal stripes instructing the engineer on the appropriate horn blasts: thick stripe for a long blast, thin stripe for a short toot.

- Around 6 miles, watch for traffic when the bike path crosses County Road 234, which leads to the antiques-laden town of Micanopy. On the right is Rochelle, a tiny settlement that dates back to one of Alachua County's first plantations.

- Shortly before 7 miles, there's a portable toilet on the right side of the trail. Beyond the rest stop, the trail passes a simple white Baptist church before entering the Lochloosa Wildlife Management Area where, during hunting season, cyclists may encounter hunters and hounds.

- Around 9 miles, the trail crosses County Road 325, which leads to Cross Creek, former home of Marjorie Kinnan Rawlings. Watch for traffic at that intersection.

- Near the 12-mile mark, the path crosses Little Lochloosa Creek before reaching the SE 152nd Street intersection. Grove Park, a town of about 150 residents and one convenience store, is to the left on SE 152nd Street.

- As the trail passes through a wooded section beyond 152nd Street, watch on the left for a ramshackle backyard bicycle repair shop. Advertising "reconditioned" bikes, the backyard is filled with used and rejuvenated bikes. A girl's pink bicycle hangs from the limb of an oak.

- After crossing the long wooden Lochloosa Creek Bridge, the trail enters a corridor of trees. Watch out for a sandy road crossing about a mile east of the bridge.

- The Lochloosa Trailhead at 15 miles offers paved parking, bike racks, benches, and information kiosk. There is neither water nor rest rooms at the trailhead.

- The last mile of the trail is a straight shot through the edge of the Lochloosa Wildlife Management Area with its towering pines to the town of Hawthorne. About a half mile from the trailhead, the path crosses Dry Creek before reaching Hawthorne Junior and Senior High School, home to the fighting Hornets.

The Hawthorne Trailhead, accessible from U.S. 301 via Johnson Street and SE 2nd Avenue, has parking, an information kiosk with trail maps, and a historical marker, but no water or rest rooms at this time.

The Gainesville-Hawthorne State Trail allows cyclists to retrace a tranquil rural route forged by locomotives long ago, and which has remained largely unchanged over the years. It's a path that invites contemplation of vistas, sunsets, and lakes that disappear overnight.

Something you should know: Plans are under way for a 1.5-mile "downtown connector" paved bike path that will connect the Gainesville-Hawthorne State Trail with Gainesville's 4.5-mile-long Depot Avenue/Waldo Road Greenway trail. Construction is scheduled to begin in 2001.

The narrow rail bed now occupied by the bike path was once a three-foot-wide railroad extending from Palatka to Gainesville. Its locomotives often crashed with intersecting trains on what is now the CSX railroad at Waits Crossing, where there were no crossing signals. The narrow-gauge railroad tracks were removed in the 1980s, but the CSX tracks still carry trains rumbling through Hawthorne.

Hawthorne was created by the merger of two adjacent settlements in 1880. The combined town was named Hawthorn after James M. Hawthorn, a local landowner. So many people misspelled the town's name, adding a final *e*, that the town conceded to illiteracy and changed the name to Hawthorne with an *e* in 1950.

Hawthorne was home to the first phosphate mill in Florida, opened in 1879 by Dr. C. A. Simmons, who is credited with first identifying the existence of phosphate in the state. The mining of phosphate helped bring in the railroads that linked Hawthorne to Gainesville, then Gainesville to Ocala and Palatka in the 1880s. The trains transported the area's main agricultural commodities of sea island cotton and turpentine.

Today Hawthorne is a town of 1,400 residents where only a dozen people still make their living on the farms and in the forests. One of the major employers builds septic tanks.

For more information, call the Gainesville-Hawthorne State Trail, (352) 466-3397, and the Gainesville Bike/Pedestrian Coordinator, (352) 334-5074.

Depot Avenue/Waldo Road Greenway

The Bike Memorial Ride

Length: 4.5 miles.
Location: Gainesville. From Interstate 75, take exit 75. Go east on Archer Road six miles. The Depot Trail starts at the corner of Archer Road and Newell Drive.
Amenities: parking, convenience stores, restaurants, wheelchair access.
Surface: 8-foot-wide asphalt without mile markers.

One mile east on the Depot Trail, just beyond the decrepit remains of a train depot, six jagged pillars form a stark and somber memorial. The pillars are in a row pointing east, like a pace line of cyclists riding down the side of a road. Embedded in the columns are broken bicycle parts from a six-person pace line that was struck by a truck on December 26, 1996, while riding on a road in Clay County. Doug Hill, a bicycle mechanic, and Margaret Raynal, a state bicycle safety coordinator, were killed.

There are wheels with broken and twisted spokes, disjointed sprockets, cranks, red plastic reflectors, front forks, handlebars, sections of frames, and bits of broken asphalt pressed into a mixture of earth and cement. Dirt taken from the crash site and Gainesville and Raynal's home state of West Virginia was mixed together to make a primitive form of building material called rammed earth. The imprint of a sprocket on one pillar, the embedded bike chain on another, look like fossils from the present. On the red frame of a Trek is a sticker that says, Girls Kick Ass!

"They almost look like large grave markers," said Brad Guy, one of the memorial's organizers. "But at night, when car lights hit the reflectors, it sparkles."

The memorial's presence beside the Depot Trail is a silent testimony to the inherent risks of cycling in Florida. And a reminder that even paved bike paths are not risk-free. Stay alert, ride safely, take care crossing streets.

Gainesville is one of the most bike-friendly cities in Florida, with bike lanes included on many streets in and around the University of Florida. Cycling is a main means of transportation in this college town.

Depot Trail/Waldo Road

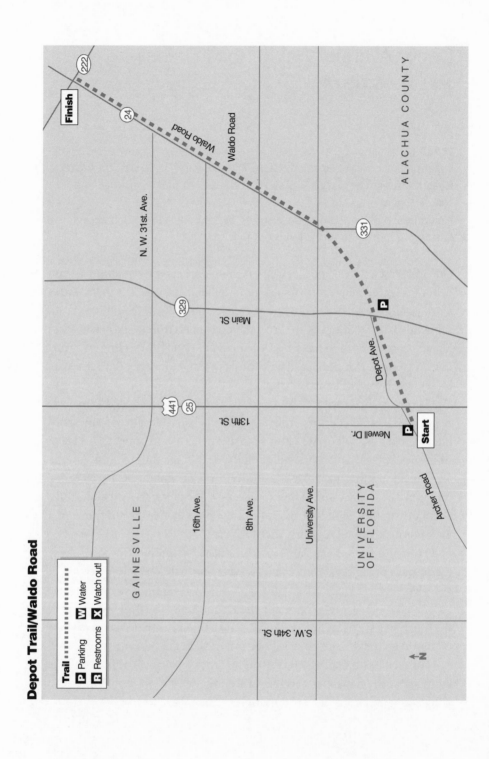

Fig. 3. Depot Trail bike memorial

The two-mile Depot Trail is like a crosstown expressway, linking the campus with the east side of town and the 2.5-mile Waldo Road bike path. The Depot path begins on the west side, across Newell Drive from the University Center Hotel and across Archer Road from the Shands Hospital parking garage. There is no dedicated trail parking, but you can use the hospital garage, side streets, and an unpaved lot at the train depot memorial.

Heading east, here's what to look for on the Depot Trail bike path:

- Within the first tenth of a mile, the Depot Trail leaves the campus when it crosses a bridge over SW 13th Street, one of the four streets that bound the university.

- Around .8 mile, watch out for gravel and sand on the path when it passes a recycling company.

- At 1 mile, the bike trail reaches South Main Street, a five-lane intersection. Be fast—the crosswalk light has a short timer. On the other side of the intersection, the Depot Trail passes the old train station and the silent memorial to the fallen cyclists. The 1907 depot, listed in the National Register of Historic Places, served the railroad that linked Fernandina Beach with Cedar Key. The passenger station had segregated waiting rooms for blacks and whites right up until it went out of service in the

1950s. Since then, the building has been used as an appliance ware-house, a hardware store, and the headquarters for a group advocating the legalization of marijuana.

- Beyond the depot, watch for cars when crossing SW 4th Street. The trail then weaves through a drab industrial district decorated in the spring with blooming dogwood trees that dress up the area like giant white bouquets.
- After crossing SW 7th Street, the path veers to the left and at 1.5 miles passes through an African-American neighborhood where gardens grow in many backyards.
- At 2 miles, the trail emerges from a canopy of trees at Williston Road and East University Avenue.

The Waldo Road Trail picks up beyond the Walgreens on the northeast corner of University Avenue and SE First Street, kitty-corner from where the Depot Trail ends. The Waldo Road Trail begins at University Avenue and runs parallel to Waldo Road until it reaches NE 39th Avenue. There are no parking lots at either end of the trail—the Walgreens serves as the unofficial trailhead.

Benches, flowers, and landscaping are sprinkled along the bike path, add-ing some relief for the eyes. If you get tired, pairs of facing benches are spaced about .2 mile apart. There are convenience stores and restaurants along the trail, but all are on the opposite side of Waldo Road.

Heading north, here's what to look for on the Waldo Road Trail:

- On the left look for the tanks and artillery that serve as front-lawn statu-ary for a VFW post.
- On the right, occupying the middle of the Waldo Trail, is the Department of Children and Families Tacachale community, a facility for people with developmental disabilities. Opened in 1921 as the Florida Farm Colony for the Epileptic and Feeble Minded, the institution was the dumping ground for anyone with a birth defect or disability. In the 1970s, when the facility was one of the state's Sunland Centers, the population reached 1,500 residents. The complex was a self-contained community with its own power plant (notice the dual brick smokestacks), water facil-ity, and stores. Residents lived in army-style barracks. With the deinstitu-tionalizing of the state's mental hospitals, the population shrank to 500. The name was changed in 1985 to Tacachale (toc-a-cholee), which means "lighting a fire" in Timucuan. The barracks were converted into

group homes with six to twelve bedrooms in each building. Most of the residents work within the facility making everything from artificial flowers to silk-screened T-shirts.

Together, the Depot Trail and the Waldo Road bike path provide a nine-mile round-trip poor man's tour of industrial and low-income neighborhoods of Gainesville. It's not the most scenic ride, but the remarkable memorial to the fallen cyclists makes it a memorable journey.

Something you should know: The memorial to dead cyclists might be the beginning of the rebirth of an area of Gainesville that has fallen on hard times. The soil around the depot is contaminated with industrial pollutants. The Sweetwater Branch creek that runs through the area carries street runoff to Paynes Prairie and into the aquifer that provides Gainesville with its drinking water.

The City of Gainesville has plans to change that by fixing up the old depot, removing the contaminated soil, and creating a thirty-eight-acre park around a fifteen-acre lake where the earth has been removed. The old depot, scheduled for renovation around 2004, will become a visitors center and trailhead for a park called Depot Junction. Construction on a 1.5-mile "downtown connector" bike path linking the Depot/Waldo path with the Gainesville-Hawthorne State Trail is scheduled to begin the same year. Gainesville also plans to acquire four miles of railroad right-of-way from 23rd Boulevard along Sixth Street to the abandoned train depot.

Adjacent to Depot Junction, the city plans to build a transportation center for crosstown buses, shuttle buses to the Amtrak station, and bike commuting facilities that would include lockers and showers. Completing the transformation would be an environmental center, a cafe, and small businesses.

For more information, call the City of Gainesville Bicycle/Pedestrian Coordinator, Planning Department, (352) 334-5074; the Gainesville Greenway Coordinator, (352) 334-2236; and Gainesville Parks and Recreation, (352) 334-5067.

Withlacoochee State Trail
The Small-Town Florida Ride

Length: 46 miles.
Location: Hernando, Citrus, Pasco Counties. From Interstate 75, take exit
61. Go east 2 miles on State Road 50. Trailhead entrance is on the left.
From Orlando, take State Road 50 west for fifty miles.
Amenities: parking, rest rooms, water, maps, bike shops, restaurants,
convenience stores, pay phones, equestrian trail.
Surface: 12-foot-wide asphalt with mile markers painted on the pavement
and on steel fence posts.

Over an embankment off the Withlacoochee State Trail, in a no-name cemetery scattered beneath tranquil pines, is the grave of Arthur Norton—a man
whose life parallels the railroad that laid the foundation for Florida's longest
rails-to-trails bike path.

Born on March 10, 1877, Norton was sixteen years old when the railroad
tracks extended into Floral City, bringing with them loads of prospectors
and phosphate miners who swelled the town to ten thousand people and
turned it into one of Florida's largest cities. By the time of Norton's death on
February 10, 1986, just one month short of his 109th birthday, the phosphate
boom was over and Floral City had shrunk back down to just another dot on
the map. Three years after Norton's death, the tracks disappeared with the
last train to leave Inverness.

The tracks have been replaced with a strip of asphalt that takes cyclists on
a tour of small-town rural Florida touching three Gulf Coast counties. With
few busy cross streets and plenty of rest stops, this is an excellent bike path
for young and novice cyclists. And with its length and long stretches of
empty asphalt, it is perfect for experienced cyclists who want to get out and
ride hard, head down, without fear of running into baby strollers.

Trailside benches and shelters are spaced regularly along the trail.

The best place to start on the Withlacoochee Trail is at the Ridge Manor
Trailhead off State Road 50. The trailhead has parking, rest rooms, water
fountain, and covered picnic area. Ridge Manor is five miles from the south-

Withlacoochee State Trail

LEVY CO.

Citrus Springs **W** **P** **R**

Finish

(200)

MARION CO.

X **W** **R**
Hernando

Withlacoochee River

SUMTER CO.

Trail ·······················
P Parking   **W** Water
R Restrooms   **X** Watch out!

(41)

X **W** Inverness
R **W**

(44)

(44)

(19)

(98)

(491)

Withlacoochee
State Forest

W Floral City
R **P**

N

CITRUS CO.

W **P**
R
Townsen Lake
Regional Park

(19)

(98)

I-75

Brooks-
ville

(50)

W **P**
R
(301)

Weeki
Watchee

(41)

Manor
Ridge
(50)

HERNANDO CO.

PASCO CO.

P

Start

ern end of the trail, which is a blunt dead end that stops short of U.S. Highway 301.

Head north from the trailhead for a 41-mile ride to the northern terminus in Citrus Springs. For extra distance, or a 10-mile ride, head south.

From the southern terminus, here's what to look for on the Withlacoochee State Trail:

- At 1 mile, the path crosses County Road 575. To the right is what remains of Trilby, a town named by the wife of railroad baron Henry Plant for a novel popular in the 1890s. A true storybook town, Trilby's original streets were named after characters in the book. In its heyday Trilby was the crossroads for three railroads and contained the third largest railroad yard in the state. The town included sawmills, grist mills, a bank, hotel, blacksmith shop, school, tuberculosis sanatorium, doctor's office, and Masonic lodge. A fire in 1925 wiped most of Trilby off the map and, with the passing of the railroads, the town never regained its prominence. About all that remains of the old railroad town is the white frame post office, the Masonic Hall, and the Little Brown Church of the South, built in 1897. The town's depot, rebuilt after the fire, has been moved to the Pioneer Museum Park in nearby Dade City. Although lacking its train depot, Trilby does have two convenience stores and a restaurant for hungry, thirsty cyclists.

- At 2 miles, the bike path leaves Pasco County as it passes through woods and pastureland sprinkled with black-and-white dairy cattle. The only thing disturbing the pastoral panorama is a huge Wal-Mart warehouse to the left.

- At 5 miles, the trail crosses a pale green bridge over State Road 50 to the Ridge Manor Trailhead.

- Around 5.5 miles, watch for a triangular cement post on the right. These posts, left over from the railroad, were mile markers—some still have their metal plates attached—that measured the distance from the railroad's headquarters in Richmond, Virginia. Also be on the lookout on the Withlacoochee Trail for whistle markers, those round-topped flat posts painted white with black stripes that instructed engineers to blow the train whistle—a thick stripe for a long toot, a thin stripe for a short one.

- Around 8 miles, just after the path crosses the two-lane Croom-Rital Road, the bike trail enters a section of the Withlacoochee State Forest. The 21,000-acre Withlacoochee State Forest—and the Croom Wildlife Management Area contained within the forest—offers camping, canoe-

Fig. 4. Whistle marker on With-lacoochee Trail

ing, hiking, horseback riding, off-road motorcycling, and mountain biking. During the winter months, when hunting is allowed in the management area, watch out for persons with rifles. For information on recreational facilities in the Croom Wildlife Management Area, contact the Withlacoochee Forestry Center in Brooksville, (352) 754-6896.

· At 9 miles, just before the bike path dips beneath Interstate 75, several of the Croom campgrounds are accessible to the Withlacoochee Trail via a dirt road on the right.

· At 10 miles, the trail crosses through the remains of Croom, another railroad town that downsized to tiny after the trains stopped running. Two reminders remain from Croom's railroad days: an old train bridge that is now the Iron Bridge Day Use Area, and a two-story white house on Croom-Rital Road where black track maintenance crews stayed. Known as gandy dancers, the crews sang rhythmic songs to the cadence of their track repair work.

• Around 10.5 miles is an abandoned railroad spur on the left that goes through Croom toward Brooksville. Efforts are under way to create a ten-mile bike path called the Good Neighbor Trail linking Brooksville with the Withlacoochee State Trail.

• Near the 11-mile mark is another covered shelter. These come in handy in the heat of summer and during the sudden thunderstorms that pop up along the trail.

• After 14 miles the trail leaves the state forest as it crosses Edgewater Avenue and reaches the small town of Nobleton. At the east end of Edgewater Avenue you will find a convenience store, canoe rentals, and a riverside park on the Withlacoochee River. The Canoe Outpost was built in 1925 as a hunting lodge and tourist inn by Harry Nobles, the town's founder.

• At 15.5 miles, the bike path passes Townsen Lake Regional Park on the left, hidden in the trees. The park has rest rooms, water, picnic shelters, playgrounds, bike racks, and a soda machine. It is also a trailhead for horses, with equestrian parking, water troughs, and hitching posts.

• At 16 miles, as the bike path crosses Magnon Drive, is the small community of Istachatta, with a cul-de-sac downtown of library, city hall, and community center. The town is believed to have been a stopping point for Spanish explorer Hernando de Soto in 1539; its name means "red man."

• Watch for Hampton's Edge Trailside Bikes on the left after the bike path crosses Peterson Camp Road and enters Citrus County. Nestled beneath a crown of shade trees, the bike shop rents, sells, and repairs bikes, specializing in recumbent bikes. The owner, who operates out of his house, also sells cold drinks and snacks. Unlike many bike shops, Hampton's Edge is usually open on weekends.

• At 17.5 miles, watch for one of two windowless brown blockhouses left standing on the bike trail from the steam locomotive days. The blockhouses were used to store railroad equipment to check the tracks for defects.

• At the 21-mile mark, the trail crosses Floral Park Drive. Floral Park, with rest rooms, water, a playground, and picnic tables, is to the left.

- Look to the right around 22.5 miles—almost midway on the Withlacoo-chee State Trail—for the cemetery where Arthur Norton is buried.

- At 23 miles, Floral City's nod to its railroad heritage is painted in a mural on the side of a store where the trail crosses East Orange Avenue. The painting portrays the town's old train depot. Where the depot once stood is a bike-path gazebo with benches, water fountain, bike rack, portable toilet, and parking lot. To the left, on U.S. Highway 41, there's a conve-nience store, gas station, pub, and antiques store. To the right is a conve-nience store, and a bar and grill in a beautiful stretch of ancient shade trees known as the Avenue of Oaks. The huge oaks have been around since the early 1800s when the town was founded. Originally a steam-boat town, Floral City switched to trains in the 1890s and ballooned to a city of substance at the peak of the phosphate-mining era.

- At 25 miles is the Wishing Stone Tavern, a watering hole that caters to cyclists with a canopy for shade from the sun or shelter from the rain, and a bike rack for those needing rest and refreshment.

- At 27 miles, Fort Cooper State Park is on the right. The 710-acre state park, which has swimming, hiking trails, canoe rentals, and RV and tent camping, is named for a Major Mark Anthony Cooper, who built a crude fort near Lake Holathlikaha in 1836 during the Second Seminole War. Cooper and 380 men withstood attacks by the Seminoles at the fort be-fore being rescued by General Winfield Scott. The entrance to the park is off Old Floral City Road, which loops around the park before rejoining the trail around 28 miles. Park admission is $2 per car. Contact Fort Coo-per State Park, (352) 726-0315, for more information.

- Just before the 28-mile mark, watch for parking, a picnic table, and an information sign on the left side of the trail. The sign describes the route taken through this part of Florida by Hernando de Soto in 1539.

- Around the 29-mile mark, the Withlacoochee State Trail crosses Eden Drive and reaches Inverness. The origins of Inverness go back to 1868, but the name, Gaelic for "at the foot of the ness," comes from a Scots-man who purchased the community in 1889. The town is wrapped around several lakes that reminded the Scot of Loch Ness, the location of Inverness, Scotland. Inverness expanded with the phosphate mining boom and became the county seat of Citrus County in 1891. The town's courthouse, built in 1912 and under renovation, is listed in the National Register of Historic Places.

- At 29.5 miles, the trail squeezes between Cooter Pond on the left and Big Lake Henderson on the right. Scenic Wallace Brooks Park, on the shore of Big Lake Henderson, has rest rooms, water, picnic tables, parking, and a fishing pier. From Wallace Brooks Park you can take a right on Dampier Street to reach downtown Inverness, anchored by its historic courthouse. There's a sidewalk along part of Dampier Street, but you will have to ride in the street to reach the restaurants, bars, cafes, gift shops, and antiques store. There is an ATM at the Bank of Inverness.

- At 30 miles, the trail passes the Inverness Depot, built in 1892, just before crossing North Apopka Avenue. On the other side of the street is the Withlacoochee State Trail office, a little brown building beside a parking lot. Trail information is available whenever a trail ranger is present.

- Next door to the trail office is Sun Coast Bicycles, which sells, rents, and repairs bikes and in-line skates. It also has maps, trail info, T-shirts, vending machines, picnic tables, and a rest room.

- Around 30.5 miles, watch out for traffic when the path intersects with Turner Camp Road.

- At 31 miles, the bike trail passes beneath the U.S. 41 overpass where paintings of boats and palm trees decorate the concrete supports.

- If fresh fruit is what you want on a bike ride, try the produce stand on the right at 34.5 miles.

- If it's ice cream you prefer, at 35 miles there's an ice cream shop, diner, and convenience store. You are now in the heart of Hernando, a quiet retirement community that in its younger days was a rough-and-tumble railroad and mining town. Named for the Spanish explorer, the town was founded by three Confederate veterans in 1881.

- Just beyond the 35-mile mark, watch out for cars and take care crossing busy Novell Bryant Highway.

- More produce stands and restaurants are on the right, strung along U.S. 41. Nobody needs to go hungry on the Withlacoochee State Trail.

- The landscape between 38 and 39 miles is so desolate, you'll find cactus.

- Passing a phosphate mining pit around 39 miles, the path angles eastward until rejoining U.S. 41 at the 40-mile mark at the former phosphate boomtown of Holder. Today a few small homes with backyard gardens and a couple of stores are all that remain. Holder, like other phosphate towns, lost much of its prosperity when World War I cut off the phosphate industry from its biggest customer, Germany. After the war, the industry relocated from Citrus County to Polk County where phosphate, a chemical used in fertilizer, was easier to mine.

- Just before the trail crosses Lecanto Highway at 40.5 miles, there's a deli on the right side of the bike path. A produce stand, restaurant, and convenience store are to the right on Lecanto Highway. Look for the second of the old brown railroad blockhouses on the right after the trail crosses Lecanto.

- At 41.5 miles, the bike path reaches Citrus Springs Boulevard and the Citrus Springs Trail Center with parking and a portable toilet. The next mile and a half takes cyclists past the empty streets of a subdivision that failed to materialize—a ghost town without houses.

- As the trail nears 43 miles, it enters Citrus Springs. After a tour of former phosphate boomtowns, Citrus Springs is the first community on the Withlacoochee State Trail with a suburban face. When the bike path crosses North Citrus Springs Boulevard around the 44-mile mark, you're in the middle of a middle-class subdivision. Watch out, though, for cars that speed down the boulevard as if it were a highway.

- After crossing Haitian Drive, the Withlacoochee State Trail ends at the Citrus Springs Trailhead, where there are rest rooms, water fountains, parking, and picnic benches.

The forty-six-mile rails-to-trails bike path is the closest thing to time travel, taking cyclists through a rural, small-town Florida that no longer exists in much of the state, and visiting the remnants of an era when fertilizer, not tourists, built the boomtowns.

Something you should know: Arthur Norton's life spanned the boomtown times of phosphate mining that changed Hernando, Pasco, Citrus, and Polk Counties forever. The discovery of phosphate in the 1800s had the same effect on Florida as the discovery of gold had on California. Towns like Floral City, Inverness, Hernando, and Holder sprang up overnight. At one time, Citrus County had thirty-four phosphate mines in operation, many of them lined up alongside the railroad tracks.

The counties traversed by the Withlacoochee State Trail that relied on phosphate, turpentine, logs, citrus, and cattle are now attracting retirees, campers, and ecotourists. In the past twenty years Hernando County, located roughly midway between Tampa and Orlando, has experienced a second population boom as a retirement destination.

The first stretch of the forty-six-mile bike path, an eleven-mile strip from State Road 50 to the Citrus County line, was opened in 1992. The path is paved with a mixture of asphalt and ten thousand pulverized tires from the Polk County landfill.

For more information, call the Withlacoochee State Trail office, (352) 394-2280, and the Rails to Trails of the Withlacoochee, (352) 726-2251.

General James A. Van Fleet State Trail in the Green Swamp

The Nature Lover's Ride

Length: 29 miles.
Location: Polk, Lake, Sumter Counties, with southern trailhead in Polk City. Take Interstate 4 to exit 21. Turn north on County Road 559. Turn left on County Road 33 into Polk City. Trailhead is on the right.
Amenities: parking, rest rooms, maps, water, shelters, benches, equestrian trail, wheelchair access. Restaurants, convenience stores, pay phones in Polk City.
Surface: 12-foot-wide asphalt marked in miles and kilometers on the pavement.

The gator is about six feet long. It floats, semisubmerged, amid the swamp scum that disguises it from all but the sharpest-eyed cyclist. Still and silent, the gator doesn't flinch or flee when bicyclists stop to stare. It just rests there as if posing for a postcard.

The General James A. Van Fleet State Trail in the Green Swamp is a ribbon of asphalt so long, straight, and flat that it's easy to miss the secrets and surprises nature has planted alongside. But no other rails-to-trails bike path in Florida offers such a panoramic view of nature as the Van Fleet. There is an abundance of wild life—otters, eagles, ospreys, blue herons, sandhill cranes, red-bellied woodpeckers, wild turkeys, hawks, vultures, bobcats, white-tailed deer, gopher tortoises, rattlesnakes, indigo snakes—and a total absence of towns and traffic.

The trail cuts through ancient stands of bald cypress, loblolly bay, longleaf pine, sweet gum, Southern red cedar, wax myrtle, morning glory, and nature's bouquet of wildflowers.

The Van Fleet Trail crosses through several habitats along the southern edge of the 460-square-mile Green Swamp. You will see swamp, marsh, wet and dry hardwood hammocks, pine flatwoods, blackwater streams, and river floodplains.

General James A. Van Fleet State Trail

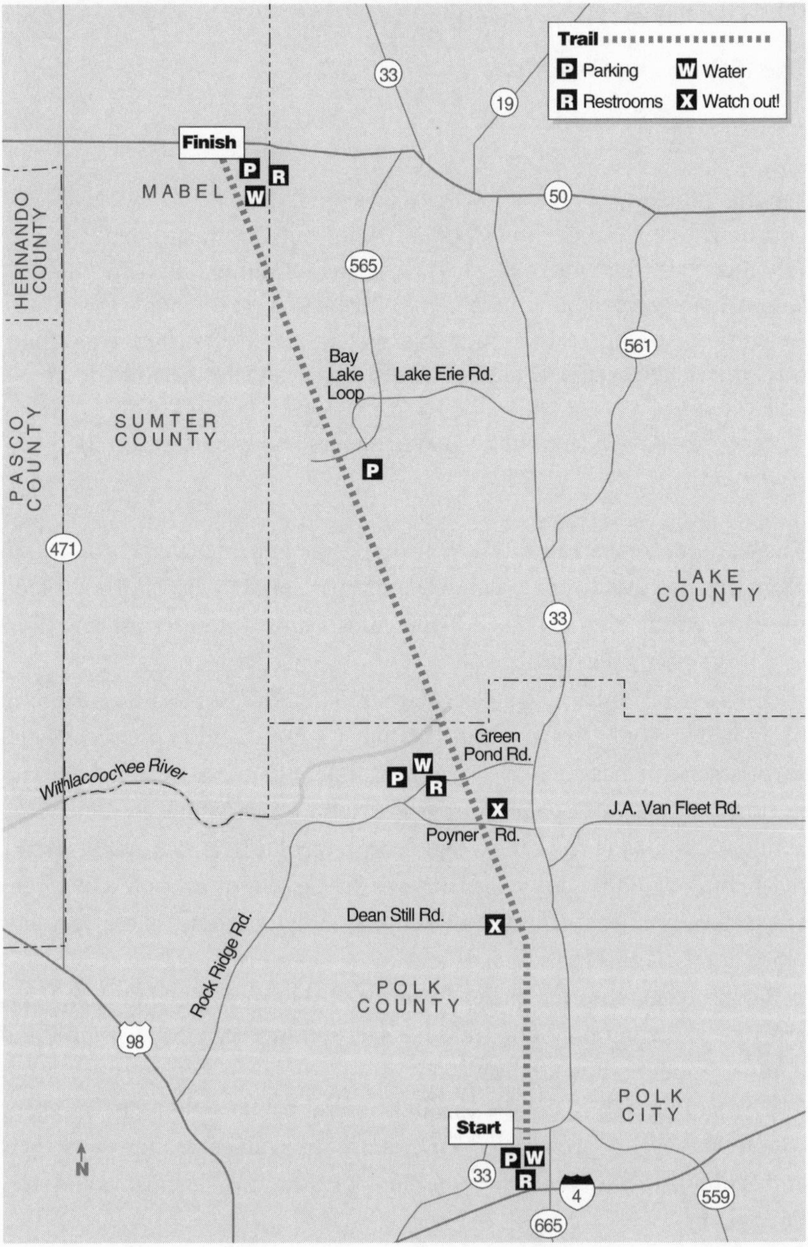

The length, linear layout, and isolation of the Van Fleet Trail make it a great trail for serious cyclists who like to get out and ride hard without getting blown off the road by gravel trucks.

Polk City, at the south end, offers small-town civilization and a solitary traffic light, but there is nothing between it and Mabel—a town in name only—on the north end. The Polk City terminus has an unpaved parking lot and a nearby park with picnic tables, a war memorial, and a playground. There is a building at the park with water and rest rooms, but it is not always open. The first trailhead with water and rest rooms is ten miles up the trail at Green Pond Road. Trail maps are available inside a black metal mailbox at both ends of the trail.

Much of the trail, especially in the afternoon, is unshaded. Be sure to pack the sunscreen. And, this being after all a swamp, cyclists should pack insect repellent. As the only water on the Van Fleet is at the Green Pond Road trailhead ten miles up and at the Mabel trailhead on the north end, bring along plenty of water and refill your bottles. Also remember to carry snacks, since there is nowhere to purchase food along the trail.

Heading north from the Polk City end, here's what to look for on the General James A. Van Fleet State Trail in the Green Swamp:

- Within a tenth of a mile is the first of a series of wooden benches. Constructed by volunteers, more than a dozen of these double-sided, covered benches along the trail provide shade no matter where the sun is in the sky. There are also four covered shelters with benches.
- The first five miles are the most heavily used section of the Van Fleet. It's where you are most likely to encounter walkers, joggers, and rollerbladers as the trail passes by farms and pastureland.
- Covered benches are located near 3.5 miles and 4.5 miles. At 5 miles, the asphalt curves westward in the only bend of the bike path, shaped like a broken arrow. Just as it curves, there is the first of four covered shelters that jut off the trail and into the trees.
- Nearing 5.5 miles, the path crosses Dean Still Road.
- The trail reaches a dense hammock just beyond the 7-mile mark and another trail shelter on the edge of the woods at 8.3 miles.
- After 8.5 miles, the trail intersects Poyner Road.
- At 10 miles, the path reaches the Green Pond Road trailhead with park-

ing, covered picnic tables, an information kiosk, and, a bit farther down the trail, rest rooms with a water fountain.

• Just beyond the third trail shelter, around 11 miles, the trail leaves Polk County and enters Lake County. The pastureland has also been left behind, replaced by a pinewood forest thick with palmettos.

• Less than a mile inside Lake County, the Van Fleet passes the first of three concrete bridges. When the season is wet and the water flows beneath the bridges, these are good spots to watch for wildlife. Covered benches are spaced between the second and third bridges, and right after the last bridge at 12.5 miles.

• After the bridges, the woods retreat from the trail. You are now in the middle of the 460-acre Green Swamp, which feeds the Peace, Hillsborough, Withlacoochee, Ocklawaha, and Kissimmee Rivers. Those five rivers span nearly the whole state from Jacksonville to Fort Lauderdale. With a high point of 130 feet, the Green Swamp also serves as a natural water tower for the Floridan Aquifer, which supplies 70 percent of Florida's groundwater.

• Beginning around 13.5 miles, a legion of tall bald cypress trees crowd both sides of the Van Fleet. In the summer months, the trees sprout fine light green needles, thirty feet above the ground. But in the winter months, when they shed their leaves, the gray, bare limbs of the bald cypress draped with shaggy Spanish moss look like the skeletal remains of a tattered army.

• There's another two-sided covered bench at 15 miles—the first in a series of four covered rest stops over the next four miles. Along this stretch enough pines commingle with the Green Swamp cypress to give the air a Pine Sol scent.

• At 19 miles, the Van Fleet meets Bay Lake Road where a trailhead is planned for the future. Right now all that exists is a grassy parking area, and a mailbox full of trail maps.

• Around 20.5 miles, watch for a family of river otters that sometimes frolic in the water beneath a series of bridges along a three-mile stretch of woods. A six-foot alligator lives around the wooden bridge at 23.5 miles. Gopher tortoises are sometimes found in a clearing beyond a covered bench at 24 miles. After passing another shade-covered bench at 25 miles, look to the left where the trees end and the land slopes away from the trail. In the mud and swamp water below is the home of an eight-foot gator.

Fig. 5. Van Fleet Trail, heading north

- Towering power lines cross above the trail at 25.5 miles. When the leaves are off the bushes and trees, herds of deer can sometimes be seen grazing on the green power-line right-of-way.
- For the last 3.5 miles, dark, dense woods follow the path to its conclusion at Mabel. Gators sometimes sun themselves in the swamp-water scum where the trees part at 26 miles.
- A good place for nature watching is the covered bench at 27 miles and again at 28 miles. Another opening in the trees at 28.5 miles is also a likely spot for gator gazing.
- The Mabel trailhead at 29 miles offers the welcome respite of shaded picnic tables, rest rooms, and water. There are also information kiosks, maps, paved parking, and a little cul-de-sac corral for the horses that use the Van Fleet's nineteen miles of equestrian trails.

Nature lovers who can differentiate bird warbles, identify plants, and bring a keen eye for spotting wildlife should love the Van Fleet. So should experienced cyclists who like to ride hard for long distances. But this is also a trail for children and novice cyclists who don't need to go a long way, yet don't want to contend with cars either.

The trail closes at sunset. As the day nears dusk, the sunlight reflects on the waters of the Green Swamp like a lighthouse beacon following the cyclist home. The fading light paints the sky with plumes of pink, orange, and purple cloud. From behind the foliage, the lonesome lowing of a cow announces the end of the day on the Van Fleet Trail.

Something you should know: Originally the Green Swamp Trail, the name was changed by the Florida Legislature in 1992 to honor General James Alward Van Fleet on his hundredth birthday. A Polk County war hero, West Point classmate of Dwight Eisenhower, and University of Florida football coach, Van Fleet led the Eighth Infantry on its D-day landing on Utah Beach and commanded the U.S. Eighth Army in Korea. He died six months after the trail was renamed.

Polk City remains a small Florida town without fast-food franchises or ATMs seventy-five years after its founding by Isaac Van Horn, an entrepreneurial dreamer from Boston who created the community in 1924 under the delusion that it sat atop a wealth of oil. Van Horn also planted orchards of tung trees, whose nut produced a varnish being imported from China at the time.

The town prospered, with a golf course, train depot, airport, busy sawmill making crossties for the railroad, and 600 residents. Soon after realizing there is no oil beneath Florida's sandy soil, Van Horn learned that the state's climate is not conducive to South American tung trees—the nuts of which are poisonous. On top of the dry oil wells and poisonous nuts came the Depression. Van Horn joined the exodus of people from his dream-town-gone-bad in 1931. Polk City shrank to 200, but rebounded in the 1990s to 1,700 residents when it became a bedroom community for commuters to Tampa and Orlando.

In the mid-1990s another dreamer, Kermit Weeks, came to Polk City and opened the Fantasy of Flight aviation museum just off Interstate 4 at exit 21. Weeks, a millionaire aerobatics champion, brought to Polk City visions of a tourist attraction as popular as Universal Studios stuck midway between Tampa and Orlando. The museum includes more than twenty vintage aircraft, flight-simulation rides, and a tethered hot-air balloon ride. Open daily 9 A.M.–5 P.M. Admission is $21.95 for adults, $19.95 for senior citizens, and $10.95 for children. Phone: (941) 984-3500.

For more information, call the General James A. Van Fleet State Trail in the Green Swamp, (352) 394-2280.

Lake Minneola Scenic Trail

The Ed Harvey Memorial Ride

Length: 3.5 miles.
Location: Lake County. Take Highway 50 to Clermont, north on 8th Street to western trailhead.
Amenities: parking, water, rest rooms, playground, beach, bar/restaurant, pay phones, bike shop, wheelchair access.
Surface: 14-foot-wide asphalt without mile markers.

A half mile from the eastern end of the Lake Minneola Trail is a shelter for cyclists and a reminder of the hazards of bicycling on Florida highways. The shelter sits in the middle of a flat stretch of woods on the edge of a ridge that descends to a playground and parking lot. With its thick timbers, brick foundation, green tin roof, and cupola, it looks like something that belongs in the mountains—a chalet without walls, an unfinished cabin.

The existence of the shelter and, to a large extent, the bike path itself is owed to the man memorialized on a bronze plaque mounted on a pillar of brick. Ed Harvey Jr., a thirty-three-year-old cycling enthusiast who rode the hills of south Lake County, was struck and killed by a car not far from his home in 1993. Harvey's death spurred the development of paved bike paths that offer a safe alternative for cyclists.

"This shelter was designed to provide a safe haven for all bicyclists and others who pass this way along the South Lake County Trail and to encourage the continued development of safe recreational trails for the enjoyment of all," says the plaque on the shelter dedicated on March 26, 1994.

The 3.5-mile bike path that immortalizes the spirit of Ed Harvey is one of the shortest but most scenic paved bike paths in Florida. The path is anchored on the western end by Clermont's lakeshore park on the edge of Lake Minneola. The park has a beach with volleyball courts, playgrounds, train-depot-style rest rooms, showers, pay phones, picnic facilities, a basketball court, benches facing the water, a boat ramp, and plenty of parking. Signs solicit $2 parking donations.

Lake Minneola Scenic Trail

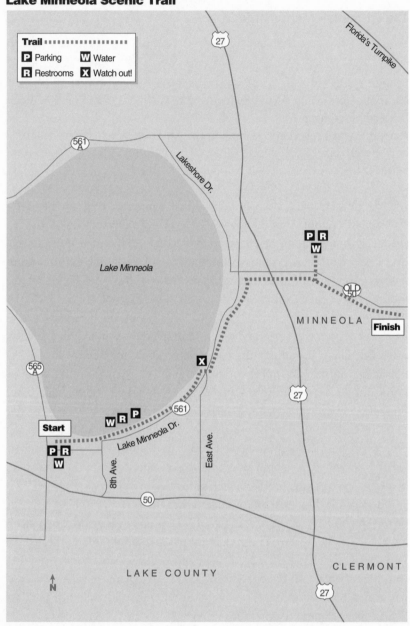

The western end of the trail actually begins one mile from the park at 12th Street and Minneola Avenue, where there is another depot-style rest room facility, a bike rack, and unpaved parking.

Starting from the west end, here's what to look for on the Lake Minneola Scenic Trail:

- At .5 mile, the path goes by an old train depot, caboose, and passenger car that have been converted into a funky restaurant called Hobo's Barbecue. The restaurant, decorated with antiques, serves ice cream, barbecue, and beer—something for everyone.

- After 8th Street, the fourteen-foot-wide asphalt bike path narrows to eight-foot-wide concrete as it passes through an industrial area. Beyond the warehouses, the path jogs to the left and enters the lakefront park.

- The path along the lakeshore is about one mile long, passing the playground, rest rooms and showers, gazebolike covered picnic facility, and volleyball nets stretched across the beach.

- At 1.2 miles, be careful when the path crosses busy East Avenue. There's a stop sign for cyclists on the path, and for good reason—cars come roaring around the road that curves along the lake.

- On the other side of East Avenue, the path parallels Lake Minneola Drive along the lakeshore. South Lake Bicycles is one block to the north of the bike path at 121 West Washington Street. The shop sells, repairs, and rents bicycles.

- At 2 miles, the path passes under the overpass of U.S. Highway 27 and into the straight section of woods leading to the Ed Harvey Station. There are lampposts along this stretch of the path—a rarity on Florida bike paths. Just before reaching the Harvey safe haven, there is a wooden deck on the left overlooking the woods. Immediately after the rest stop, a .3-mile side path curves and descends on the left to another depot-style rest room at the bottom, along with playground equipment shaped like a train.

- Beyond the Harvey shelter, cyclists emerge from the trees with an elevated view of the woods stretching to the shores of Plum Lake before the path curves downhill and ends abruptly at Mohawk Road.

Although short, the Lake Minneola Scenic Trail offers lakeshore scenery, a shady stretch through the trees, a safe-haven sanctuary on one end, and a place that serves beer on the other. What more can you ask for in a bike path—except more of it.

Something you should know: The Lake Minneola Scenic Trail is often referred to as the South Lake County Trail—the name etched in the stone memorial to Ed Harvey. By either name, the trail is the first phase of a 21-mile paved bike path that will eventually link with the West Orange Trail to the east and the General James A. Van Fleet State Trail in the Green Swamp to the west. The next phase is a five-mile connector to the West Orange Trail. When completed, the Lake Minneola Scenic Trail will connect the cities of Minneola, Clermont, Groveland, and Mascotte.

South Lake County, much like west Orange County, is undergoing a transition from agriculture to subdivisions. The gentle hills around Clermont that once flowed with neat rows of deep green orange trees are being stripped down to Tang-colored sand and replanted with neat rows of pastel-painted houses. The town's two-hundred-foot Citrus Tower, a tourist attraction built in 1956 to capitalize on the beauty of the countryside dotted with orange and grapefruit trees, now provides visitors with a bird's-eye view of rooftops. Devastating killer freezes in the 1980s wiped the citrus trees from the hillsides, replacing them with pine tree farms and subdivisions.

Clermont began its existence in 1884 as a "model town" with large lots spread around fifteen lakes. Named after Clermont-Ferrand, France (birthplace of the development company's general manager), the town promised new residents "all the advantages which the name implies . . . a location which is absolutely free of malaria . . ."

The Lake Minneola Trail follows the tracks of the narrow-gauge Orange Belt Railroad that was extended in 1887 from Oakland to Minneola, Clermont, and the town of Trilby, now on the Withlacoochee State Trail. When completed, the railroad extended from Sanford to St. Petersburg, but was plagued with problems from the start—including going broke in 1889, freezes that wiped out agriculture in 1894–95, and the end of passenger service because the railroad couldn't afford to keep paying farmers for all the cows that were killed on its tracks.

For more information, call the Lake County Public Works Department at (352) 253-4900.

West Orange Trail

The Former Farm Towns Ride

Length: 18 miles.
Location: Orange County. From Orlando, take State Road 50 west. Turn
right on County Road 438 at Deer Island Road. Turn left at the entrance to
the County Line Station Trailhead, the western terminus.
Amenities: parking, water, rest rooms, maps, convenience stores, restaurants, bike shops, ATMs, picnic facilities, shelters, playgrounds, equestrian
trail.
Surface: 15-foot-wide asphalt with miles marked on posts.

Three miles east of the County Line Station is a landmark unique to the West
Orange Trail. A short stretch of railroad track, retained from the days when
trains hauling oranges and other crops rolled through the small farm towns
of Oakland and Winter Garden and Ocoee, is punctuated by five towering
oak trees that have grown up between the rails and ties of that railroad remnant. The trees between the crossties symbolize the passing of the old days,
which cyclists can see for themselves as they pedal from one end of the eighteen-mile paved bike trail to the other. Time, weather, and population
growth have changed west Orange County from farms and groves to subdivisions and golf courses.

One of the most popular paved shared-use recreational trails in Central
Florida, the West Orange Trail starts on the west where Orange and Lake
Counties meet. County Line Station offers parking, rest rooms, water, an air
pump, playground, covered picnic pavilion, and the West Orange Trail Bikes
and Blades shop that rents and repairs bicycles and rollerblades.

Starting from the west end, here's what to look for on the West Orange
Trail:

- Within the first mile, the West Orange Trail crosses two roads and a
bridge that spans Florida's Turnpike, and passes close enough to the Deer
Island Nursery that cyclists are sometimes sprinkled by the fine spray
used to water the plants.

- As the trail approaches the tiny town of Oakland, it passes remains of the
groves that gave Orange County its name. Around 1.6 miles, look to the

West Orange Trail

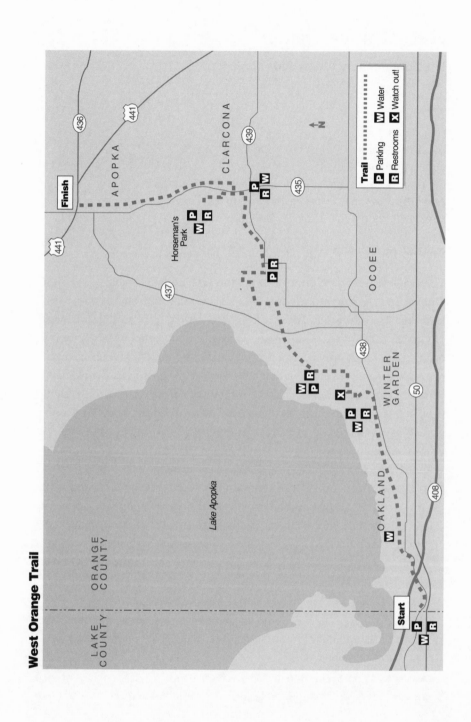

left for an old rusty-topped wooden water tower—vines crawling up its legs and sky showing through missing boards—that pokes above the trees near a cluster of farm labor houses. On the right, look for the house with a yard full of whirligigs made of discarded fan blades.

- At 2 miles, the path enters Oakland with its small frame houses and circular brick rest stop with benches and water fountain; soft-drink vending machines are available about .1 mile down the trail. Oakland is known for its large old oaks with Spanish moss dripping from the limbs. Dating back to 1844, the town was started by a group of wealthy men from South Carolina who brought along their slaves to clear the land for cotton, corn, and sugarcane. By 1860 Oakland was home to grist mills, cotton gins, sugar mills, and lumber mills. The town incorporated in 1887 and became the headquarters of the Orange Belt Railroad after local pioneer and power broker James G. Speer offered the railroad 180 acres of free land if the tracks came through Oakland.

- Although Oakland is a small town of 750 people, the trail crosses several streets as it goes through town. Cyclists should be alert for cars and some loose sand where the trail crosses dirt roads and driveways.

- As the bike path exits Oakland, look to the right just beyond the 2-mile mark for one of those long, thin cement posts left behind by the railroad. The triangular mile markers were used as reference points for track repairs and usually marked the number of miles from the railroad's headquarters.

- At 2.7 miles, the trail passes a little rest stop with a portable toilet and a covered bench. To the left, beyond the dirt road and fields, you can catch a glimpse of Lake Apopka, the fourth largest lake in Florida.

- As the trail passes the 3-mile mark, there's a little deck with a ramp to the left. It's just .2 mile from the trees-inside-the-railroad-tracks oddity, which offers benches on each side of the trail. To the right of the tracks is a sign of the new economy of west Orange County—the Meadow Marsh bed-and-breakfast. And just beyond that is the Xeriscape experimental water-conservation and butterfly garden using flowers and landscaping plants that require little watering. The garden, with green plastic-coated wire-mesh benches, is a cooperative effort between the Orange County's Water Department and Parks and Recreation.

- Up ahead is a survivor of the old days—a gray, tin-sided citrus plant. After the bike path crosses Tildenville School Road at the citrus plant, the trail winds through a tree-lined stretch that takes cyclists past Lakeview

Middle School (built in 1927 as a high school), a fenced-off orange grove preserved like a museum for citrus, and a shed decorated by a Florida State University fan with the Seminole mascot painted on the tin roof and Gator effigies below.

- At 4 miles, the path enters the industrial outskirts of Winter Garden. Here the path parallels the railroad tracks that still bisect the town. Watch out when the path crosses the railroad tracks before Central Avenue on the west side of downtown and at the Winter Garden Station on the east side. Also use caution when crossing Park Avenue and Dillard Street, two busy roads in a town whose economy has been boosted by more than forty thousand trail users a month. Hardware and feed stores have been replaced by antique shops and sidewalk restaurants.

- The West Orange Bike Shop on Plant Street, across from the Winter Garden Heritage Museum, sells, repairs, and rents bikes. Also on Plant Street, there's an ATM available at the First Union Bank on South Boyd Street.

- The Winter Garden Heritage Museum, housed in an old Atlantic Coast Line depot, is open 1–5 P.M., Tuesday through Sunday. Admission is free, but donations are appreciated. Phone: (407) 656-5544. The depot was built in 1918, back when there were two passenger waiting lobbies—one for blacks, one for whites. Today the museum contains artifacts from Winter Garden's agricultural past, including a collection of citrus crate labels. Exhibits in the museum tell the story of Winter Garden: its incorporation in 1903, its rebirth in 1910 after being destroyed by fire, its boom and bust in the 1920s, and its glory years as a packing and shipping center for oranges, grapefruit, tomatoes, cucumbers, carrots, lettuce, sweet corn, celery, even bananas.

- A second train depot, containing an extensive railroad museum, is located one block to the west on South Boyd Street. The National Railway Historical Society Museum, owned by the Central Florida chapter, is open 2–5 P.M. on Sunday and by appointment. Phone: (407) 277-5719. The depot, built in 1913, belonged to the Tavares and Gulf Railroad. The thirty-eight-mile-long T&G was derisively called the Turtle and Gopher, Tug and Grunt, and Try and Go in its day.

- At 5 miles, the Winter Garden Station is a shady oasis on the trail with parking, rest rooms, drinking fountains, vending machines, a playground, pay phones, and the trail office with a supply of maps.

- Leaving the Winter Garden rest stop, the path weaves up a slight incline and over a boardwalk before rewarding riders with a downhill coast

Fig. 6. Tree canopy on West Orange Trail

around 6 miles. But be careful, because the bottom of the hill intersects with Davidson Street and then takes a steep right-hand turn. Watch out at this corner not only for cars but also for runaway in-line skaters headed downhill.

· Watch for cars crossing Hinnis Road around 6.5 miles. The trail continues through more of West Orange in transition landscape before reaching Chapin Station with its rest rooms, water (including a drinking fountain for horses), parking, and a really spiffy playground. The park also has tennis and basketball courts nestled amid a grove of oaks.

· At 8.5 miles, the trail reaches Ocoee-Apopka Road. Stop and hit the crosswalk button. Equestrians have a second crosswalk button positioned at horse height.

· Around 9 miles, the bike path passes under an entrance ramp for the Central Florida Greenway, whose toll booths loom over the horizon like monoliths.

· Near 10 miles, the West Orange Trail reaches the Forest Lake Country Club. For the next two miles, the trail bends itself around the periphery of the golf course. Towering cyclone fences protect cyclists from bad shots and channel golf balls back onto the course.

- At 10 miles, the bike path passes under the twin spans of the Greenway tollroad, which in the summer offers an oasis of shade for cyclists.

- Around 10.5 miles, look to the right for the headless statue—patron saint of cyclists without helmets—as the West Orange Trail passes a memorial park.

- At 11.5 miles, the trail passes a horse stable with red barn, bare dirt corrals, and a sign that begs bikers not to feed the horses.

- At 12 miles, there's a parking lot and a portable toilet at the Ingram Outpost, a rest-stop-in-progress. Watch for loose sand where the trail crosses Ingram Road.

- The next half mile is one of the most beautiful sections of paved bike path in the state. Trees arching over the path form a scenic tunnel of shade. Its only rival on the trail is another couple of miles down the West Orange Trail, after the trail crosses busy Clarcona Road.

- At 14 miles, the path reaches the Apopka-Vineland Outpost, a rest stop with parking, water fountains, a sheltered picnic area, and a portable toilet a little bit farther down the trail. The rest stop is right behind the Baoan Buddhist Center, a sign of Orange County's changing population. The Buddhist temple is just across the street from the Clarcona Community Center, a gathering place for residents of the rural community quickly becoming suburbanized.

- From the rest stop, the trail runs uphill alongside unscenic Clarcona Road. Where the trail crosses Clarcona Road—with another set of cyclist and equestrian crosswalk buttons—cyclists can either turn right toward Apopka or continue straight for another .7 mile to Clarcona Horseman's Park. Horseman's Park includes parking, stables, an equestrian ring, rest rooms, water, pay phones, a playground, a soda machine, and picnic facilities nestled beneath a canopy of shade trees. On the way to Horseman's Park, take care crossing McCormick Road, which does not have a crosswalk light.

- Where the trail crosses Clarcona Road and heads toward Apopka, cyclists pass through a cathedral of trees as scenic as on any paved bike path in the state.

- The scenery ends when the path emerges from the trees and becomes a cement sidewalk that runs alongside Clarcona Road. Passing mobile-home parks, plant nurseries, and warehouses for the next mile, cyclists should take care at cross streets and be aware of trucks pulling into and out of the businesses.

· The final mile and a half takes cyclists past the Easter-egg-colored houses and small churches of Apopka's black community. After crossing the railroad tracks at 8th Street, the trail ends at 6th Street and the Forrest Avenue Baptist Church. This temporary eastern terminus has no parking or facilities.

Even without the Horseman's Park side trip, which makes the ride nineteen miles long, the West Orange Trail is the longest, most scenic paved bike path in Central Florida. It has the length to satisfy cyclists who want a longer ride and enough places to start for those cyclists who don't want to ride the whole trail.

Something you should know: Plans are under way to extend the West Orange Trail another nine miles north through Apopka into Wekiva Springs State Park and to a final destination at Kelly Park by 2005. There are also efforts under way to link the trail with the South Lake Trail five miles to the west.

Much of the trail follows the tracks of the Orange Belt Railroad, a narrow-gauge line that stretched from Jacksonville to St. Petersburg. The railroad was owned in the 1880s by rail baron Henry B. Plant, whose name remains stamped on Winter Garden's main east-west thoroughfare.

Winter Garden and its neighboring communities have long owed their existence to Lake Apopka, the 31,000-acre lake that forms the town's northern boundary. The lake's waters produced cooling breezes in the summer and warmer breezes in the winter that protected the crops from droughts and freezes in the 1800s. The lake's trophy-size bass made Winter Garden a sportsman's paradise for many years. After World War II, levees along the lake created muck farms that produced carrots, tomatoes, corn, and other vegetables.

But by the 1980s, catastrophic freezes had wiped out the citrus groves, and runoff from the muck farms had poisoned the fish and lake vegetation with fertilizer and pesticides. In the late 1990s, the state purchased the muck farms in a $103.5-million project to bring Lake Apopka back to life. Today, with the West Orange Trail and the lake restoration, the town of ten thousand residents is undergoing a gradual transition from farm town to recreation destination.

For more information, call the West Orange Trail: (407) 654-5144 or 654-1108.

Cady Way Trail

The Old Navy Base Ride

Length: 3.5 miles.
Location: Orlando/Winter Park. From Lakemont Avenue, turn east on Whitehall Drive, left on Greene Drive, right on Cady Way to Ward Park on the left.
Amenities: parking, water, picnic tables, bike racks, emergency phone, shopping mall, wheelchair access.
Surface: 12-foot-wide asphalt with mile marker posts.

Just 3.5 miles long, the Cady Way Trail is one of the oldest and most popular paved bike paths in Central Florida. The trail links a Winter Park park with an Orlando shopping mall, cutting though suburban backyards and around the decommissioned Orlando Naval Training Center.

Often crowded with rollerbladers, bicyclists, joggers, walkers, stroller pushers, and dog walkers, Cady Way helped pave the way for other multiuse paths in Central Florida. A white line down the middle of the path directs bikers and bladers to the left, walkers and wheelchairs to the right. Expect multiuse traffic from the start, and warn people when you are coming up from behind. Keep a wary eye for oncomers. If you have to stop, step off the path and leave the pavement clear for other people.

The path's north end at Ward Park offers parking, water fountains, bike racks, picnic facilities, and a community swimming pool.

Starting from Ward Park, here's what to look for on the Cady Way Trail:

- Watch for traffic when the path exits the park and crosses Cady Way. As it enters the first neighborhood, the path splits around a grassy median with trees in the middle. The paths converge and then split again for the first half mile as the Cady Way Trail passes through a corridor of houses with big shade trees and small backyards. The path crosses several residential streets along this stretch. Traffic is light, but cyclists are expected to stop.

- Around the half-mile point, the path reaches the edge of the old Orlando Naval Training Center, a military base that was closed in 1998 and subse-

Cady Way Trail

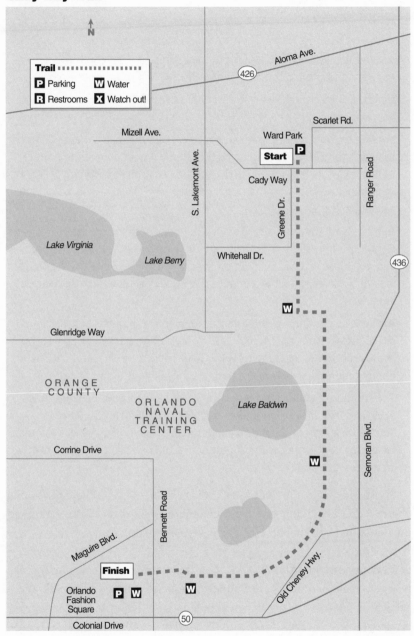

quently sold by the city to a redevelopment company that plans to create a new community on the land.

- At .7 mile, the path passes a rest area with benches, water, and trash cans.

- Around the 1-mile mark, you have the abandoned navy golf course on the right and the still thriving Winter Pines Golf Course on the left.

- Near the 2-mile mark is a rest area with covered bench, water fountain, and emergency phone.

- Veering to the right, the path crosses a couple of streets where you need to watch for traffic. Cutting through a shady wooded area, the path switches to concrete for a stretch and back to asphalt before reaching another older neighborhood around 2.5 miles. The cross streets carry light residential traffic.

- Approaching 3 miles, Cady Way Trail reunites with the old Naval Training Center, passing acres of asphalt parking, empty yellow brick classrooms, and a glimpse of Lake Baldwin on the right. The view gives cyclists a clear look at a military ghost town that once ranked as Orlando's third largest employer.

- At the 3-mile mark is another rest stop, with water, grills, benches, and picnic tables. After the trailside rest stop, the bike path takes cyclists on a boardwalk across the edge of Lake Gear. There's a bench and emergency phone on the right before the path reaches Bennett Road at 3.4 miles.

- The southern trailhead has a parking lot, water, covered benches, trash cans, and bike racks. Across the street is the parking lot for Fashion Square Mall, one of Orlando's earliest malls. Fashion Square has the major department stores, a second-story mezzanine food court, and plenty of stores—but no bike shops.

Short and scenic, the Cady Way Trail is excellent for families with young children and beginning cyclists. A couple of laps on Cady Way is a good introduction to cycling on Florida's paved bike paths.

Something you should know: Cady Way Trail is the linchpin in plans for bike paths stretching across Orange and Seminole Counties. If bike-path advocates have their way, Cady Way will be linked to the Little Econ Greenway Trail to the east and the Cross Seminole Trail to the north, creating a twenty-eight-mile network of bike paths. In 1999 a five-mile bike route was dedicated, joining Cady Way with Winter Park's Meade Gardens Park. The bike

Fig. 7. Multiuse
recreation on
Cady Way Trail

route is not a paved bike path but uses bike lanes and signs to get cyclists
from one park to the other.

The Cady Way Trail curves around the 1,110-acre Orlando Naval Training Center. Opened in 1968, the base trained more than 600,000 navy recruits in its thirty years of operation. Among its graduates were the first
women in the navy to train alongside men. Just as the Cady Way Trail gave
cyclists a view through the chain-link fence of officers on the golf course and
recruits in rows of white, it now will provide a front-row seat to the transformation of the base into a planned community under a proposal approved
by the Orlando City Council that calls for 2,000 houses and condos, 1,300
apartments, a million square feet of office space, 350,000 square feet of shops
and stores, and more than two hundred acres of parks.

For more information, call the Orlando Transportation Planning Bureau, (407) 246-
2775, and Orange County Parks and Recreation, (407) 836-6200.

Cross Seminole Trail

The Suburban Backyard Ride

Length: 3.5 miles.
Location: Oviedo. Eastern terminus is one block north of State Road 426 on State Road 434. Blackwater Hammock Trailhead is on the south side of State Road 434 west of the Greenway Expressway overpass; equestrian parking is available at this trailhead.
Amenities: parking, water, shelter, equestrian and hiking trail, wheelchair access. Convenience stores, restaurants, and pay phones in Oviedo.
Surface: 12-foot-wide asphalt with mile markers on posts.

The First Baptist Church of Oviedo sits atop a hill at the corner of Broadway Street and Central Avenue, lording it over the eastern terminus of the Cross Seminole Trail like some antebellum mansion of red brick and white pillars. From its perch the church has witnessed the change that has taken Oviedo from the marketplace for fields of celery and carrots to the epicenter of subdivisions that serve Orlando and the University of Central Florida.

Opened in May 1998, the 3.5-mile Cross Seminole Trail that starts at the base of the church links the newly suburban Oviedo to Winter Springs, another Seminole County city of subdivisions that grew up in the 1980s. The trail cuts behind the backyards of homes with screened pools and satellite dishes peeking over fences and through the trees.

Dedicated trail parking is located on the west side of Central Avenue before Broadway Street. More parking is available at the Oviedo Shopping Center. The Oviedo Quick Stop convenience store serves as the unofficial eastern trailhead for cyclists needing water, Gatorade, or a Moon Pie before or after their ride.

Starting from the east end, here's what to look for on the Cross Seminole Trail:

- Early on the trail, look to the left to catch a glimpse of a backyard orange grove—a small reminder of Oviedo's agricultural past—and quickly to the right for Antiqua Pools' boxcar reminder of the railroad that preceded the bike path.

Cross Seminole Trail

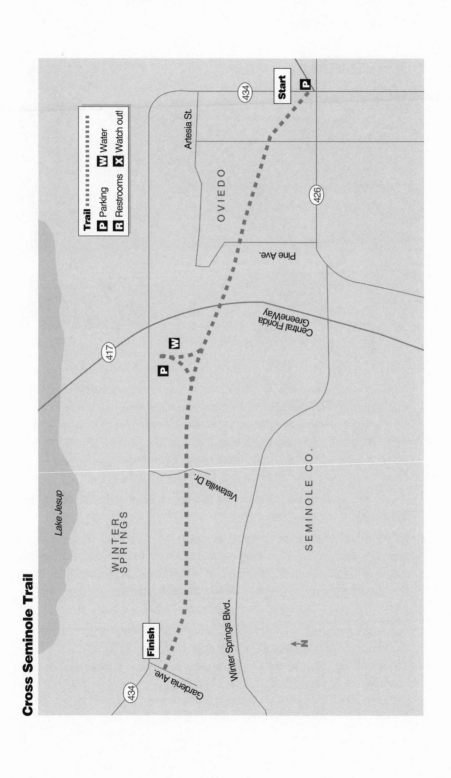

Fig. 8. Cross Seminole Trail trestle bridge

• Nearing .4 mile, two yellow no-passing stripes on the asphalt alert cyclists that the path is crossing North Jessup Avenue. Although not very long, the Cross Seminole Trail intersects five streets, each marked with a stop sign aimed at cyclists. Do not ignore the signs. While none of the intersections involves a major road, there's enough traffic along the way to cause cyclists to pause and look both ways before crossing.

• A sign at .6 mile marks the start of a hiking and equestrian trail that goes the length of the bike path.

• At 1.2 miles, where the trail passes beneath the Greenway Expressway overpass, split-log benches offer a place of rest in the sun beneath the sound of traffic overhead. Just beyond the overpass, a footbridge off to the left leads hikers on a short side trip through woods dense with the palmettos, palms, and pines that line both sides of the bike path.

• When the path reaches 1.5 miles, it branches off to the right on the Blackwater Hammock cutoff, a short spur that leads to a parking lot, gazebo, benches, and the start of the equestrian trail. The parking lot provides spaces for horse trailers, and a hitching post. This little oasis has a water fountain for people, a water spigot for dogs, and a water trough for horses. The Blackwater Hammock spur adds half a mile to the ride.

- At 2 miles, the bike path runs through a sunny stretch before crossing Vistawilla Drive and the subdivisions of Winter Springs.

- At 2.5 miles, the path reaches the signature point of the Cross Seminole Trail—the Howell Creek Trestle. Here you can hop off the bike and, from wood-rail alcoves with benches built into the bridge, peer down at the dark water flowing below and watch the creek disappear into the cool green woods. This spot is as picturesque as any place you'll find on Florida's paved bike paths.

- Crossing Tuscora Drive at 3 miles, the bike path runs through the middle of a subdivision. On the other side of Tuscora Drive, look to the right for a rare souvenir left behind by the railroad—a concrete mile marker that says 782.

The bike path ends, for now, at Gardenia Avenue. Across the street you can see the right-of-way where the trail will eventually extend. At present, the cleared land is used as a hiking trail.

Short yet scenic, the Cross Seminole Trail is a popular multiuse path with rollerbladers, families with young children, dog walkers, joggers, and strollers. With the extensive trees and canopy of shade, it is one of the most pleasant paved bike paths around.

Something you should know: Plans call for the Cross Seminole Trail to span fourteen and a half miles, linking three parks and five schools. The western end of the trail will extend to the Central Winds Park in Winter Springs and eventually to Soldiers Creek Park at Spring Hammock Preserve. Heading east, the Cross Seminole Trail will link with the Little Big Econ State Forest. Plans also call for joining the Cross Seminole Trail with the Cady Way Trail in Winter Park and the Lake Mary Trail. The six-mile-long Lake Mary Trail will also connect with the fourteen-mile Seminole-Wekiva Trail via a bridge over Interstate 4. Eventually, Seminole County hopes to have a network of paved bike paths that can be used for commuting as well as recreation.

Oviedo is not so long removed from its farm-town origins that chickens can't still be found pecking around the Popeye's restaurant at the Oviedo Shopping Plaza across the street from the trail. The freelance roosters and hens have become the unofficial mascots of the town and the trail. A T-shirt promoting the trail features the chickens in its design. The Old Downtown Development group—ODD—uses a rooster in its classic car shows. Nobody claims ownership of the chickens, who roam freely around the Oviedo shopping center, but anyone who tries to have them removed runs into save-our-chicks opposition from local residents who feed the poultry as if they were squirrels in the park.

For more information, call Seminole Parks and Recreation, (407) 788-0405, and Seminole County Greenways and Trails, (407) 665-1130, extension 7351.

Little Econ Greenway Trail

The Riverside Ride

Length: 4 miles.
Location: Orange County. From Highway 50 take Dean Road north to Jay Blanchard Park on the right.
Amenities: parking, rest rooms, water, maps, picnic area, playgrounds, ball fields and courts, fishing, canoeing, kayaking, equestrian trail, bike and in-line skate rental concession on weekends, wheelchair access.
Surface: 14-foot-wide asphalt with mile marker posts.

There are plenty of blue benches sprinkled along the Little Econ Greenway Trail facing peaceful vistas of the Little Econlockhatchee River. But there is one spot in particular worth stopping for a minute just to enjoy the view.

It comes a mile and a half down the four-mile trail when the bike path takes a left-hand turn. Behind you is a dense, cool woods. In front of you is a split-rail wooden fence and the placid, shiny dark water of the river. And beyond that, across the water, a parade of bicyclists, rollerbladers, dog walkers, joggers, kids riding bikes with training wheels, and couples just out for a stroll. People on the other side have a similar view—mirror images where the bike path bends around the water and over a wooden bridge in an elongated U.

For some people, the Little Econ Greenway Trail is a linear nature park where you might catch a glimpse of an osprey, eagle, turtle, or alligator. But for most folks, it's a people-watchers trail where young and old, on wheels or afoot, get their exercise on a multiuse path wide enough for everyone.

In addition to benches and picnic tables scattered along the path, there are also three water-cooler stops along the way.

Starting from the east end, here's what to look for on the Little Econ Greenway Trail:

· The first half mile of the bike path passes the parking lot, rest rooms, pay phones, playgrounds, picnic tables, tennis and basketball courts, soccer fields, and baseball diamonds of Jay Blanchard Park. Running along the southern shore of the Little Econlockhatchee River, the path meanders past picnics in progress and couples contemplating the water.

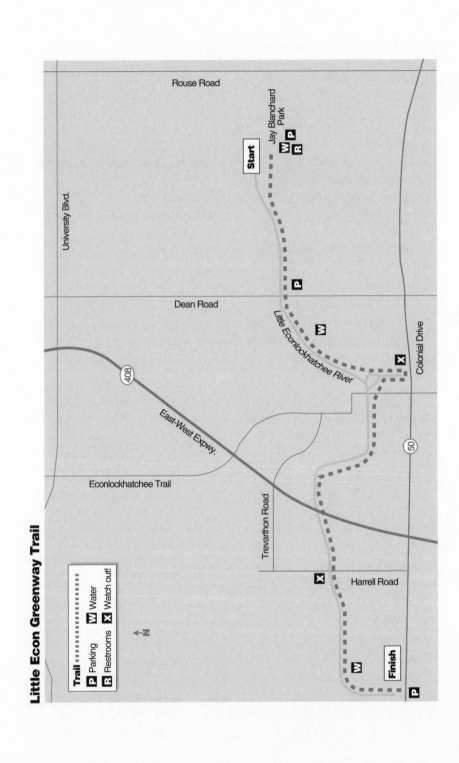

Little Econ Greenway Trail

Rouse Road

Jay Blanchard Park

Start

University Blvd.

Dean Road

Little Econlockhatchee River

408

East-West Expwy.

Econlockhatchee Trail

Colonial Drive

50

Trevarthon Road

Harrell Road

Finish

Trail
P Parking
R Restrooms
W Water
X Watch out!

←N

• At .7 mile, the path reaches a second parking lot. On most weekends, the Bikes and Blades concession stand rents bikes and in-line skates, as well as selling cold drinks and snacks. Beyond the concession stand, the bike path turns from asphalt to concrete as it dips beneath Dean Road.

• At 1 mile, the Little Econ Trail passes the first water stop, just before the soccer fields of Union Park Middle School.

• At the 1.4-mile mark, there's a colorful butterfly garden to the left and a covered picnic pavilion to the right that overlooks water as smooth and dark as black ice.

• As the path takes that left turn to bend itself in half, cyclists ride along a corridor of untouched nature, headed toward the cars backed up on State Road 50. A sign posted on the bridge warns that the wood boards rumbling beneath your wheels can be slippery when wet. The semicircular bridge takes cyclists over the river to the other side.

• A second water stop is located at 1.8 miles, shortly before the bike path crosses Econlockhatchee Trail. A parking lot waits on the other side of the road.

• For the next half mile there are picnic tables and benches placed in the shade of aged oaks or facing the water. Curving left past a sign warning against swimming or diving, the bike path crosses another small wooden bridge at 2 miles.

• Around 2.5 miles, the surface turns to concrete and dips downhill beneath the roar of traffic on the Greenway Expressway.

• Be careful at 3.1 miles when the trail crosses Harrell Road without a traffic light. The two-lane road is not heavily traveled, but there is nothing to stop the cars either. Unpaved parking is available off Harrell Road.

• At 3.2 miles, the path curves again and then hits a half-mile straight stretch of pavement that passes a marsh of cattails to the left and woods reflected on the river to the right.

• The third water stop is on the left at 3.5 miles.

• At 3.9 miles, the Little Econ Trail runs into a paved parking lot and then cuts to the right over a small dam where a blue post and a simple bench mark the temporary terminus to the trail.

Although short, this is a rare paved bike path that gives cyclists a riverside view the whole way. Whether enjoying the scenery or watching the people, there's plenty to see on the Little Econ Greenway Trail.

Something you should know: The four-mile segment is the first phase of a ten-mile bike path that will reach eastward to the University of Central Florida and eventually connect with the Cady Way Trail to the west. The next phase, a two-mile extension, will take the Little Econ Trail west to Goldenrod Road around 2002.

The 412-acre Jay Blanchard Park is home to alligators, otters, turtles, raccoons, possums, and the occasional gray fox. Fishing is permitted along the river, and people with fishing licenses catch bass, bluegills, speck, gar, catfish, mudfish, and the rare chain pickerel.

An equestrian trail cuts through the woods on the north side of the river opposite the bike trail. Information on stables and trail rides, as well as businesses that rent kayaks and canoes, is available at the park.

The park, which dates back to the 1960s when it was called the Little Econ Park, is named for Orange County's first parks and recreation director. Before Jay Blanchard took over Orange County's parks in the early 1970s, he was head of Winter Park's park department—which explains why there is another Blanchard Park in Winter Park.

For more information, call Jay Blanchard Park, (407) 249-6194.

Kissimmee–Neptune Road Bike Path

The Cowpastures-to-Subdivisions Ride

Length: 5.5 miles.
Location: Osceola County. From Interstate 4, take exit 25B. Go east on U.S. 192 to Main Street in Kissimmee. Turn right on Main Street, right on Broadway, left on Ruby Avenue, right on Lakeshore Drive.
Amenities: parking, rest rooms, water, pay phone, convenience stores.
Surface: 8-foot-wide asphalt and concrete without mile markers.

There are more scenic spots along the Kissimmee bike path, but just a hundred feet or so from the Bertha Partin Memorial Reststop and across a wooden bridge there is a view that gives you a simultaneous glimpse of both the past and the future of Osceola County. To the right is a wide marshy area alive with the sounds of unseen insects and animals. To the left, across the two-lane blacktop, cattle graze in a pasture. And up ahead is the jagged rooftop outline of a subdivision with backyard swimming pools pushing against the edge of marsh and cattle land.

Osceola was once, not so long ago, the Wild West of Florida where cattle ranches and cowboys filled the flat, empty spaces between barbed wire fences. Osceola remains the most rural of Central Florida counties, but those ranchlands are filling fast with homes and shopping centers. Its proximity to Walt Disney World and other Orlando attractions has transformed Osceola from the land of cattlemen to a suburban appendage of the tourist industry.

Unlike other trails intended for recreational use, Osceola's paths are designed for transportation of people on bicycles from one point to another. The Kissimmee–Neptune Road path is a two-part paved trail linking the lakefront parks and marina of Kissimmee with Neptune Middle School. The first part is a mile-long asphalt path along the shoreline of Lake Tohopekaliga. The second part is the wide concrete sidewalk that parallels Neptune Road until it reaches the middle school.

In between, there is enough to see to make the ride enjoyable and few enough busy cross streets to make it a good route for families and inexperienced riders. Longer than the Cady Way in Orlando and the Cross Seminole in Oviedo, the Kissimmee trail doesn't attract the heavy-use traffic of com-

Kissimmee-Neptune Bike Path

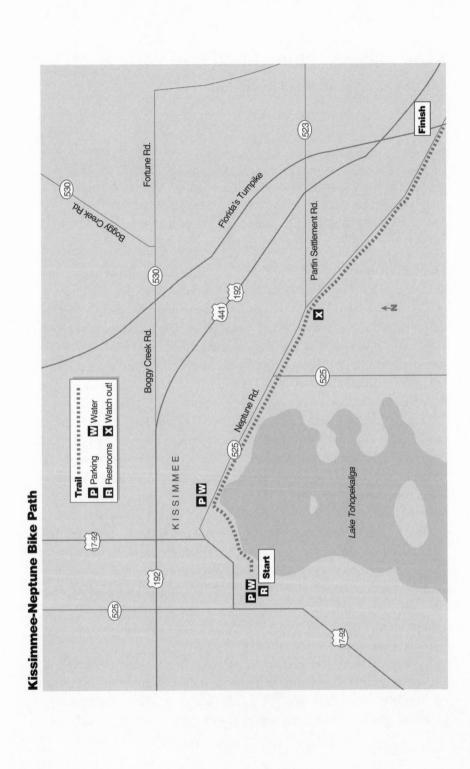

peting rollerbladers, bikers, joggers, and walkers of those more popular paths.

The bike path starts at the lakefront park and Toho Marina on Kissimmee's Lakeshore Drive. There are two parking lots, water fountains, and rest rooms at the park, which also has a playground anchored by a red train caboose, picnic tables, a volleyball court, and covered picnic areas. The Toho Marina sells food, beverages, and live bait. For local color, try the marina snack bar.

Starting from the marina, here's what to look for on the Kissimmee–Neptune Road Bike Path:

- Within the first mile, the path crosses five streets and several driveways. Although the streets are not busy, watch for cars nonetheless when the path veers away from the water and crosses Lakeshore Drive at .2 mile. It passes the Tohopekaliga Yacht Club, the American Legion post, and a row of monuments to war dead, death-march survivors, and retired city employees.

- At .7 mile, the path crosses back over Lakeshore Drive (watch for cars) and takes a right at Neptune Road. There's a water fountain at Brinson Park and an aluminum fishing pier. Additional parking is available across Neptune Road. From here the path provides a panoramic view of Lake Toho.

- At 1 mile, the path crosses a little bridge over a canal and changes from asphalt to concrete. There's a good view of the lake before the water starts playing peekaboo between the trees and houses.

- Look to the left for the mailbox shaped like a church. Big old oaks draped with Spanish moss force the path to detour around their trunks.

- At 1.5 miles, nice lakefront homes line the shore to the right. Watch out for people pulling into and out of driveways along this stretch of Neptune Road.

- At 1.7 miles is the Bill Johnson Reststop with its covered bench and bike rack, but no water or rest rooms.

- At 2 miles, the path reaches Aultman Road on the right. Take a little half-mile detour off the path down the two-lane road to Sunset Pointe, an upscale, walled lakeside subdivision. The lightly traveled road crosses a bridge over a canal and then treats the cyclist to a beautiful view of the lake.

- Before 2.5 miles, the path crosses Kings Highway where there is a light and crosswalk. Cyclists can take a two-mile side trip down Kings Highway to Pine Island Road on a five-foot-wide shoulder. This is not a bike path, but it's more than a bike lane, since cyclists are separated from cars by a raised rib in the road.

- Partin Road, at 2.5 miles, is named for Osceola County's pioneer ranching family. The Partins are credited with starting Kissimmee's cattle industry by importing and breeding livestock that could stand up to Florida's heat. The hump-backed Brahmas you see along the bike trail were among the first heat-tolerant cattle raised in Kissimmee. The Partin family's presence is stamped all along the path, including the rest stop dedicated to Bertha Partin at 3.5 miles and another road named for Henry Partin around the 4-mile mark.

- At 3 miles, the path passes a Texaco station and convenience store where Neptune Road meets Partin Settlement Road. The convenience store has rest rooms, a pay phone, and refreshments for sale.

- Beyond the convenience store, watch for the house on the right side of the path selling "potheads"—clay flowerpots shaped like human heads.

- After Bertha Partin's rest stop, the path returns to asphalt and runs along a three-rail fence for about a half mile to the subdivision you saw on the horizon from the rest stop.

- There is a nice shady stretch before the path passes the Osceola Children's Home and crosses back over Neptune Road at 5 miles. There is no light or crosswalk, so take care crossing Neptune.

- The last half mile of the path is a straight line to Neptune Middle School, passing through pastureland on both sides of the road. Street lights tower over the path at this point—illumination for students going to school in the dark during the winter months. The path ends suddenly at the entrance to the school.

A return trip gives you an eleven-mile bike ride on a path that is smooth, underutilized, and free of debris and broken glass.

Something you should know: Efforts are under way to expand the Neptune Road bike path beyond Neptune Middle School, across Florida's Turnpike and the St. Cloud Canal, to link it with a 2.5-mile bike path along St. Cloud's East Lake Tohopekaliga lakefront. When complete, the two paths would comprise a nine-mile bike path linking St. Cloud and Kissimmee.

There are also plans for a spur off the Neptune Road bike path two miles to Chisholm Park.

Kissimmee has always been more West than South. Cowboys and cattle gave the town its start in the 1840s. Kissimmee's cattle pens became collection points for livestock being shipped to Cuba. Steers sold for thirteen dollars, and cowboys paid for their drinks in Kissimmee bars with Spanish gold doubloons. In the 1870s the rough-and-tumble cowtown was home to a ride-through saloon where cowboys could buy a drink without dismounting from their horses.

An early attempt to civilize Kissimmee failed when a vote to incorporate was defeated in January 1883—an election that was later tossed out when someone pointed out that forty-four votes were counted but only thirty-six people were registered to vote. The next referendum, held two months later, passed when thirty-three of the thirty-six eligible voters approved incorporation.

Cattle continued to roam freely through the streets of Kissimmee into the early 1900s. The town kept its rural roots until the 1980s, when tourism began to replace agriculture and Osceola County became a commercial extension of Disney World.

In the 1990s the town and Osceola County became a destination for Puerto Ricans moving to Central Florida for hospitality jobs at the area attractions. More ethnically diverse than ever, Kissimmee still pays homage to its past every year with the Silver Spurs Rodeo in July.

For more information, call the Osceola County Engineering Department, (407) 343-2600.

Pleasant Hill Road Recreational Pathway
The Clothing-Optional Ride

Length: 7 miles.
Location: Osceola County. From Interstate 4, take exit 24A. Take U.S. 192 east to John Young Parkway. Turn right and follow John Young Parkway/ Bermuda Avenue (U.S. 17-92) to Pleasant Hill Road.
Amenities: drugstores, convenience stores, ATM, wheelchair access.
Surface: 8-foot-wide asphalt without mile markers.

Perhaps the best scenery on the Pleasant Hill Road Recreational Pathway is unseen. At the very end of the bike path, behind a ten-foot-high fence of sheet metal, is the Cypress Cove nudist resort.

Visitors welcomed.

Anyone riding naked on this seven-mile bike path risks not only arrest but severe sunburn. The path passes plenty of woods but offers little shade. The trees are far enough away from the path to put it just beyond the reach of their shadows.

On the plus side, the path runs for seven miles without crossing a major street. For cyclists who like to get out and ride hard, never stopping for traffic lights or worrying about cars, this bike path was made for you.

There is no designated parking for the bike path. The Walgreens on the southeast corner of the Pleasant Hill Road–Bermuda Avenue intersection is the unofficial trailhead, with parking, rest rooms, water fountains, drinks, and food. The intersection also has an Eckerd's, Chevron and Citgo convenience stores, and a NationsBank with an ATM.

Please, if you use the parking, patronize the businesses—even if it's just to buy a bottle of Gatorade. You'll be glad you did. There are no convenience stores, rest rooms, or water stops on the bike path.

Much like the Kissimmee–Neptune Road Bike Path, except longer, the Pleasant Hill Road Pathway provides a bike's-eye view of a landscape in transition from pastures and groves to houses and streetlights. Ride this bike path, come back a year later, and you'll see something different.

Starting from the north, here's what to look for on the Pleasant Hill Road Recreational Pathway:

Pleasant Hill Recreational Pathway

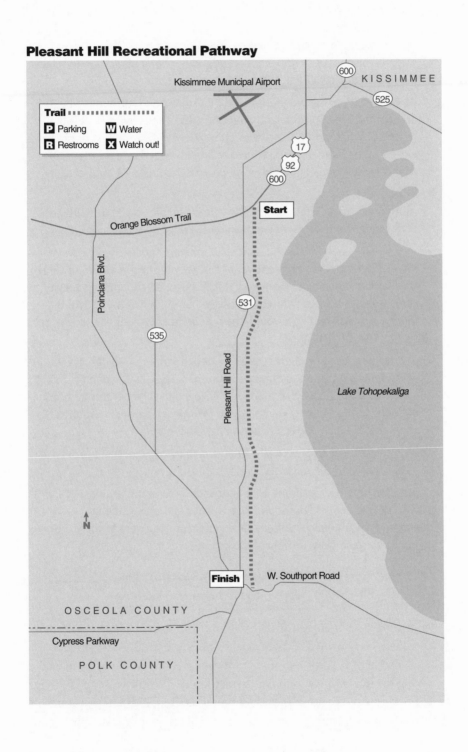

- At 1.5 miles, a pair of large old oaks wearing tatters of Spanish moss spread a blanket of shade over the ground next to a placid pond—all encased behind a chain-link fence, like a zoo for pastoral beauty.

- At 4 miles, there is a wonderful vista of a small pond surrounded by 392 acres of flat green pastureland ringed in the distance by trees. It is the picture of what most of Osceola County looked like for much of its existence. On the edge of that pasture is a large wooden sign that says the land is for sale and zoned for development. Past, present, future, all in one place.

- Around 4.5 miles, listen for the thin whine of radio- controlled airplanes performing stunts over a toy airfield on the edge of the woods.

- At 5.5 miles, look for the Pleasant Hill Cemetery sandwiched between rows of deep green orange groves—another vanishing remnant of Central Florida's agricultural heritage. Despite being an endangered species, citrus growers are not without a sense of humor. A half mile down the road, a dirt road cutting through the orange trees is identified by a street sign as Villa Gorilla Lane.

- At 6.5 miles, trees reaching over the wooden fences of Wilderness subdivision homes provide the only shade on the bike path. Beyond the subdivision, look for the whimsical folk-art yellow dancing man just before the entrance to the Merry D Campground. At the campground entrance, you'll find a bench nudged against a nice shade tree.

- At 7 miles comes Cypress Cove with its privacy fence of metal woven like a basket around the naturists' campground.

- Just after Cypress Cove, the bike path ends in a vacant lot. Beyond the lot and across West Southport Road is a deli and pizza shop in the Oakbridge Commerce Center, and a water fountain next to the storefront Poinciana New Testament Church of God.

The Pleasant Hill Road Recreational Pathway is just that—a pleasant recreational pathway that gives witness to a changing landscape.

Something you should know: The Cypress Cove resort has been around for thirty-five years, owned and operated by the same family. With three thousand members, it is the second largest nudist resort in Florida and ranks among the top ten most popular destinations for people without clothing. The twenty-six-acre resort includes a nine-hole chip-and-putt golf course, a fifty-acre lake, a campground, six tennis courts, a volleyball court, pool tables, darts, a souvenir shop, a restaurant, and a poolside bar and grill called Cheeks.

Visitors are welcomed, and can receive a free tour of the facilities. Gawkers have never been much of a problem, says co-owner Barbara Hadley: "Voyeurs don't come to look at people playing tennis."

Of course, when Cypress Cove opened in 1954, it was an island of skin surrounded by cows and oranges. All that started to change in 1972 when the first homes were being built at the Poinciana development to the west. Poinciana now has 6,500 homes and 19,000 residents, with 600 new homes going up every year. Set on 47,000 acres that straddle Osceola and Polk Counties, the development has room for a quarter million residents before it is done. Right now, Poinciana includes its own retail center, two golf courses, recreational facilities, a community center, a high school, two elementary schools, a middle school, and an "intermediate" school for grades four through eight. The community's rapid growth required the creation of that intermediate school when the elementary schools started overflowing with kids.

One of the community's primary developers, Avatar, has its welcome center and sales office at the foot of the southern end of the Pleasant Hill Road Pathway. Buy a house and you can use their rest room.

For more information, call the Osceola County Engineering Department, (407) 343-2600.

Flagler County Trail
The Shade and Seashore Ride

Length: 19.5 miles.
Location: Flagler County. From Interstate 95, take exit 93. Turn east on County Road 206. Turn south on State Road A1A and go eight miles to the north end of the trail at Marineland.
Amenities: parking, rest rooms, water, ATM, convenience stores, restaurants, state parks, beach access, wheelchair access.
Surface: 10-foot-wide concrete without mile markers.

No other bike path in Florida shows cyclists as much of the Atlantic Ocean as the concrete trail that extends the length of Flagler County. Seven miles of the trail offer bicyclists an unobstructed view of the wide blue ocean. Along much of the rest of the trail that runs alongside State Road A1A, the ocean is felt, if unseen, just beyond the dunes and oceanfront homes.

At the northern end, where the path swerves away from the ocean, it dips and weaves through woodsy alcoves and brushes against a wall of vegetation, offering cyclists a welcome wall of shade.

Along the way, the trail passes by four parks before it ends at the Volusia County line. For a ride through a coastal county not yet walled in by beachfront developments, strip malls, and subdivisions, start at Marineland and head south on the Flagler County Trail.

From the north end, here's what to look for on the Flagler County Trail:

- For a trip back in time to Florida tourism before theme parks, try Marineland, "the world's first Oceanarium." Started in 1938, the attraction is incorporated as its own municipality with a population around twenty. Florida's most popular commercial tourist attraction in 1951, Marineland couldn't compete with Orlando's high-powered theme parks. The attraction closed in 1999, but reopened in a condensed form later that year with its low-tech exhibits, aquarium, and marine shows featuring explosions of leaping dolphins. Future plans include a River-to-Sea Preserve that will replace Marineland's hotel and campgrounds with a back-to-nature restored beachfront, hiking trails, primitive camping, and historical and interpretive facilities. The park is open Wednesday–Sunday,

Flagler County Trail

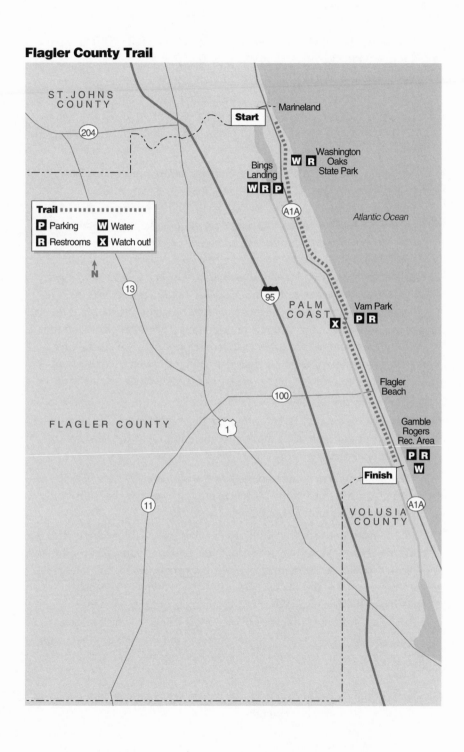

9:30 A.M.–4:30 P.M. Admission is $12 for adults, $8 for children aged 3–11, free under 3. Phone: (904) 460-1275.

- The first glimpse of the ocean comes at 1.5 miles when the path turns a corner and passes the Granada Campground and RV Park. Ocean winds and salt sculpt the vegetation along this stretch of undeveloped land to create a bony-fingered canopy of protection for fox, bobcats, snakes, and birds.

- At 2 miles, the path reaches the entrance to Washington Oaks State Park, which charges $2 to park on the ocean side, where there is a portable toilet and a boardwalk to the beach. On the other side of A1A, the charge is $3.25 for cars, $1 for bicyclists, for admission to the four-hundred-acre preserve that includes parking, rest rooms, a hiking trail, ornamental gardens, and a tree-shaded picnic area. The preserve was once part of the Bella Vista Plantation owned by General Joseph Hernandez, Florida's first delegate to the U.S. Congress. Washington Oaks takes its name from Hernandez's son-in-law George Washington, a distant relative of the president of the same name. Hernandez gave the plantation to Washington and his daughter as a wedding present. The plantation's groves and gardens were purchased in 1936 by Owen D. Young, chairman of General Electric, and donated to the state by his widow in 1964. The present visitors center was Young's house.

- Near 3 miles, the path turns away from the road to dip beneath the trees that form a dark tunnel of shade over the entrance to the Sea Colony gated community.

- After a covered picnic area on the left, the path merges back with the road at 3 miles, passing the Motel Dolores, an old-style roadside motel with rooms that offer air conditioning and color TV!

- At 3.5 miles, the path reaches Bings Landing Park, a tree-shaded oasis on the Intracoastal Waterway that offers free parking, water, rest rooms, and picnic facilities. An archeological dig at the park is uncovering remnants of its existence as the Mala Compra Plantation owned by Joseph Hernandez. Once a supporter of the Seminole Indians, Hernandez went to war against them after they burned Mala Compra (which means "bad purchase") in 1836. Both Mala Compra and the Washington Oaks plantation were used to produce salt for the Confederacy during the Civil War.

- Across from Bings Landing is the Seabreeze Sweet Shoppe in the unincorporated community of Hammock.

- Beyond Bings Landing, the Flagler County Trail dips back into the woods, where it wiggles and weaves through the trees on a path almost obscured by leaves and pine needles. A covered picnic shelter marks the 4-mile point on the trail.

- At about 5.5 miles, watch out for a sandy road that crosses the path, and another one right after it.

- At 6.5 miles, the path crosses the entrance to Hammock Dunes, an exclusive golf resort developed by ITT Development Corporation, which also created Palm Coast, the largest community in Flagler County.

- At 7 miles, after a bridge underpass, a trail splits off to the left, leading cyclists into Palm Coast, a community with twenty-six miles of paved bike paths and another fourteen miles of bike lanes. For a three-mile scenic side trip, take the Palm Coast bike path over a high-arching bridge spanning the Intracoastal Waterway. Cyclists are separated from cars on the bridge by a two-foot concrete barrier. Off the bridge, follow the path as it loops back under the bridge. At the first bike path intersection, take the trail to the right. At the intersection of Palm Harbor Parkway and Clubhouse Drive, take a right to cross the parkway. Continue straight toward the Harborside Inn, then curve to the right around the hotel toward the water. Where the path intersects with another bike path, take a right. The path will lead you along the water and beneath the shade of a thick hardwood canopy that forms one of the most scenic stretches of bike path in the state. Continue following the bike path under the bridge overpass and along a canal. The path will cross several roads, which require some care in crossing. There are no crosswalks on the bike path until you reach Palm Coast Parkway. Cross the parkway and turn right on a bike path that will take you back to the foot of the bridge.

- Another alternative for cyclists here is the eight-mile Palm Coast bike path that runs from Colbert Lane in Palm Coast to State Road 100 in Flagler Beach.

- Continuing straight on the Flagler Trail, note the yellow tractor-style mailbox on the right. The Artesian Gardens Indian River Fruit Stand and Gift Shop—another artifact of roadside Florida—is on the right, with an orange concrete man standing sentinel in front of the parking lot as the path curves left around 7.5 miles.

- Watch out for cars when the bike path crosses over A1A at 9.5 miles. On the left, before the bike path crosses the road, is Varn Park, a county park with beach access, free parking, and rest rooms.

- Around 11 miles, the path passes through unincorporated Painter's Hill, followed by a bait and tackle shop, cafe and lounge, and the oceanfront Sharkhouse Seafood Restaurant on the left.

- Around 12.5 miles, the ocean begins peeking between the homes, restaurants, and RV campgrounds of Beverly Beach. Small concrete picnic tables line A1A on the beach side as the ocean comes into full view.

- As the bike path reaches the Flagler Beach city limits around 13.5 miles, cyclists have an unrestricted view of the Atlantic Ocean on the left. On the right is the Jose Gaspar Treasure Company, offering three "American-made" T-shirts for ten dollars, and a pile of conch shells for thirty-nine cents apiece.

- Flagler Beach's row of restaurants, outdoor cafes, bars and grills begins around 14 miles. Take your choice: Louisiana cooking, pizza, seafood, hamburgers, but you might want to save a spot for Sally's Ice Cream at 15 miles.

- Around 15.5 miles, the trail reaches State Road 100, Flagler Beach's main street. There's a city park on the right, and on the left a pier extending into the ocean from an A-frame building bearing the town's name. Off-street parking lines the beach side of A1A. The town offers more restaurants with outdoor dining, surf shops, swimsuit boutiques, souvenir and gift stores, gas stations, and convenience stores on the other side of State Road 100. If you need cash, there's a NationsBank with an ATM on the left about two blocks north of Highway 100.

- Beyond the commercial district, wood, stone, plaster, and ceramic pelicans decorate homes along this residential stretch of A1A. See how many you can count on balconies, driveways, and front lawns on the final four miles of the path.

- At 18.5 miles, just before the entrance to the Gamble Rogers Memorial State Recreation Area, is the Hightide restaurant, squeezed so close to the ocean and road that it offers valet parking in lieu of a parking lot. Next door is the Ultimate Intimate motel, built for romance with rooms that include ocean views, fireplaces, and Jacuzzis.

- The Gamble Rogers Memorial State Recreation Area is another of those places where you can park on the beach side for $2 or inside the park for $3.25. The 145-acre park contains rest rooms, water fountains, picnic facilities, a nature trail, camping, fishing, swimming, and a boat dock. Sea turtles nest in the dunes in the summer months.

• The path dead-ends at the base of a sign that says Entering Volusia County.

The nineteen and a half miles covered by the Flagler County Trail have enough historic and scenic significance that the county is trying to get the state to designate that stretch of A1A a "scenic corridor."

Something you should know: With its Flagler County Trail along A1A and its network of Palm Coast bike paths, Flagler is one of the most bike-friendly counties in the state. The county also has added five-foot bike lanes on both sides of Highway 100 from Flagler Beach to Interstate 95, with plans to extend those lanes to Bunnell. Palm Coast has plans for an additional ten miles of bike paths within the community over the next five to ten years. By the year 2007, Flagler hopes to build the seven-mile-long Lehigh Greenway Rail Trail that will link up with the Palm Coast bike path at Colbert Lane.

All this bike-path planning comes as Flagler County ranks among the fastest-growing counties in Florida. Retirees and commuter residents moving in from Daytona Beach to the south and Jacksonville to the north almost doubled the county's population in the 1990s. Much of that growth has been in Palm Coast—the largest town in Flagler that isn't a town. Envisioned by ITT in the 1970s as a future city of 700,000 on 38,000 acres, the unincorporated planned community has about 28,000 residents, or about two-thirds of Flagler's total population.

Flagler Beach, with about 4,300 residents, began in 1915 as a town on the west side of the Intracoastal Waterway called Ocean City. The name was changed to honor Henry Flagler, whose railroad became vital to the shipment of cattle, timber, turpentine, potatoes, and citrus produced in the area during the 1880s.

For more information, call the Flagler County Planning Department, (904) 437-7484.

Brevard/A1A Bike Path

The Beach Life Cross-section Ride

⁣

Length: 15 miles.
Location: Melbourne Beach. From Interstate 95, take exit 71 east. Follow U.S. 192 across the Melbourne Causeway. After the bridge, turn right on Riverside Drive, left on Ocean Boulevard, right on A1A. Spessard Holland Park is on the left after Oak Street, across from the golf course.
Amenities: parking, rest rooms, water, picnic areas, restaurants, convenience stores, ATMs.
Surface: 8-foot-wide asphalt without mile markers.

All that remains of the airstrip is some broken asphalt, rotting boards, and chunks of concrete scattered among the mangrove trees and palmettos. Beside an abandoned building, a rectangular slab of concrete rises next to the Brevard/A1A Bike Path near the midway point of the fifteen-mile trail. A faded white arrow on the pale blue slab points to the Sea Dunes Resort across the road. In even more weather-worn paint are the faint images of a Coast Guard ship, a palm tree, and a Piper Cub.

In May 1968, during the tyrannical reign of Haiti's Papa Doc Duvalier, a Brevard County soldier of fortune by the name of Jay Humphrey owned a Piper Cub and the little airstrip across from the Sea Dunes. He also owned a World War II B-25 that he kept at the Melbourne Airport. Sympathetic to Duvalier opponents, Humphrey handed his bomber to a handful of Haitian exiles who, from an airstrip in the Bahamas, dropped bombs on the palace of Papa Doc. Nice try, but no coup: The dictator was unharmed, the rebels were captured, and the bomber never returned to Brevard County.

The A1A Bike Path itself is nothing special. It's a skinny strip of asphalt running alongside a busy two-lane road and blocked by dunes and development from views of either the Atlantic Ocean or the Indian River. There are way too many cross streets, far too few funky beachside bars, and precious little shade. But sprinkled along the length of Brevard's south beaches are enough points of interest, local legends, and stretches of unspoiled barrier island to make the ride interesting. And there's a bonus at the end: the Sebastian Inlet State Recreation Area.

Brevard/A1A Bike Path

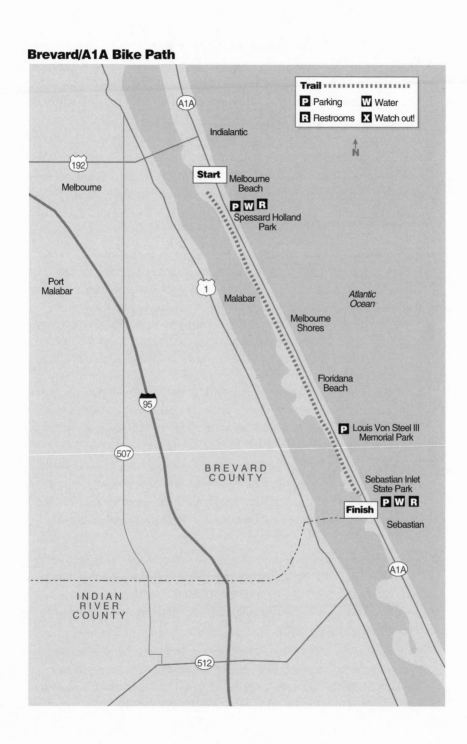

Trail ••••••••••••••••••••
- **P** Parking
- **R** Restrooms
- **W** Water
- **X** Watch out!

N

A1A

Indialantic

192

Melbourne

Start Melbourne Beach

P **W** **R**

Spessard Holland Park

Port Malabar

1

Malabar

Atlantic Ocean

Melbourne Shores

Floridana Beach

95

507

B R E V A R D
C O U N T Y

P Louis Von Steel III Memorial Park

Sebastian Inlet State Park

P **W** **R**

Finish

Sebastian

A1A

I N D I A N
R I V E R
C O U N T Y

512

A word of caution: There are many driveways and residential side streets along this path. Watch out for cars, because they might not be watching out for you. There is also a tendency for landscapers and yard-sale patrons to park on the bike path. On this beach-community bike path, cyclists may find themselves competing for asphalt with sidewalk surfboard sales.

There are no shelters along this "multiuse" paved path, but there are plenty of opportunities to get off the bike and the bike path—short side trips through subdivisions, across-the-road views of the ocean, restaurant rest stops, beach-funky bait shops, and convenience store/gas station rest rooms.

From the northern end, here's what to look for on the Brevard/A1A Bike Path:

• The bike path begins inauspiciously on Oak Street at the entrance to the Harbor East subdivision at Driftwood Avenue, across from the Grace Lutheran Church parking lot. At 1 mile, where Oak Street meets A1A at the Spessard Holland Golf Course, is a globe-shaped radar tracking station that monitors launches from the Kennedy Space Center. The tracking station occupies the former site of a "house of refuge." From the 1880s through the turn of the century, the Brevard County coastline was dotted with houses of refuge where shipwrecked sailors could find shelter and food. Some of the houses were occupied by families whose duty it was to help search for shipwreck survivors. Other houses of refuge were unoccupied buildings that contained food and bedding for shipwreck victims fortunate enough to wash ashore alive.

• Immediately south of the tracking station is the beachside Spessard Holland Park. The park provides parking, rest rooms, water fountains, and showers. It's a good place to start, especially if you want to take a dip in the ocean. But be careful crossing busy A1A to reach the bike path on the other side.

• Beyond the park, the bike path parallels A1A like a linear cross-section of beach life. There are the mom-and-pop motels, old mobile home parks, and bait shops advertising live pigfish. And there are the showcase beachfront homes with Spanish tile roofs, the pastel condominiums, and the new gated subdivisions.

• At 1.5 miles, the path merges with the road, from which it is separated by a white line. The lane is wide enough to safely separate cyclists from cars, but bicyclists also need to be aware of cars using the bike lane as a turning lane into the Hampton's Rental Community on the right.

- The black and white rectangular markings on the pavement, starting around 2 miles, are survey markers used for aerial mapping.
- Nearing 3 miles, the A1A bike path reaches the Archie Carr Wildlife Refuge—a swatch of thick, bristly saw palmettos that has been saved from development by the county. Across the highway is the beachside Coconut Point Park with parking, rest rooms, water, showers, and picnic areas.
- At 3.5 miles, the path reaches the Driftwood Plaza Shopping Center, where there are bike racks, a Publix grocery, and an ATM.
- After the plaza, the landscape returns to nature with thick, impenetrable palmettos, mangroves, and dunes on both sides of the road. The surviving stretch of mangroves offers a little glimpse of the maritime forest that once ran the length of Florida.
- A classic contrast between the past and the future arrives at 5.5 miles with the old-style oceanside Sandgate Motel on the left and the Turtle Bay development on the right, where rooftops and pool screens peek over the wall that encircles the subdivision. There's another mom-and-pop motel, the Ocean Pines, at 6 miles, followed by another roadside relic, the Sea Chest shell shop.
- At 6.5 miles, cyclists will pass the Sea Dunes Resort, Loggerheads Restaurant, and the remnants of the once-famous airstrip. Just beyond that point, the bike path merges with the road—cyclists and motorists separated by the white stripe of a bike lane. Again, watch for cars using the bike path as a turning lane.
- Same warning applies at 7.5 miles when the path merges with the road as it reaches the town limits of Melbourne Shores.
- At 8.5 miles, the A1A bike path enters Floridana Beach, a community started by a New York developer in the 1940s. The beach community is a little bit funkier than its neighbors, best characterized by the whimsical mailboxes shaped like conch shells, giant lizards, and Baby Huey–sized turtles breaking out of their eggs.
- Near the 9-mile mark you will find a bait and tackle shop and a convenience store with a sub shop. After that, watch out for a jarring dip in the pavement around Medina Street.
- Just beyond the Floridana Beach town limits, at 9.5 miles, the path reaches Honest John's Fish Camp and Marina on Mullet Creek Road. Robert Smith, Honest John's father, was one of the pioneers of Brevard's south beaches. Robert Smith's talent was growing green beans. His sta-

tionery carried his motto In Beans I Trust. So famous were Robert Smith's green beans that Franklin D. Roosevelt had them flown to the White House on special occasions. The Smith family's old homestead house is preserved within the confines of Honest John's fish camp.

• Across from Honest John's is another barrier island landmark, the Sebastian Beach Inn. One of the oldest buildings on the beach, the rambling wooden restaurant and bar occupies the site where the Coast Guard built a station during World War II. Part of the station's mission was to watch for German submarines trying to land spies on the beaches of Brevard. Men on horseback patrolled the beaches during the war looking for Germans.

• Beyond the 10-mile mark, south of Sunnyland Beach, is the sprawling Aquarina—a two-hundred-acre "ocean-to-river community" that spreads out on both sides of A1A with high-rise condos, beachfront Windows On The Sea restaurant, golf course, tennis courts, and gated subdivision. Deep inside the development, beyond the access of nonresidents, is a historical marker where Oak Lodge once stood. Built in the 1880s as a boarding house, the capacious wooden lodge burned down and was rebuilt in 1910. The lodge was a favorite residence for scientists, naturalists, and researchers who came to study the flora and fauna of Brevard's barrier islands. The lodge lasted until Aquarina arrived in 1982.

• Exiting Aquarina at 11 miles, the path passes the classy compound of homes belonging to Dick Catri, a successful Brevard businessman whose name is listed second from the top at the East Coast Surf Legends Hall of Fame at Sebastian Inlet. Catri is the living rebuttal to all those parents who told their surfer kids, "You'll never amount to anything."

• At 12 miles, there is an abandoned steak house with a gravel parking lot and a wood-rail fence. The building and thirty acres of undeveloped land on both sides of A1A were donated to Brevard County by the Richard King Mellon Foundation. The property is the future site for the Barrier Island Ecosystems Center for the study and management of barrier island wildlife, including the sea turtles that nest on Brevard beaches. Adjacent to the ecocenter-in-the-making is the beachside Louis Von Steel III Memorial Park, with a parking lot and a boardwalk to the beach but no facilities. Opposite the park is a nature sanctuary of mangroves and sea grapes that is part of the county's endangered-land program.

• Near the 12.5 mile point, the barrier islands are as skinny as they get—a quarter of a mile across. To the right, catch a glimpse of the Indian River.

- At 13.5 miles, the Long Point Bait and Tackle Shop sells beer, bait, and convenience-store food. There is also an ATM at the bait shop. Down Long Point Road is a boat ramp, fishing, and a campground.

- Around 14 miles, the path reaches the Sebastian Inlet State Recreation Area marina and administration complex. Down a hard-packed gravel road is the marina, which offers powerboat, canoe, and kayak rentals, pay phones, picnic tables, and soda machines. The marina is also the site of boat tours of the area's marine life—including dolphins, manatees, and sea turtles—conducted by park rangers. The tours cost $15 for adults, $10 for children under 12, and require advance reservations; call 1-800-952-1126.

- At 15 miles, the Brevard/A1A Bike Path takes you inside the eight-hundred-acre Sebastian Inlet State Recreation Area. Admission is $1 for bicyclists, $3.25 for cars. The park includes rest rooms, water fountains, showers, and a snack bar where you will find the East Coast Surf Legends Hall of Fame with a roll call of the men, and some women, who called the waves that break beyond the jetty their personal playground. Food, camping supplies, fishing licenses, bait and tackle, and beach equipment rentals are available at the concession stand.

The tree-shaded park sits at the foot of the arching bridge that spans the inlet canal separating Brevard and Indian River Counties. The recreation area is a favorite of surfers, shrimpers, snorkelers, scuba divers, boaters, anglers, and nature lovers. While the first facilities were opened to the public only in 1971, the inlet was created back in the 1920s when voters approved a special tax district. A lack of maintenance during World War II allowed shifting sands to close the inlet. After the war, however, surplus explosives were used to open a new inlet at its current location.

On the south side of the bridge is the McLarty Treasure Museum, an exhibit of artifacts and history recounting a 1715 hurricane off the Florida coast that sank a fleet of Spanish ships returning from Mexico and Peru loaded with gold and silver. The museum sits on the site of a "shipwreck survivors" camp. Hours are 10 A.M.–4:30 P.M. daily. Admission is $1, children under 6 free. Phone: (561) 589-2147.

A campground with fifty-one campsites and a boat dock and ramp is also located on the south side of the inlet bridge. For camping information and reservations, call (561) 589-9659. For other information about the recreation area, call (407) 984-4852.

Wildlife is abundant on both the seashore and riverfront of the recreation area, including nesting sites for loggerhead and green sea turtles. Osprey, rare species of wading birds, and the occasional migrating whale are also found around the recreation area. With advance reservations, visitors can accompany a ranger during a nighttime hunt for loggerhead turtles during the nesting season.

Sebastian Inlet can serve as a starting point for camping bicyclists or as a turnaround destination for day riders. Either way, it provides a natural respite from a paved bike path that takes riders on a geographic time trip through the evolution of beach life from untamed wilderness to golf-resort villas.

Something you should know: In the future, Brevard County plans to develop paved and unpaved spur trails off the A1A bike path leading into wooded parks being developed along the south beaches. The parks will provide relief from the lack of shade along the trail.

On the north end, cyclists can extend their ride about one mile by following white arrows painted on the pavement and bike route signs through Harbor East subdivision. The residential streets, with little traffic, take cyclists to Ocean Boulevard where, turning left, a sidewalk will lead you into the picturesque town of Melbourne Beach. Riverfront Ryckman Park offers parking, rest rooms, water fountains, a playground, picnic facilities, basketball courts, shuffleboard, horseshoes, and pay phones. Melbourne Beach, founded in 1883, has as its focal point the town pier that extends into the Indian River. Built in 1889 and restored in 1985, the pier served as a dock for ferryboats that connected Melbourne and the mainland with the beaches before the causeway bridge was constructed over the Indian River.

Back in the 1800s, when pineapple plantations lined the barrier islands where the bike path now goes, Melbourne Beach was the point for shipping the pineapples by rail and boat. The railroad followed the Indian River contours now occupied by the tree-shaded, scenic Riverside Drive. Freezes around 1910 and competition from Cuban pineapple growers wiped out the plantations, although a few pineapple trees remain on the islands.

Experienced cyclists might want to follow the narrow, two-lane Riverside Drive a mile and a half to Douglas Park at the foot of the Melbourne Causeway. A two-mile-long bike path goes over the bridge, where cement barriers separate cyclists from cars, and into the city of Melbourne.

For more information, call the Brevard County Bicycle/Pedestrian Coordinator, (407) 690-6890, and Melbourne Beach Town Hall: (407) 724-5860.

Pinellas Trail

The Neighborhood to Neighborhood Ride

Length: 34 miles.
Location: Pinellas County. From Interstate 275, take exit 12. Go west on 22nd Avenue. Turn left on Highway 19. Turn right on Fairfield Avenue to reach trailhead parking. The trail starts south of Fairfield Avenue across the street from Gibbs High School.
Amenities: parking, water, rest rooms, bike shops, convenience stores, restaurants, ATMs, pay phones, wheelchair access.
Surface: 15-foot-wide asphalt with mile markers on posts.

Dunedin is the poster child for rails-to-trails communities. Cafes, gift shops, galleries, antique stores, bars, and restaurants abound in this quaint little town resurrected by the ribbon of asphalt that replaced abandoned railroad tracks in the early 1990s. Dunedin is what Tarpon Springs is on the way to becoming, what Winter Garden, Oviedo, Floral City, Branford, Baldwin, and a half dozen small towns hope someday to be.

For some cyclists, Dunedin is the ideal starting point. It has plenty of parking, rest rooms, water, bike shops, and convenience stores. The Tarpon Springs terminus is twelve miles north; the southern end is twenty-two miles in the other direction. And when you are done cycling, Dunedin is the kind of place that rewards outdoor recreation with a cold beer, stacked sandwich, or ice cream cone. The town of 35,000 embraces cyclists with the open-arms hospitality of folks who don't mind if you walk around wearing a bicycle helmet and sweat-stained T-shirt.

In fact, the Pinellas Trail is a model for counties in the process of, or thinking about, building long-distance bike paths. The trail is the longest urban paved bike path in the state. Pinellas County is shaped like a foot wearing a floppy sock, and the thirty-four-mile path goes almost from toe to top. Along the way, it takes cyclists through about every kind of neighborhood you can find in a city.

The southern end starts at U.S. 19, next to the Pinellas Tech Education Center and across the street from Gibbs High School. A sidewalk links the

Pinellas Trail

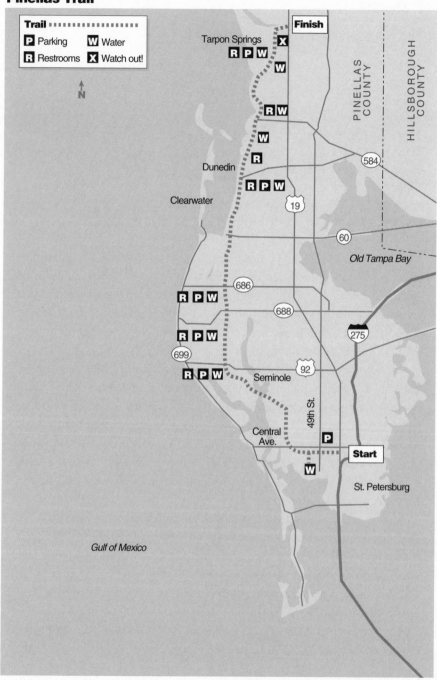

Trail ·················
P Parking   W Water
R Restrooms X Watch out!

N

Tarpon Springs X Finish
R P W
W
R W
W
R
Dunedin
R P W
Clearwater
19
686
688
275
699
R P W   92
R P W
R P W   Seminole
49th St.
Central
Ave.   P
Start
W
St. Petersburg

Old Tampa Bay

PINELLAS COUNTY
HILLSBOROUGH COUNTY
584
60

Gulf of Mexico

end of the trail with convenience stores, gas stations, and pay phones to the north.

Starting from the south end, here's what to look for on the Pinellas Trail:

- The trail begins with a tour of the Childs neighborhood, a working-class industrial area that has prettied itself up with bright, life-affirming murals on the back sides of warehouses, and small trees planted along the bike path.

- The trailhead park on Fairfield Avenue between 37th and 40th Streets is a nice wooded place to park, but lacks facilities.

- At 1.8 miles, after entering Gulfport, a bike path spur on the left points you toward Gulfport Beach. The .3-mile Gulfport spur takes you past a water fountain and Boca Ciega High School before ending at a sign that gives bike route directions to Gulfport Beach.

- Watch out for cars at busy 58th Street S before the path passes a pretty little lake on the left and crosses a concrete bridge over Bear Creek.

- Just beyond 3 miles, the trail plays a little trick on cyclists when it seems to dead-end at Pasadena Avenue. Take a right on the sidewalk at the Texaco station and cross Pasadena and 1st Avenue S to pick up the path.

- Around 4 miles, the Beach and Trail Bike Shop, which sells, rents, and re-pairs bikes and rollerblades, is on the left just before the path crosses 9th Avenue S.

- At 5 miles, the bike path goes past Tyrone Mall on the right and beneath the Tyrone Boulevard overpass decorated with Egyptian-style paintings.

- Around the 6-mile mark is a water fountain in front of another uplifting mural painted on the back of a building.

- A pedestrian overpass across busy Park Street, scheduled for completion before 2001, should furnish the last missing link on the Pinellas Trail. The overpass will join the trail with a bridge over Boca Ciega Bay finished in 1999.

- At the southern end of the Boca Ciega bike bridge is Trail Sports, which rents, sells, and repairs bikes and in-line skates. There are also two parks that offer respite for traffic-weary cyclists. Abercrombie City Park is to the left off Park Street. On the north end of the bridge, experienced cyclists might want to peel off the trail and take 95th Street N on the left for wa-ter, rest rooms, picnic tables, and a cool army tank at War Veterans' County Park on Boca Ciega Bay. A crosswalk on 95th Street helps you cross Bay Pines Boulevard.

- Near 8 miles, the KOA campground offers tent camping and cabin rentals, a convenience store, pay phone, and water. Beyond the campground, the trail heads through a residential neighborhood where a grassy median with trees separates the asphalt into one lane for bicyclists and rollerbladers and another for walkers, joggers, and strollers.

- At 9 miles, there's a small lakeview park on the left with shade and picnic tables. Just beyond the mile marker, the path crosses a bridge over six-lane Seminole Boulevard. Gear down to get over the bridge, which is steep enough to reroute rollerbladers.

- At the 10-mile mark, the bike path reaches Seminole City Hall Park, which offers shade, parking, rest rooms, pay phones, water, and picnic tables. The next five miles—from Seminole City Hall to Taylor Park—comprise the first segment of the Pinellas Trail, completed in December 1990.

- After skirting an upscale subdivision, the Pinellas Trail reaches 102nd Avenue just before the 12-mile mark. To the left, Walsingham County Park offers parking, water, rest rooms, and picnic tables.

- Around 13 miles is Mickie's Bike Shop, which rents and repairs bikes, on 117th Street, on the right one block west of the trail after it crosses Walsingham Road. D&S Bikes, on the east side of the trail just north of Walsingham Road, sells, rents, and repairs bikes.

- To the left off Walsingham Road is Heritage Village and Historical Museum, a recreated Victorian town with a barn, school, train station, general store, and homes moved from throughout the county. Salvaging a part of Pinellas lost forever, the park was started on twenty-one acres in 1976, the nation's bicentennial. It is open 10 A.M.–4 P.M., Tuesday–Saturday, and 1 P.M.–4 P.M. on Sunday. Admission is free, donations appreciated. Phone: (727) 582-2123. Heritage Park has rest rooms, water, and picnic facilities.

- The history village is located, most appropriately, in Largo, a former farm town now a city of 66,000. Just as Heritage Village preserves what is left of Pinellas's past, Largo keeps the name of a five-hundred-acre lake that no longer exists. Lake Largo, for which the city is named, was drained for development. The only trace of the lake reappears when heavy rains cause flooding on East Bay Drive.

- At 14 miles, the trail passes over Ulmerton Road. Ridgecrest Park is off Ulmerton Road to the left. The park has rest rooms, parking, and picnic tables.

- At 15 miles, the trail cuts through a wooded stretch before reaching a bike path spur on the left that leads to Taylor Park. The waterside park offers tall pine trees, picnic pavilions, parking, rest rooms, water, and a playground for the kiddies. The park is a restful, shady oasis overlooking Taylor Reservoir.

- After crossing 8th Avenue SW with its blinking light and stop sign, look to the right for the trailside botanical garden planted by Mildred Helms Elementary School students. On the left side, watch for Lou the Bike Guru's bike shop before the trail crosses the bridge over West Bay Drive. Mike's Cycle City is a couple of blocks to the right on 16th Avenue NW.

- Around 17.5 miles, the fifteen-foot-wide asphalt bike path ends when the Pinellas Trail crosses Fort Harrison Avenue at Belleview Boulevard. On the other side of Fort Harrison, the Pinellas Trail becomes a wide concrete sidewalk with curb cuts. The asphalt trail resumes around 18 miles.

- To the left, the Belleview Biltmore Resort, built in 1897, boasts of being the world's largest continuously occupied building. The hotel was built by railroad magnate Henry Plant, the Gulf Coast's answer to Henry Flagler. Surrounding the hotel is the Belleview Golf Course that attracted golf legends Bobby Jones and Babe Didrikson Zaharias.

- For the next 2.5 miles, the trail weaves through the back side of Clearwater's business district. The city has beautified the Pinellas Trail along this stretch with marine murals, old-style street scenes, and wildlife paintings.

- Crossing busy Chestnut Street, the path passes Freedom Park on the right and a train-station restaurant with bike racks and the promise of serving breakfast all day. There's a bike and skate rental shop to the east on Cleveland Street across from the post office.

- North of Cleveland Street a fire in 1910 destroyed much of downtown Clearwater. The town, started in 1891 and named for the clear water of its harbor in 1906, rebuilt—and bought its first fire engine. When the Florida Legislature created Pinellas County (formerly known as West Hillsborough) in 1912, Clearwater residents built a courthouse almost overnight to become the first county seat—temporarily winning a race against the eventual champ, St. Petersburg.

- After 19 miles, the path turns left on Drew Street and then right, crosses Jones Street, and returns to asphalt as it passes through a black neighborhood.

- A nice wooded stretch leads to a bridge crossing Stevenson Creek around 20.5 miles. There's a park without facilities off Stevenson Creek Road and another with a playground at the end of Granada Street just beyond the 21-mile marker.

- Just beyond 22 miles, the Pinellas Trail reaches downtown Dunedin. The town is a natural pit stop on the Pinellas Trail. Rest rooms, water, and bike racks are available at the old train depot, which houses the town's historical museum. Main Street will take you east to Pioneer Park or west to Edgewater Park, situated on Clearwater Harbor, with rest rooms, water, and picnic facilities. The Energy Conservatory bike shop is a couple of blocks to the right on Main Street. There are also stores in town that rent and repair rollerblades.

    Long popular with wealthy residents from the north—W. K. Kellogg had a mansion here—Dunedin incorporated in 1899 to control its hog population. An ordinance was passed to keep stray pigs out of the city limits. The first hogs impounded in the new municipality became the object of a jailbreak orchestrated by their owners, who chopped down the pound's fence rather than pay the dollar-per-pig fine.

- North of Dunedin, the bike path resumes its tour of suburban backyards, fences, and screened pools. Hammock Park on the right at 24 miles offers rest rooms, picnic tables, and historic Andrew Chapel, a church built in 1888.

- Around 25 miles, after crossing Curlew Creek Road, there's a water fountain, and benches line a trailside park. A sky blue pedestrian bridge zigzags over Bayshore Boulevard, giving cyclists an elevated view of the Gulf before depositing the trail on the west side of Bayshore Drive. Immediately after the bridge there is a fruit stand/cafe with rest rooms.

- Just before the path crosses Florida Avenue, look to the right for an osprey nest on a tall platform. You are now passing through Ozona, a community that began its existence in 1870 as Yellow Bluff. Sounding a little too much like "yellow fever," the name was changed to Ozona on the advice of a couple of doctors who thought it evoked the image of healthy Gulf breezes. Ozona possesses one of the rare concrete railroad mile markers left on the Pinellas Trail. Watch for it around 26.5 miles.

- Near the 27-mile mark, an ornamental ironwork business has erected a sign that says Welcome Pinellas Trails, featuring what looks like an old-fashioned big-wheel bicycle chasing a frantic rollerblader.

Fig. 9. Pinellas Trail: Dunedin depot

- Beyond 27 miles, Stansell Park, with rest rooms, water, picnic tables, and shade, is to the left of the trail off Florida Avenue. Turn right on Florida Avenue for a residential street tour of the older homes, restaurants, and businesses of Palm Harbor. The oldest streets in the town were named for states back when the community was called Sutherland in 1888. Residents changed the name to Palm Harbor in 1925 in the belief it would remind people of Palm Beach.

- Look for another osprey nest on the right before 29 miles and a glimpse of the Gulf of Mexico on the left after the mile marker.

- Near the 30-mile mark, the trail passes some upscale homes and some undeveloped land before going under Bayshore Boulevard. The overpass offers cyclists a respite from the sun—or shelter from the rare rain.

- Nearing 30.5 miles, on the right you will pass Chimp Farm Inc., a sanctuary for unwanted primates started in 1951 by Bob and Mae Noell. Of the two gorillas, three orangutans, twenty-seven chimps, and twenty-one monkeys, the star reject is Otto, a thirty-three-year-old, 550-pound gorilla who couldn't make it in a zoo. The farm is a nonprofit organization. There is no admission, but donations are appreciated.

- Take care crossing busy Klosterman Road as the trail nears 31 miles.

- Around 31.5 miles, there's a rest stop with water fountain, bike racks, and shade. A half mile up the trail, the bike path enters Tarpon Springs, passing through the town's older neighborhoods. The bike path runs down the old railbed median between two streets before reaching downtown Tarpon Springs, filled with cafes and antique and curio shops. Don't get too distracted by the shops—watch out for cars when crossing busy Tarpon Avenue. Just before Tarpon Avenue is Neptune Cyclery to the right, across from the town's old depot. The bike shop sells, rents, and repairs both bikes and in-line skates.

- Long known for its fleet of sponge-fishing boats, Tarpon Springs retains a strong Greek heritage. Nearing 33 miles, the Pinellas Trail passes one of the town's sponge companies before reaching Tarpon Springs's elementary school and garden club, which cultivate flowers and butterflies.

- Watch out when the path crosses Pine Street where there is no crosswalk light.

- For the last mile, the path runs alongside the marshland of the Anclote River. It ends at the white-and-orange-striped barricade before an underpass at U.S. Highway 19. There is no parking at the temporary trail end where the asphalt dissolves into a stretch of weeds, stones, and dirt patiently waiting to be paved.

A bench facing the marsh and the water beyond offers a chance to rest and contemplate before turning the bike around and heading back. Road-savvy cyclists may want to get on the road and follow the signs pointing to the city's sponge docks, where fishing boats are docked beside Greek restaurants, pastry shops, bars, gift stores, T-shirt and souvenir shops, and an aquarium attraction that promises Shark Encounters!

Whether by bike or car, the Tarpon sponge docks are worth visiting for their blend of history, food, and tourist kitsch. The town takes its name from the days when the Cedar Key area was known for its fishing. According to one version of the town's origin, tarpon swimming up the Anclote River to spawn inspired a woman to exclaim, "See the tarpon in the springs!" In the 1900s the sponge industry attracted Greek sponge divers, who brought their families and created an ethnic community that survived even after synthetic sponges and disease wiped out the sponge crop in 1947.

From toe to top, no other bike path in Florida dissects a county—its geography, communities, and history—as thoroughly as the Pinellas Trail.

Something you should know: Opened in 1990, the Pinellas Trail is one of the oldest in the state—and it's not done yet. When completed, the Pinellas Trail will form an eighty-mile loop through the county. Plans call for extending the north end of the trail another four miles, linking the existing trail with a six-mile section of bike path along East Lake Road. A twenty-mile stretch, built by Florida Power for $15 million, will hook up the East Lake Road section with the Friendship TrailBridge bike path. On the southern end, another three and a half miles of bike path will take cyclists into St. Petersburg. Other spur routes are planned along the Pinellas Trail in Clearwater, Largo, and Dunedin Beach. All told, Pinellas County has two hunded miles of bike paths on the ground or in the works.

"It has just been so accepted as a way of traveling around the county, you can't put enough of them in," said Brian Smith, Pinellas director of planning.

Long known for its sizable retirement population (St. Petersburg has been called "God's waiting room"), Pinellas County has hosted Spanish explorers, pirates, land barons, and railroad magnates. But the route covered by the Pinellas Trail was once the private domain of one man. Hamilton Disston, a Philadelphia playboy, borrowed a million dollars in 1881 to buy four million acres of Florida swampland. The largest individual landowner Florida has ever seen, Disston built an extravagant hotel in Tarpon Springs and started a model community he named for himself—Disston City—at present-day Gulfport. Disston City died when the railroad bypassed the community and the economy took a nosedive in 1896. Hamilton Disston himself died three years later by committing suicide in his bathtub.

For more information, call the Pinellas County Planning Department, (727) 464-4751, and the Pinellas Trail Park Ranger, (727) 549-6099.

Fort De Soto Park Trail

The Old Fort Ride

Length: 4 miles.
Location: Pinellas County. From Interstate 275, take exit 4. Follow Pinellas Bayway to County Road 679. Turn left on 679. Toll for Fort De Soto County Park is 85¢ per car. Turn left at Anderson Boulevard. East Beach parking is on the right.
Amenities: parking, water, rest rooms, picnic facilities, playground, showers, snack bar, gift shop, old fort, wheelchair access.
Surface: 14-foot-wide asphalt with miles marked on posts.

Grass grows on top of the bunkerlike gray remains of Fort De Soto, witness to more than a century of sunsets on the Gulf of Mexico. Tourists stop their sightseeing and couples gather on the slim white beach to watch the day end with clouds painted fluorescent orange and lavender.

Once the first defense against an invasion of Tampa Bay, the fort now anchors a 1,136-acre playground for camping, swimming, fishing, boating, kayaking, rollerblading, and cycling.

Heading west from East Beach, here's what to look for on the Fort De Soto Park Trail:

- The bike path runs alongside Anderson Boulevard, but does so by weaving and curving between live oaks, cabbage palmettos, and strangler fig trees. Look for informational signs along the way that describe the vegetation on the island.

- At .2 mile the path reaches the administration building and the intersection with County Road 679. Take a right and cross Anderson for a one-mile spur trail that takes cyclists to the park's campgrounds.

- Continuing straight, at mile 1 the trail reaches Bay Pier with its five-hundred-foot fishing pier, parking, rest rooms, and water. Bay Pier offers fishing in Tampa Bay, while its thousand-foot cousin south of the old fort juts into the Gulf of Mexico.

- At 1.5 miles, the path reaches the fort with its gift shop, snack bar, and 1898 artillery cannons. De Soto is an example of the concrete Endicott Period forts that replaced the Civil War–era brick forts. The concrete fort,

Fort De Soto Park Trail

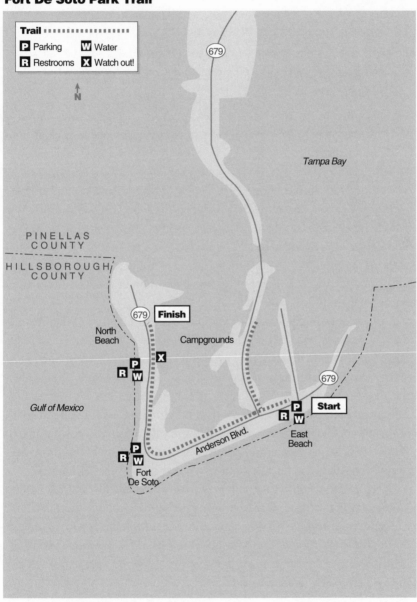

with walls as thick as twenty feet, is covered with 72,000 cubic yards of sand.

· The best view of sunsets is just beyond the fort—or on top of the fort.

· Near 2 miles, the path reaches more beach parking. A bench beneath an Australian pine offers a bit of shade and rest.

· At 2.8 miles, the path crosses Anderson Boulevard. It ends at 3 miles when it reaches North Beach with more parking, rest rooms, water, and picnic facilities.

A pleasant meandering beach-to-beach ride that takes you past a century-old fort, the De Soto Park Trail gives you plenty of reasons to stick around until the sun goes down.

Something you should know: Fort De Soto County Park, created in 1963 with a dedication ceremony that included the Guy Lombardo Band, was built to repel Cuba-based Spanish forces during the Spanish-American War. The fortification included beachside barracks, laundry, lavatory, bakery, and mess hall to support 125 personnel. Armed with the most advanced weaponry of its day, the fort never fired a shot. Four months into its construction, the Spanish-American War ended.

Fort De Soto remained an active military base until 1910, when its soldiers were transferred. Its cannons, with a range of seven miles, were removed in 1917, and much of the base was removed by the Army in the 1940s. What remained was destroyed by hurricanes, rot, and beach erosion. When the property became a park, the county removed what was left of the ruins. The layout of the small town of wood-frame structures is outlined just south of the old fort. Visitors can walk for free through the empty powder magazine and ordnance rooms, and climb the stairs to the top of the fort where twenty-five-cent binoculars give them a closer view of the setting sun.

Fort De Soto County Park, comprised of five islands, attracts 2.7 million visitors a year to beaches that have been rated the seventh best in the nation. Guided nature and history tours are available on weekends and by request during the week. One of the largest boat ramps in Florida launches fishermen who angle for tarpon, sea trout, redfish, whiting, and snook off the shores guarded by an abandoned fort.

For more information, call Fort De Soto County Park, (727) 866-2484.

Friendship TrailBridge

The All-Water Ride

Length: 2.5 miles.
Location: Hillsborough/Pinellas. From Interstate 275, take exit 21. Turn south on West Shore Boulevard. Turn right on Gandy Boulevard. Trail parking entrance is on the right before the Gandy Bridge.
Amenities: parking, portable toilets, fishing boardwalks, lights, wheelchair access.
Surface: 30-foot-wide concrete without mile markers.

We make an exception to this guidebook's three-mile-minimum rule for the Friendship TrailBridge because, well, it's an exceptional trail. The only paved bike path in Florida that is entirely above water, the Friendship occupies a bridge linking Tampa with St. Petersburg.

Opened in late 1999, the trail is popular with cyclists, rollerbladers, walkers, and joggers. It's one place training-wheel cyclists can ride in the road without cars. The old bridge still contains the lane-dividing black and white stripe running down the middle, but all the traffic has been diverted to its Gandy Bridge replacement that runs alongside to the south. Old-style lampposts line the bike path, which is open during daylight hours for exercisers but available twenty-four hours a day for fishing.

The experience of riding across Tampa Bay on a bicycle is exhilarating with the smell of salt in the air and the sun sparkling off the water. Pleasure boats pass below, tugging plumes of white spray behind. The skyline of downtown Tampa is a jagged outline against the horizon.

Starting from the east end, here's what to look for on the Friendship TrailBridge:

- Portable toilets are available at both ends of the trail, but there's no water, so bring your own.

- Wooden catwalks for fishermen and -women extend on both sides for the first .3 mile at each end of the bridge.

- At the .5-mile mark, the trail rises in a half-mile-long hump that allows large boats to pass below the bridge.

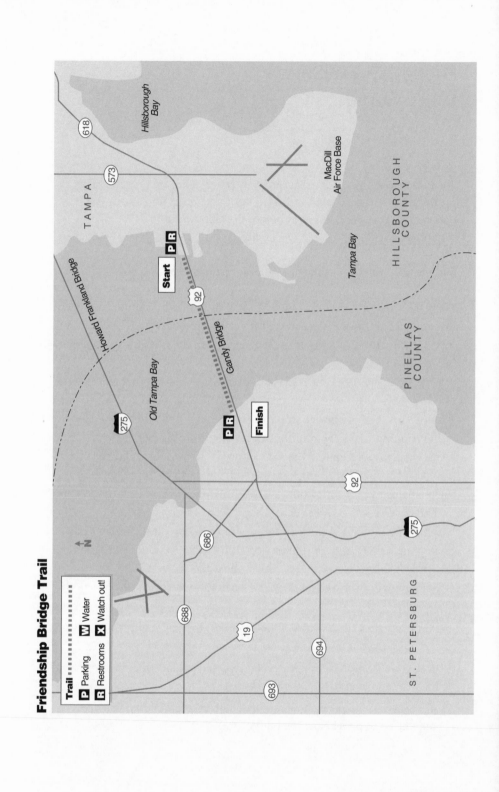

Friendship Bridge Trail

Trail ░░░░░░░░░
- **P** Parking
- **R** Restrooms
- **W** Water
- **X** Watch out!

N

TAMPA

Hillsborough Bay

618

573

Howard Frankland Bridge

275

Old Tampa Bay

92

P **R** Start

Gandy Bridge

P **R** Finish

MacDill Air Force Base

Tampa Bay

HILLSBOROUGH COUNTY

PINELLAS COUNTY

686

668

19

92

275

693

694

ST. PETERSBURG

· Trash cans are available at .5 mile and 2 miles on the bridge. There are no benches on the trail, but you can sit on the curb of the bridge's railing.

Short, sweet, and spectacular, the Friendship TrailBridge is truly unique among Florida's paved bike paths.

Something you should know: Plans are to extend the Friendship Trail in both directions, linking the bridge with Weedon Island nature preserve in Pinellas and Picnic Island Park in Hillsborough, for a total of fifteen miles.

The original Gandy Bridge was opened in 1924 as a toll road linking Hillsborough and Pinellas Counties for the first time—reducing the commute between Tampa and St. Petersburg from forty- three miles to nineteen. Built and financed by George S. "Dad" Gandy, the bridge took two years and $3 million to complete. The bridge, which also had a trolley line, charged a toll of 75¢ per car and 10¢ per passenger. The tolls were eliminated when the federal government took over the bridge in 1944, citing national security reasons. The trolley tracks were paved over in 1949, and the two-way bridge became westbound-only when a companion was built in 1954. The original "Dad's bridge" was demolished after a third bridge was built in 1975. The current Gandy Bridge, opened in 1997 at a cost of $31 million, occupies the site of Dad Gandy's original bridge.

The Friendship TrailBridge occupies the westbound span built in 1954. Slated for demolition, the bridge was saved by a grassroots effort in 1997 to convince state Department of Transportation, Hillsborough, and Pinellas officials it might be a better idea to spend the $7 million it would take to knock the bridge down for preservation instead. The Council to Save the Gandy prevailed when officials changed their minds seventeen hours before the demolition order deadline.

For more information, call the Pinellas Department of Recreation, (727) 464-3347, and the Friendship Trail Corporation, (813) 289-4400, extension 303.

Bayshore Trail

The Bay and Beautiful Homes Ride

Length: 5 miles.
Location: Tampa. From Interstate 275, take exit 23. Take Dale Mabry Highway south. Turn left on Gandy Boulevard. Take a right on Bayshore Boulevard. Veer left on Interbay Boulevard to Ballast Point Park. Park entrance is on the left. Or take the Crosstown Expressway Toll Road south to exit 1 at Gandy Boulevard and proceed as above.
Amenities: parking, rest rooms, water, picnic facilities, playground, snack bar, wheelchair access.
Surface: 9-foot-wide concrete without mile markers.

For cyclists on the Bayshore Trail, there is beauty on both sides. Across Bayshore Boulevard, gracious homes provide a cross-section of architectural styles: colonial, Spanish, Tudor, Mediterranean, Italian, Victorian. On the other side are the smooth, sparkling waters of Hillsborough Bay.

The trail takes you on a waterfront ride from Ballast Point Park on the south end into the heart of downtown Tampa on the north. With no cross streets until the very end, the trail is ideal for families with young cyclists.

Heading north from Ballast Point Park, here's what to look for on the Bayshore Trail:

- Ballast Point Park was a tourist recreational destination in the 1890s when it featured a dance pavilion, water slide, fishing pier, and gazebo.

- From Ballast Point Park, the first half mile takes cyclists through a tree-shaded residential area on a five-foot-wide concrete sidewalk.

- The nine-foot-wide section of the Bayshore Trail starts one block north of Gandy Boulevard at Hawthorne Road and Bayshore Boulevard—site of a Civil War skirmish in 1863 that killed six Confederate and three Union soldiers. Look left for the abstract stainless steel sculpture in the median of Bayshore Boulevard.

- Much of the balustrade running the length of the Bayshore Trail was built in the 1930s. Alcoves with benches are built into the concrete railing. Some have benches facing the bay with steps leading down to the water.

Bayshore Trail

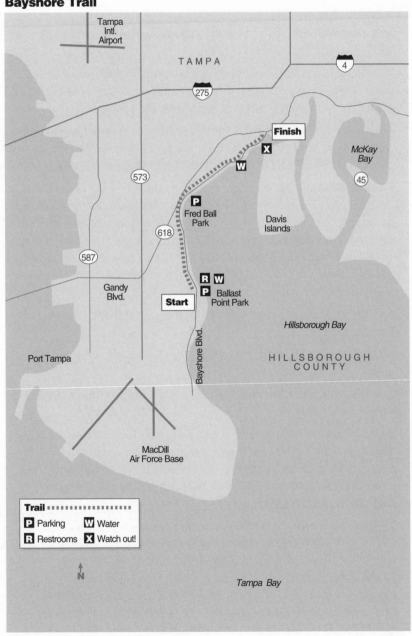

Tampa Intl. Airport

TAMPA

275

4

Finish

X

McKay Bay

W

573

45

P
Fred Ball Park

Davis Islands

618

587

R W
P Ballast Point Park

Gandy Blvd.

Start

Bayshore Blvd.

Hillsborough Bay

Port Tampa

HILLSBOROUGH COUNTY

MacDill Air Force Base

Trail ▪▪▪▪▪▪▪▪▪▪▪▪▪▪▪▪▪▪
P Parking   W Water
R Restrooms X Watch out!

N

Tampa Bay

Others have circular benches facing the road and curving around trash receptacles.

- Around mile 2, the path passes the Academy of the Holy Name, a private girls' school founded by nuns in the 1890s and moved to this location in 1928.

- Near 2.5 miles, after the path passes a sculpture that looks like a large white Slinky, it reaches Fred Ball Park at Rubideaux Street. The park, named for a city commissioner, offers shade and parking.

- Around 3 miles, watch for the metal sculptures of grazing horses in the road median. Across the bay is Davis Islands, an upscale Mediterranean-style development built in the 1920s for $30 million by David Davis.

- Historic Hyde Park and its chichi shopping district is down Rome Street at 3.5 miles. Be careful crossing busy Bayshore Boulevard, as there are no traffic lights or crosswalk signs. Hyde Park, one of Tampa's oldest neighborhoods, was developed by Alfred Swann and Eugene Holtsinger during a building boom from 1905 until the 1920s. Swann and Holtsinger were responsible for the creation of Bayshore Boulevard and many of the mansion-style homes that line the roadway.

- At 4 miles is the only water fountain on the trail, at the foot of North Boulevard.

- Watch for traffic when the trail crosses the Davis Bridge on-ramp at 4.5 miles.

- Same warning when the trail crosses the Plant Bridge within a tenth of a mile.

- Beyond Plant Avenue, the bike path passes the site of Fort Brooke where Tampa got its start in 1824, then a statue honoring Christopher Columbus, and the dockside pirate ship of Ye Mystic Krewe of Gasparilla. The pirate ship reenacts the invasion of Tampa that kicks off the city's Mardi Gras–like Gasparilla Days.

- The path ends beneath the Tampa South Crosstown Expressway at Tony Jannus Park, dedicated to the pilot of the first commercial flight, which went from Tampa to St. Petersburg in 1914. Watch out crossing Channelside Street to reach the park. There is no crosswalk to help cyclists across the street. A pedestrian walkway along the Channelside Bridge will take you into downtown Tampa and the convention center. On the left at the intersection of Channelside Drive and Franklin Street is the Tampa Bay History Center, featuring a one-hour tour of the city's history. Admission is free, but donations are appreciated. Hours are 10 A.M.–5 P.M., Tuesday–Saturday. Phone: (813) 228-0097.

On a cool sunny day in Florida, there may not be a more pleasant ride anywhere in the state than Tampa's Bayshore Trail.

Something you should know: The Bayshore Trail boasts of being the world's longest continuous sidewalk. Known as the Boulevard of Dreams, Bayshore was first developed by Emelia and Chester W. Chapin, a pair of New Yorkers who bought 110 acres of Hillsborough Bay shoreline in 1891. The couple formed the Consumers Electric Light and Street Railway Corporation to bring electricity and trolley cars to the area in 1893. Emelia Chapin enjoyed her personal trolley car, dubbed Fair Lady, for trips to Ballast Point and the pavilion that once dominated the park. The Chapins' dream exploded on 2 October 1899 when somebody blew up their electricity-generating dam. Nobody was ever arrested for the explosion, but the most likely suspects were cattlemen who objected to the flooding of pastureland caused by the dam. The Chapins never recovered. They sold their property and trolley line and left Tampa, never to return.

For more information, call the Tampa Parks Department at (813) 931-2121.

Flatwoods Loop
The Round-Like-a-Wheel Ride

Length: 9 miles.
Location: Hillsborough County. From Interstate 75, take exit 55. Go east on Morris Bridge Road for five miles. After crossing the Hillsborough River, turn left into Flatwoods Park at the orange sign. Entrance fee is $1.
Amenities: water, rest rooms, bike racks, drink machines, picnic tables, pay phones, maps, mountain bike trails, wheelchair access.
Surface: 10-foot-wide asphalt with yellow mile markers on the pavement.

The Flatwoods Loop runs circles around other wilderness paved bike paths. The Van Fleet is longer, the Starkey is shorter, but neither ends back where it began. The seven-mile loop is just the right length for young and novice cyclists. Add another four miles on the two-mile spur for those who want a little bit more distance. Complete a couple of laps and you have long-distance cycling without the interruptions of cross streets and traffic.

The bike path is wide enough for cyclists to ride side by side or to share the path with rollerbladers and joggers. Since all the traffic is moving in the same direction, clockwise, there is no oncoming multiuse traffic to worry about. You do have to be aware of cyclists coming up from behind, because it is a place ideal for riding hard and fast, with the head down and the legs pumping.

The geography of Flatwoods Park is just as it sounds: flat and woodsy. This is the land of saw palmettos and slash and scrub pines. It is wide open to the sun, so bring along the sunblock. In the rainy season, when pine flatwoods become close cousins to the swamp, don't forget the bug repellent either.

There is a parking lot off to the left of the park entrance that has water, rest rooms, drink machines, picnic tables, trail maps, and other information. A two-lane road leads bicyclists a half mile from the first parking lot inside Flatwoods Park to the start of the loop, where there is a second parking lot and a water stop. Although cars are sparse, remember you are sharing the road.

Flatwoods Loop

Trail ▪▪▪▪▪▪▪▪▪▪▪▪▪▪▪▪▪▪▪
P Parking   **W** Water
R Restrooms   **X** Watch out!

N

PASCO
COUNTY

HILLSBOROUGH
COUNTY

75

275

Bruce B. Downs Blvd.

Morris Bridge Road

P

W

W

R **W**
P

P

START

W

581

579

301

582A

502

580

75

301

TAMPA

Starting at the parking lot, here's what to look for on the Flatwoods Loop:

- The bike path curves and weaves as it circles around the park, passing scorched pine tree trunks where controlled burns keep the flatwoods habitat rejuvenated.

- The first water and shade stop is just beyond the 1-mile mark. Water coolers dispense iced water to paper cups pulled from the bottom of metal sleeves.

- Shortly after 3 miles, the path passes a second water stop and then curves to the left. The Bruce B. Downs spur continues straight, linking up with another trailhead two miles away. Watch for the birdhouses posted along both the loop and the spur trail. Hawks, turkey buzzards, white-tail deer, bobcats, foxes, raccoons, possums, and wild hogs occupy the woods of slash and longleaf pine.

- The spur takes cyclists through a series of S-curves as it passes the rolling green hills of a golf course ringed with large homes. Unlike the loop, the Downs trail has two-way bike traffic, so be careful on the curves. The spur ends with a parking lot facing the traffic of Bruce B. Downs Boulevard.

- Returning to the Flatwoods Loop, turn right to follow the southern half of the circle back to the starting point. As on the northern half of the trail, strips of asphalt lead off from the loop like spokes on a wheel to small concrete-block buildings, some with benches and picnic tables under slanting roofs. The blockhouses hum with pumps extracting drinking water for Tampa.

- Off-road trails also peel off from the Flatwoods Loop, leading mountain bikers into the woods that seem to cower away from the asphalt. The off-road trails are marked with small, numbered wooden stakes.

- Just beyond the yellow 5-mile mark is the last water stop on the trail.

- On the way back to the parking lot, you might want to take a short side trip down an asphalt spur off to the right leading to an interpretive area. At the end of the .4-mile spur you'll find a brown block building, a parking lot, shaded picnic tables, charcoal grills, and a sandy path that leads into a cypress hammock. It's a nice chance to get off the bike and out of the sun. Triangular wooden structures cover boardwalks over wetland parts of the trail. The .2-mile long path ends at a leaf-covered circle with a couple of benches for those who just want to stop moving for a moment and soak up nature's greenery.

Flatwoods Park is much like that interpretive trail cul-de-sac—an oasis of wilderness preserved from the encroachment of surrounding development. In cities, we need such sanctuaries to save our sanity from civilization.

Something you should know: The 3,600-acre Flatwoods Park is one of six parks that comprise Hillsborough County's 16,000-acre Wilderness Park created in the mid-1980s when Hillsborough County leased the land from the Southwest Water Management District. Flatwoods Park is bordered by the Hillsborough River on the south, Morris Bridge Road on the east, Interstate 75 on the west, and housing subdivisions along Bruce B. Downs Boulevard on the north. The paved bike loop was built in the early 1990s. An eighteen-mile off-road mountain bike trail cuts through the center of the paved loop and links Flatwoods with Morris Bridge and Trout Creek Parks. Those parks, situated on the Hillsborough River, offer boating and fishing facilities.

For more information, call Flatwoods Park, (813) 987-6211.

Jay B. Starkey Wilderness Trail
The Pines and Palmettos Ride

Length: 3.7 miles.
Location: New Port Richey. From Interstate 75, take exit 59 west on County Road 52 for seven miles. Turn left on Moon Lake Road (County Road 587). Moon Lake becomes DeCubellis Road. Turn left from DeCubellis onto Starkey Boulevard. Turn left on Wilderness Road to Jay B. Starkey Wilderness Park.
Amenities: parking, rest rooms, water, picnic area, playgrounds, cabin and tent camping, hiking and equestrian trails.
Surface: 12-foot-wide asphalt with mile markers in yellow paint.

Plenty of paved Florida bike trails are longer and more scenic than the one in the 3,800-acre Jay B. Starkey Wilderness Park. But not many offer cyclists nearly four miles without cross streets, stop signs, cars, clots of rollerbladers, baby strollers, and yapping dogs.

Except for a half dozen small concrete-block pumping stations sucking up drinking water for Pasco County, there are no buildings, no roofs poking above the treetops. Civilization retreats here, preserving ranch and timberland inside the largest county park in Florida. Deer, wild turkeys, squirrels, foxes, and hawks are at home in the flatwood forest of slash, longleaf, and pond pine.

The nearest parking lot is .2 mile from the start of the path. You are sharing the road with cars, but the road is wide and the traffic is light. Shade is a delicacy on this path, so apply sunscreen and bring water along for the ride.

Starting from the parking lot, here's what to look for on the Starkey Wilderness Trail:

- The trail itself curves and weaves through the pine woods, with periodic spur trails leading to the six bunkerlike concrete-block pump stations. You can add mileage to your ride by following the side paths to their dead ends and back.

- At the 2-mile mark is a shaded picnic area.

- At 2.5 miles, the bike path crosses under the huge towers and high wires of a power-line corridor—the only reminder of the civilization, with its

Jay B. Starkey Wilderness Trail

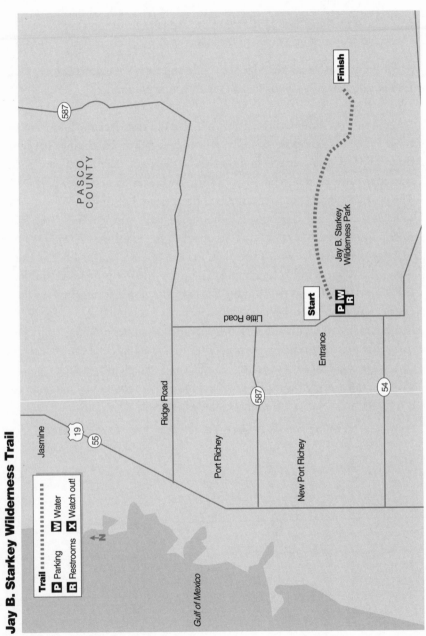

Trail ▪▪▪▪▪ **W** Water
P Parking **X** Watch out!
R Restrooms

N→

Gulf of Mexico

Jasmine

19
55

Port Richey

New Port Richey

Ridge Road

587

Little Road

Entrance

54

PASCO COUNTY

587

Start

P **W**
R

Jay B. Starkey
Wilderness Park

Finish

housing subdivisions and shopping centers, that spirals outward from this oasis of nature.

· At the end of the bike path, one of the asphalt spurs shoots off to the left, adding another .2 mile to the ride.

Given its shortness and its lack of traffic and cross streets, the Starkey bike trail is an excellent path for families with young children.

Something you should know: There are plans to resurface the bike path to make it more rollerblade-friendly, and there's talk of extending the path three miles to the western boundaries of the park. The 8,300-acre park started as cattle land purchased in 1937 by Jay B. Starkey and three partners. The pinelands and cypress swamp had been cleared of timber. What exists today is second- and third-generation trees. That, too, might have been lost to development if Starkey hadn't approached the Southwest Florida Water Management District with a proposal for its preservation. In 1972 Starkey donated 250 acres of his ranchland. The water district purchased another 8,000 acres from the Starkey family. The park, developed jointly by the water district and Pasco County, opened in 1992.

Besides the bike path, the park includes thirteen miles of hiking trails, ten miles of equestrian trails, a 1.6-mile interpretive trail, rental cabins, camp-sites, a horse corral with watering trough, two large picnic pavilions, picnic shelters, and a playground. Tent and cabin reservations can be made up to thirty days in advance, but must be made in person at the park.

For more information, call Jay B. Starkey Wilderness Park, (727) 834-3247.

Boca Grande/Gasparilla Island Rail Trail

The Island Tour Ride

Length: 6.5 miles.
Location: Lee County. From Interstate 75, take exit 34. Turn west on River Road/Highway 777. Turn left on Highway 775, called Pine Street until it crosses Highway 776 and becomes Placida Road. Stay on Placida Road/Highway 775 for fifteen miles. Turn right at the Boca Grande Causeway. There is a toll of $3.25 per car to cross the bridge onto the island. Once on the island, follow Gasparilla Road south, turn east on 5th Street, then south on Gulf Boulevard to the Boca Grande Lighthouse.
Amenities: parking, rest rooms, water, bike shop, restaurants, convenience stores, ATMs, wheelchair access.
Surface: 6- to 9-foot-wide asphalt with miles marked in white paint.

The oldest building on this island named for a pirate is the Boca Grande Lighthouse—a squat, square wooden structure that has stood guard at the southern tip of the island for 110 years. The beautifully restored Victorian-style building sits beside the assistant lightkeeper's residence, a near twin. Surrounded by sea and sand, the lighthouse and its companion have withstood hurricanes, beach erosion, and abandonment to serve as the southern anchor for a bike path that shoots six and a half miles up the spine of the island.

Along with the tarpon, the Boca Grande Lighthouse is the emblem of Gasparilla Island, a coastal barrier island that has attracted pirates, wealthy sports fishermen, and tourists for more than a century. Add bicyclists to the list, because it's hard to find a more enjoyable place to cycle in the state.

The Boca Grande/Gasparilla Trail begins outside the parking lot of the Gasparilla Island State Recreation Area. There is a $2 honor-system parking fee that includes admission to a great historical museum inside the assistant lightkeeper's house. Rest rooms, shower, water, pay phones, and picnic facilities are also available at the lighthouse park. Boardwalks over the dunes provide access to the beautiful beaches known for their seashells.

The park is open from 8 A.M. to sunset. The museum and visitor center is open 10 A.M.–4 P.M., Wednesday–Sunday. Admission is free, donations are appreciated. For more information, call (941) 964-0060.

Boca Grande/Gasparilla Rail Trail

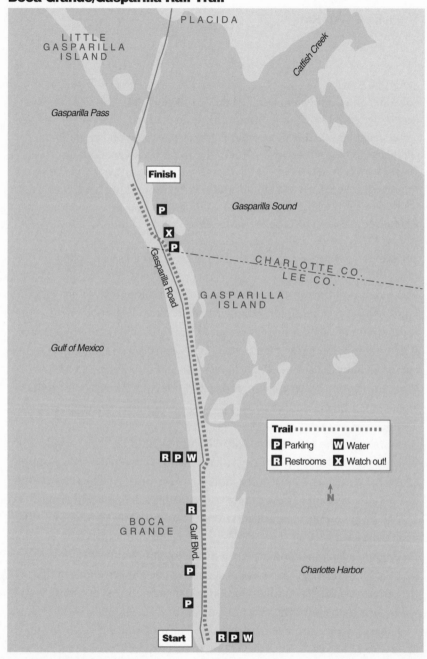

Starting from the southern end, here's what to look for on the Boca Grande/Gasparilla Island Rail Trail:

• The first mile takes you past the island's resort area, including the sprawling Boca Bay resort with its classy three-story gray-with-white-trim beach houses. There is beachside parking about .2 mile into the trail, next to the seaside South Beach restaurant where on Wednesdays you can stuff yourself with all the shrimp you can eat. More oceanside parking is available at about .4 mile.

• At .9 mile, the path begins to cross a series of residential streets. Although there is not a lot of traffic on those streets, be aware of cars along this stretch of the bike path. You're also going to encounter a lot of golf carts on the path as it parallels Gulf Boulevard. Next to bicycles, golf carts are the most popular form of transportation for people with time to enjoy the scenery.

• Nearing 1.4 miles, around Revels Court, you'll notice resort housing that mimics the architectural style of the lighthouse. Roofs topped by enclosed cupolas and widow's walks are common on the houses of Gasparilla Island, where ocean views are incorporated into the price of real estate.

• At 1.5 miles, you reach another beachside parking area, anchored by a 105-foot-tall steel lighthouse built in 1927. The Fresnel lens light was removed from the Boca Grande Lighthouse and installed in the Rear Range Light in 1966, where it remained for twenty years until it was returned to the restored Boca Grande Lighthouse. The parking lot has rest rooms, picnic areas, a bike rack, and beach access.

• The trail turns right on 5th Street at 1.8 miles, where it passes the Boca Grande Community Center, the town's old Spanish-style high school that has been converted into a recreation, education, and community-meeting center. Parking, playgrounds, rest rooms, and water are available here.

• Around 2 miles, the bike path crosses over 5th Street and continues along East Railroad Avenue. At this point, as the path widens from six to nine feet, you are entering the downtown area of Boca Grande, a town with a year-round population of 800 that balloons to 3,000 with seasonal residents in the spring.

• Boca Grande, a beautiful small town of restaurants, gift shops, boutiques, and ice cream stores, is anchored in the middle by the old train depot,

Fig. 10. Boca Grande/Gasparilla Island Trail range light

home to the popular Loose Caboose Restaurant. A row of bike racks beside the old railroad tracks invites cyclists to dismount, lock up the bikes, and look around. Across from the depot is the post office, around the corner on Park Avenue is an ATM, and across the street from the ATM is Island Bike and Beach, which rents, sells, and repairs bicycles. This is a good place to get off the bike path and just pedal around town. What you will find is quaint little white churches, a tree-lined boulevard of large houses, and short little side streets of old-style houses with tin roofs and front porches. Just be careful of cross streets, cars, and golf carts.

· Around 2.5 miles, the path crosses 9th Street, which leads to the Gasparilla Inn, one of the island's oldest and grandest resorts. The Gasparilla Inn began in 1912 as the Hotel Boca Grande, then was expanded and renamed two years later. Once the premier place for the wealthy and famous who came to fish for tarpon and to dine and dance in elegance, the Victorian-style Gasparilla Inn remains a refuge for the affluent, with a private beach club and tennis club and the only golf course on the island. The historic inn has 138 rooms and cabins available to the public.

- A sandy path for joggers runs alongside the bike path for the next four miles—leaving the asphalt for cyclists, bladers, baby strollers, and golf carts.

- Around the 4-mile mark, look for a bronze plaque on the ground to the right. The plaque marks the former site of the Boca Grande Ferry Company, which provided the only access to the island from 1927 until the causeway was built in 1958.

- Beyond 4.5 miles, look to the left for more of the lighthouse-style homes with glassed-in cupolas on their roofs overlooking the Gulf of Mexico. Vacant lots on the Gulf side—and there aren't many left—sell for a million dollars.

- Around 6 miles, watch out as the bike path crosses Gasparilla Road. On the Gulf side of the road, the bike path narrows to six feet. You are riding against the southbound traffic along this stretch. There is parking at the Gasparilla South Fishing Pier just beyond where the path crosses Gasparilla. Parking is also available across the road at Uncle Henry's Resort and Courtyard Shops with a grocery store, marina, hotel, restaurant, and pay phones.

- Don't get too distracted by Uncle Henry's or you'll slam into a telephone pole planted in the bike path at 6 miles. Watch out for another telephone pole a little way up the path. The bike path ends at Gulfshore Drive, just before the bridge leading to Cole Key.

The Boca Grande/Gasparilla Island Rail Trail has taken you almost the entire length of Gasparilla Island—a place of class, beauty, and fascinating history.

Something you should know: Most of the Boca Grande/Gasparilla Island Rail Trail is owned and maintained by the Gasparilla Island Conservation and Improvement Association, comprised primarily of homeowners on the island. The group are proud, and a bit possessive, of their bike path. They can't keep outsiders from riding on it, but they don't necessarily encourage visiting cyclists either. It's not the bikes they mind, it's the cars and the traffic that come with them.

Boca Grande calls itself the Tarpon Capital of the World and has adopted the fish as its town symbol. The sport fish migrates up the Gulf Coast and spawns in the waters off Gasparilla Island in numbers seldom found anywhere else. Since 1983 the town has hosted the World's Richest Tarpon Tournament in mid-July. The three-day festival of catch-and-release fishing pays $100,000 for the heaviest fish, $40,000 for the second-place fish, and $25,000 to the team that catches and releases the most fish. Participation is limited to sixty boats.

For more information, call the Gasparilla Island Conservation and Improvement Association, (941) 964-2667, and the Boca Grande Chamber of Commerce, (941) 964-0568.

Sanibel Island Bike Paths

The Bike-Friendly Island Ride

Length: 23 miles.
Location: Lee County. From Interstate 75, take exit 21. Go west on Daniels
Road. Turn left at Six Mile Cypress Road. After crossing U.S. 41, turn left
on Summerlin Road and follow to Sanibel. Causeway toll is $3.
Amenities: parking, rest rooms, water, restaurants, convenience stores,
ATMs, bike shops.
Surface: 6- to 8-foot-wide asphalt without mile markers.

Sanibel Island is fully stocked with things to see and do by bicycle: beaches,
seashells, shops, restaurants, bird-watching, and nature walking. But an
easy-to-miss little polished granite bench on the bike path just east of the
entrance to the Ding Darling Wildlife Refuge is worth looking for. Chiseled
into the stone bench are the words Rest Awhile.

It's good advice. Sanibel on bicycle is an experience worth savoring. It
shouldn't be rushed or squeezed. On Sanibel's twenty-three-mile network of
bike paths, the journey is as much fun as the destination.

One word of warning. Sanibel is serious about enforcing its paid parking.
Signs are posted in four languages instructing visitors how the park-and-pay
system works and reminding everyone that it's a $35 fine if you don't. The
island's park-and-pay lots charge 75¢ an hour.

The island is bisected down its length by an eleven-mile bike path that
goes from the eastern tip at Lighthouse Beach to Turner Beach on the west
end of the island. A second path, six and a half miles long, runs along West
Gulf, Middle Gulf, and East Gulf Drives on the southern edge of the island.
Connecting those two trails are five north-south bike paths—Lindgren Boulevard, Donax Street, Casa Ybel Road, Tarpon Bay Road, and Rabbit Road.

Heading west from Lighthouse Beach, here's what to look for:

- First off, check out the oldest structure on the island—the 1884 Sanibel
Lighthouse on Lighthouse Beach—before taking off on Periwinkle Way.

- Periwinkle Way is the cycle-and-shop stretch of Sanibel. The stores begin
.3 mile down the bike path at Old Town Sanibel. The site of Sanibel

Sanibel Island Trails

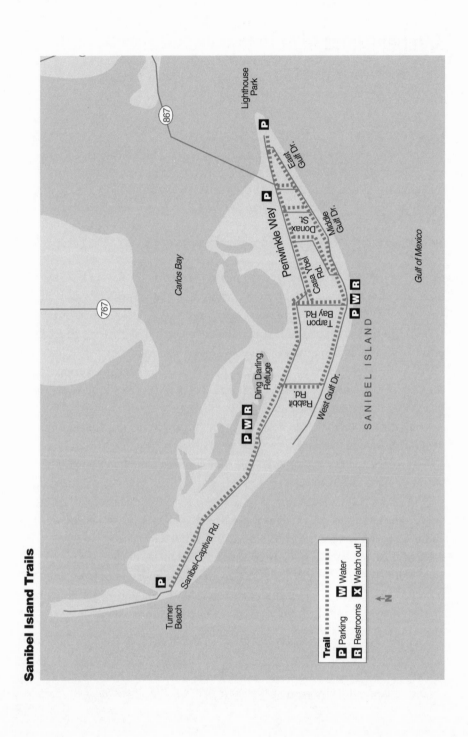

Island's first settlement in the 1860s, the area now hosts cafes, delis, ice cream shops, gift stores, shell shops, and boutiques.

- At .4 mile, Periwinkle intersects with East Gulf Drive, the eastern end of the bike path that runs along the southern edge of the island. A left turn here onto East Gulf would bring you to the island's hotel and resort district.

- At 1.3 miles, the path reaches busy Lindgren Boulevard. Lindgren is a major intersection, so take care when crossing. On the other side of the street, you can take the Lindgren bike path to the left for a half mile, passing houses that have front yards paved with rocks and mailboxes decorated to look like flamingos, Dalmatians, and manatees. Or to the right, north of Periwinkle, there's a .4-mile-long path to the Sanibel Island Chamber of Commerce and a parking lot near the causeway bridge.

- Continuing west on Periwinkle, pay attention to signs along this stretch of bike path that advise both cyclists and motorists to Look Both Ways. Cars pulling into and out of businesses along this strip cross the bike path, so beware. Cyclists also need to be careful at several points where the bike path merges with the roadway, becoming a mere bike lane, with traffic and cyclists separated only by a white line. There is plenty of room for cyclists in the bike lane, but be careful on these short departures from the bike path.

- At 1.6 miles, the path crosses the entrance to the Periwinkle Trailer Park and Campground—with $24-a-night camping, a low-cost alternative to the island's hotels and resort accommodations. Not far beyond the campground is a shop specializing in a commodity that made Sanibel famous: She Sells Sea Shells. It's worth a stop for the alliteration alone.

- Around 2 miles, the path crosses a major intersection at Donax Street. Taking a left on the Donax bike path will lead you past a half mile of modest homes, small motels, and the periphery of a golf course to Middle Gulf Drive. The Sanibel Beach Club on Donax became Florida's first time-share development in 1974.

- Beyond Donax, the Periwinkle bike path takes a little wilderness detour from the shops, passing through a tree-lined stretch that blots out the two-lane traffic on your right and offers a pastoral view of the golf course to the left. Then the path rejoins the roadside and more restaurants, cafes, convenience stores, galleries, and a bike rental store called Bikes, Boats and Beach Stuff.

- At the 2.5-mile mark, on the left, Periwinkle meets the Casa Ybel bike path, which runs south for a mile to intersect with Middle Gulf and West Gulf Drives.

- Around 3 miles, the Periwinkle path hits a pretty stretch with large casuarina trees forming a cool green canopy of shade. Here the road reaches the Periwinkle Place shopping center, which offers just about everything a cyclist/shopper could want: restaurants, gift shops, boutiques, clothing stores. And, just as important, rest rooms.

- At 3.5 miles, watch out as the path crosses Periwinkle at the Episcopal church. On the other side of Periwinkle, a .3-mile bike path branches off to take you along Palm Ridge Road. On its right is the Bike Route, which rents, sells, and repairs bikes. The bike path passes Sanibel's city hall, library, and art museum before connecting with the Sanibel-Captiva Road bike path at Tarpon Bay Road.

- Continuing west on Periwinkle, you'll find Finnimore's Cycle Shop—which rents, sells, and repairs bikes—in the Wings Plaza at the corner of Periwinkle and Palm Ridge Road. Another Bikes, Boats and Beach Stuff store is on the left just before Periwinkle dead-ends into Tarpon Bay Road at 4 miles. Next door to the bike shop is Bailey's, a grocery and hardware store that harks back to its general-store origins in 1925. On the other side of Tarpon Bay is Olde Sanibel Shoppes, a cluster of boutiques that's not that olde.

- If you turn left on Tarpon Bay, the path will take you .8 mile to the park-and-pay lot for Tarpon Bay Beach at West Gulf Drive. At the entrance to the beach there are rest rooms and water fountains. About .3 mile from its end, the path passes the Bailey Tract, a parcel of the Ding Darling Refuge that offers hiking trails.

- Turn right on Tarpon Bay and the .4-mile path will connect you with the intersection of Sanibel-Captiva Road and Palm Ridge Road.

- If you have had enough of cycling-and-shopping, the seven-mile-long Sanibel-Captiva Road bike path offers a birds-and-biking antidote. Running along a relatively undeveloped section of the island, the path passes the Bailey-Matthews Shell Museum within the first mile. A one-of-a-kind attraction, the museum is a house of worship for shells: shells in art, history, and habitat. Rare and fossilized shells share space with specimen shells gathered from the twenty miles of beaches on Sanibel and Captiva. Hours are 10 A.M.–4 P.M., Tuesday–Sunday, closed Monday. Admission is $5 for adults, $3 for children aged 8–16, free under 8. Phone: (941) 395-2233.

· One mile from the shell museum, the Sanibel-Captiva bike path hits the Rabbit Road intersection, where cyclists can turn left across Sanibel-Captiva Road, snake behind the Island House Restaurant, and follow the path south for 1.3 miles to West Gulf Drive. There's a pretty little stretch where trees form a tunnel over the bike path. The path crosses a small wooden bridge over a canal and then disappears when it reaches a short residential street. At the end of the street, the bike path picks up again as it reaches West Gulf Drive.

· Continuing west for .3 mile on San-Cap Road from Rabbit Road, the path reaches the entrance to the J. N. "Ding" Darling Wildlife Refuge. Watch for that Rest Awhile stone bench on your right. The six-thousand-acre refuge includes hiking trails, canoe rentals, fishing, and a visitor center that offers guided tours. Bikes are allowed on Wildlife Drive, a hard-packed limestone road that takes you five miles through the sanctuary named for a Pulitzer Prize–winning political cartoonist and early conservationist. Wildlife Drive is open from sunrise to sunset every day except Friday. There is an honor-system entrance fee of $1 for bicyclists and $5 for cars, which goes toward wildlife and habitat preservation. There's no better deal on the island, not even those shops that sell five T-shirts for $15. Although the Wildlife Drive is not paved, the surface is hard enough to accommodate bicycles, including road bikes with skinny tires. The ride is a pleasant trip though Sanibel's past when the twelve-mile-long island was all mangroves, marshes, tidal basins, bays, birds, alligators, and insects. (Don't forget to pack the mosquito repellent and sunscreen.)

· If you bypass the Ding Darling detour, the Sanibel Recreation Complex offers rest rooms, water, a playground, and parking.

· The next three miles of the San-Cap bike path become a roller-coaster trip on asphalt that undulates and curves as the path passes over humps, around trees, and across wood-plank bridges. On your right is the unadulterated land of the refuge, on the left subdivisions with tree-shaded entrances.

· For the last 1.5 miles of the San-Cap bike path, amuse yourself looking for the mailboxes decorated with shells, flamingos, and fish. Or imagine the houses hidden behind the trees at the end of long private drives.

· The path ends short of the Captiva Island bridge at Blind Pass. On the left is Turner Beach with its sand, sea, and sun. On the right is a little plaza with the Sunset Grill restaurant with its beer, burgers, and Sunday brunch. Either choice will please the senses.

· Turning around, take the Rabbit Road bike path connector for the return trip east. The bike paths on the south side of the island take you along resort row, as most of the island's hotels and vacation resorts are lined up shoulder to shoulder on Sanibel's southern shore.

· Headed east on West Gulf Drive, the bike path meets Tarpon Bay Road at 1.5 miles. Stop for water and rest rooms on the south side of West Gulf, where you can also park your bike to enjoy the sun and sand at a public beach.

· About .7 mile from Tarpon Bay Road, the West Gulf Drive path hits the intersection of Casa Ybel Road and Algiers Lane. To return to Periwinkle Way, take the Casa Ybel path left for a mile. To reach Middle Gulf Drive and continue along the south side of the island, take the Algiers Lane path.

· On the Algiers Lane path, watch for an old family cemetery that dates back to the 1800s on your left before the path forks. The left fork will take you to Casa Ybel Road. The right fork leads to Middle Gulf Drive.

· Middle Gulf Drive returns you to the island's beachside hotels and resorts. On the right, Sundial of Sanibel—Sanibel's largest resort complex—lines Middle Gulf with tennis courts for half a mile.

· Beyond Lindgren Boulevard, the East Gulf path passes Victoria Way, a development of beautiful plantation-style two-story houses. East Gulf returns you to Periwinkle Way and Old Town Sanibel. Across the street, Pinocchio's ice cream awaits you.

Sanibel Island has turned itself into one of the few places in Florida that can truly call itself intermodal. Whether you are visiting for the day or staying at one of the Gulf-front hotels, there is nowhere worth going on Sanibel that can't be reached via bike path. Unlike many places where bike paths are an afterthought or isolated multiuse recreational strips, the island's network of asphalt ribbons ties this island together in a way that allows transportation and recreation to take place simultaneously.

Something you should know: Sanibel Island's web of bike paths originated as a save-the-trees solution to traffic congestion. Unlike so many places in Florida where developers favor widening roads to solve traffic problems, a couple of developers on Sanibel began building bike paths in 1976 to spare the beautiful canopy of casuarina trees along Periwinkle Way. The city, incorporated in 1974, soon followed the developers' lead by building bike paths and requiring new development to include bike paths as part of the construction plans. The result is twenty-three miles of bike paths on an island that measures only twelve miles by two-and-a-half.

Tourism is big business on Sanibel, where the year-round population of 5,000 swells to 20,000 in the winter. But tourism didn't take off on the island until 1963, when the causeway was built. Before then, visitors coming to the island and residents leaving Sanibel relied on the Kinzie brothers' ferry that began operating in 1928. Part of the Kinzies' dock still exists at the end of Ferry Road, near the museum that occupies the island's first post office.

Sanibel's first inhabitants were the Calusa Indians, who had the 10,700-acre island all to themselves until Ponce de Leon arrived in 1513. The first European settlers didn't show up until 1833. Fishing and family farms dominated the island until hurricanes in the 1920s doused the land with salt water and ruined Sanibel for agriculture. Today, about two-thirds of the island is preserved as conservation land. The rest is set aside for tourists—and bicyclists.

For more information, call Sanibel City Hall, (941) 472-4135, and the Sanibel–Captiva Islands Chamber of Commerce, (941) 472-1080.

Pompano Beach Air Park Bike Path
The Loop-de-Blimp Ride

Length: 4.5 miles.
Location: Pompano Beach. From Interstate 95, take exit 35A. Go east on Copans Road to the Pompano Square Mall at 12th Terrace. The bike path is on the right.
Amenities: parking, water, food court at Pompano Square Mall.
Surface: 10-foot-wide asphalt without mile markers.

U.S. Highway 1 in Pompano Beach looks like any major road in any major city in Florida. The traffic is thick and incessant. The roadside is a solid wall of shoulder-to-shoulder commerce: sub shops, restaurants, liquor stores, pawnshops, marine shops, car dealers, one-low-price cleaners, and half-price pottery.

But at the corner of NE 10th Street, the path takes a sharp right, weaves through a stand of big shade trees, crosses a road, and delivers the bicyclist to an unexpected oasis. At a small alcove of gray benches facing a tee on the Pompano Beach Municipal Golf Course, someone has left an orange Rubbermaid cooler filled with ice-cold water.

Give thanks, and donations, to the Beach Bladers, an in-line skate club that trains on the four-mile course that circles around the golf course and municipal airport, for the water-break oasis. And remember that this bike path is a multiuse recreation facility shared by bladers, bikers, walkers, and joggers.

Essentially self-contained with few cross streets, the Pompano Beach Air Park Bike Path is perfect for fast hard riding by experienced bikers, and short enough for kids and novice cyclists. The best place to start is the parking lot of the Pompano Square Mall at the corner of Copans Road and NE 12th Terrace.

Starting at the shopping mall parking lot, here's what to look for on the Pompano Beach Air Park Bike Path:

• Following the contours of the shopping mall parking lot and the municipal golf course, the bike path reaches the first of several benches at .1 mile.

Pompano Beach Air Park

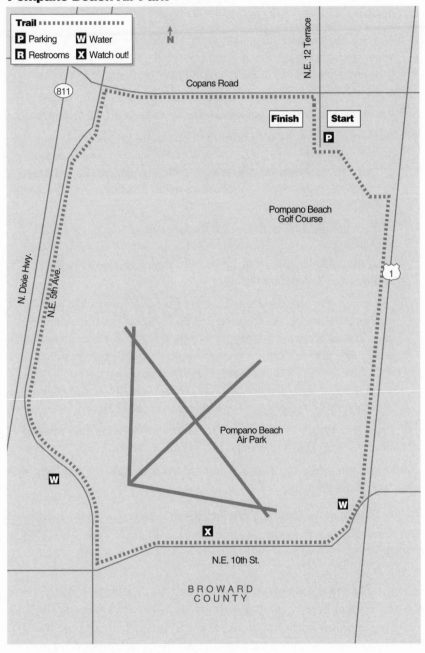

Trail ▪▪▪▪▪▪▪▪▪▪▪▪▪▪▪▪▪▪
P Parking   W Water
R Restrooms   X Watch out!

N

Copans Road

811

N.E. 12 Terrace

Finish   Start
P

Pompano Beach
Golf Course

1

N. Dixie Hwy.

N.E. 5th Ave.

W

Pompano Beach
Air Park

W

X

N.E. 10th St.

B R O W A R D
C O U N T Y

- The path turns right when it reaches U.S. 1. On the left is traffic and free enterprise. On the right is the city golf course with a golf-cart crossing at .8 mile and the course entrance at 1.1 miles.

- At 1.3 miles, the path turns right at NE 10th Street, zigzags around the water stop, and leaves the golf course behind. The asphalt path narrows to about eight feet as it curves around the perimeter of the Pompano Beach Air Park.

- Watch for cars entering and leaving the airport around the 2-mile mark.

- Nearing 2.5 miles, the path turns right at NE 5th Avenue where a sign warns: "Use Path At Your Own Risk. Walkers, skaters, cyclists beware of surface defects, debris, and vehicles at path intersections. Report unsafe conditions to Public Works, phone, 786-4107. Thank you for your cooperation."

- At 2.7 miles, the bike path reaches the Goodyear Blimp Base, a huge hangar that houses one of Goodyear's blimps used for all those aerial shots of football games. Just .2 mile from the blimp base are a water fountain and benches on the left.

- At 3 miles, after passing the entrance to the blimp hangar, the path reaches the Pompano Beach Sand and Spurs Equestrian Park, with its rows of stables behind the hedges looking like a small trailer park for horses. The park is a city-owned facility with privately owned stables—one of the few of its kind in the nation. The stables are a reminder of when Broward was rural enough for Pompano Beach to call itself home to the nation's largest winter vegetables market in 1939.

- There is another little rest area at 3.7 miles with three benches situated around a small shade tree and a bed of crushed stone.

- Beyond the benches, the path returns to Copans Road and a straight shot back to the shopping mall.

At the end of the loop, you can lock the bike and refuel at the food court in the mall. Or you might take another lap. Go ahead. Take two. They're small.

Something you should know: The Pompano Air Park began in the 1940s as a navy training base for pilots learning to land on aircraft carriers. The land, like much of Broward County before World War II, had been used to raise pineapple, tomatoes, peppers, beans, cucumbers, and squash. After the war, the airfield was passed from the Department of Defense to Florida, which gave the facility to the city of Pompano Beach with the stipulation that the land remain an airport.

Since then, Pompano Beach has added a golf course, a high school and elementary school, and the Sand and Spurs Equestrian Park to the property. In the 1960s the city sold part of the land to the developer who built the Pompano Square Mall. The life span of a mall seems to be about thirty years, and there is talk of razing the mall and replacing it with housing and a strip center.

Legend has it that surveyors from the Florida East Coast Railroad were treated to a dinner of pompano fish by locals in the 1890s. They made a note of the hospitality on their map for future surveyors. The folks who extended the railroad to the area in 1896 mistook the notation for the name of the settlement. Pompano was incorporated in 1908 and merged with the town of Pompano Beach in 1947. Longtime residents still refer to the area of the railroad tracks between Federal Highway and U.S. 441 as Old Pompano and boast that their city is the "oldest continuously named community" in Broward County.

For more information, call the Pompano Beach City Hall Planning Department, (954) 786-4600.

Palm Beach Lake Trail
The High Society Intracoastal Ride

Length: 4.7 miles.
Location: Palm Beach. From Interstate 95, take exit 52 onto Okeechobee Boulevard east. Cross the Royal Palm Bridge. Trail starts at Four Arts Plaza.
Amenities: street parking, ATM, bike shops.
Surface: 6- to 10-foot-wide asphalt without mile markers.

Henry Flagler's first Palm Beach home was a cute little Victorian cottage with stained glass in the second-story bay window and porch railings that formed the letter H. It was a modest home for a railroad baron who made one fortune in partnership with John D. Rockefeller and another building a railroad the length of the east coast of Florida. Flagler purchased Seagull Cottage from another railroad man, R. R. McCormack, in 1893. He didn't live there long. By 1902 Flagler had built his palatial mansion Whitehall and surrounded it with one of the largest, most ornate iron fences of its day.

Today the two Flagler residences stand side by side about a half mile from the southern end of the four-mile-long Palm Beach Lake Trail. The trail gives cyclists a history tour of the backyards, boat docks, and exquisite landscaping of Florida's most affluent community.

The path serves as the waterfront sidewalk for Palm Beach residents. It's their turf and the rest of us are just borrowing the pretty scenery as we pass by. Your only chance to get close to one of these mansions is to pay admission to Whitehall, now open to the public as the Henry Morrison Flagler Museum.

The just-visiting nature of the Palm Beach Lake Trail is reinforced by the lack of trail parking, rest rooms, water fountains, and convenience stores along the trail. The southern end of the bike path is behind Four Arts Plaza, whose parking lot is off limits to nonmembers of the Society of the Four Arts. But there is off-street parking near the plaza, free parking at the Flagler Museum, metered parking on Lake Street near the Palm Beach marina, and free two-hour parking on Sunset Avenue just north of Royal Poinciana Way.

(The Palm Beach Chamber of Commerce suggests you park in West Palm Beach and ride across the Flagler Bridge to catch the trail.)

Palm Beach Lake Trail

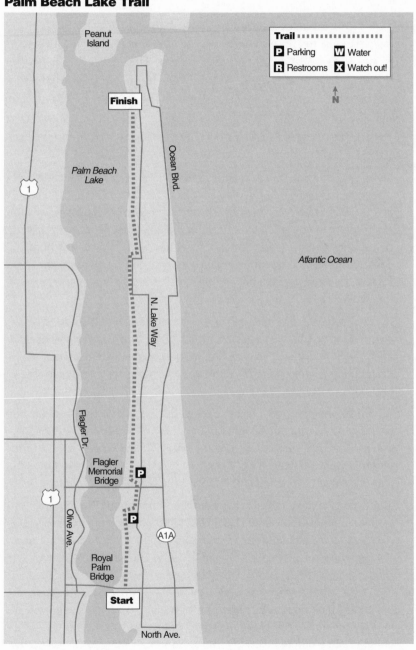

The bike path starts just north of the Royal Palm Bridge, but to the south is a half-mile asphalt bike path that goes along the waterfront of Palm Beach Marina. If you admire yachts and appreciate fine pleasure boats, it's worth the side trip just to see row after row of the boats that come in two sizes—large and larger. A word of caution, however. There is no traffic light or crosswalk at Lake Street and Royal Palm Way. It's not an easy situation for novice bicyclists crossing Royal Palm Way with traffic coming off Royal Palm Bridge.

Heading north from Royal Palm Way, here's what to look for on the Palm Beach Lake Trail:

• Right away the path begins with a sense of leisure, with someone's Adirondack chairs surrounded by a white picket fence facing the water and the skyline of West Palm Beach across the Intracoastal Waterway. All along the path you will find benches occupied by people reading, talking, or just watching the water. This is a short trail with no reason to hurry. Take your time, and a seat on a bench, to hear the waves slapping against the bank, feel the breeze, and smell the salty marine fragrance of the water.

• Planted along the first half mile of the trail you will find the odd, en-chanted-looking banyan trees with their gnarly trunks, sinewy vines, and thick shady branches. Their twisting trunks contrast with the sharp edges of the finely trimmed hedges of the houses on the opposite side of the bike path.

• At .5 mile, the bike path reaches Seagull Cottage, now serving as the par-ish residence for the Royal Poinciana Chapel. Moved to its present loca-tion in 1984, it is positioned to be exhibited. The path takes a right turn, presents you with Seagull Cottage, then takes a sharp left past a broad, ancient banyan tree and straight toward the broad side of Whitehall.

• There are bike racks outside the elaborate front gate of Whitehall, whose exterior suggests the White House, but which inside looks like a king's palace. Used as a hotel from 1925 to 1959, the mansion was restored as the Henry Morrison Flagler Museum in 1960. The museum contains Flagler memorabilia, historical exhibits, and archives. Rooms like the Louis XIV music room and the Louis XV ballroom are furnished in the opulent manner of the Gilded Age. The front foyer alone contains seven kinds of imported marble. Each of the mansion's bedrooms is furnished in a differ-ent era from a different country. Flagler's personal railroad car sits on the south lawn. Hours are 10 A.M.–5 P.M., Tuesday–Saturday, noon to 5

Fig. 11. Palms and hedges on Palm Beach Lake Trail

P.M. on Sunday, closed on Monday. Admission is $7 for adults, $3 for children aged 6–12. Phone: (561) 655-2833.

· Beyond Whitehall the path runs parallel to Coconut Row, named for the thirty-foot coconut palms that line the street like giant feather dusters. On the right, across the road, is a golf course that belongs to the Breakers Beach and Golf Club. The Breakers' pale yellow twin spires are visible in the distance beyond the rolling greens and bunkers of the golf course.

· Outside a condominium on Coconut Row a historical marker indicates the spot where Flagler's first resort hotel, the Royal Poinciana, once stood. One of the largest wooden structures in the world at the time of its construction in 1884, the rambling six-story white and yellow hotel had rooms for two thousand guests. Surrounded by fine gardens, the Royal Poinciana was occupied until 1930 and demolished in 1936.

· At 1 mile, the path crosses Royal Poinciana Way, a major intersection with a crosswalk light. To the right is a boulevard of shops, boutiques, and cafes. On the other side of Royal Poinciana Way is the Teriscope Garden Park dedicated in 1997 by the Garden Club of Palm Beach.

· Just beyond the park, take a left on Sunset Avenue, where there is on-street parking and easy access to the Palm Beach Lake Trail that picks up at the western end of the street. Palm Beach Bicycle Trail Shop, at 223

Sunrise Avenue, is one block north of Sunset Avenue. The shop rents, repairs, and sells bicycles, and rents and sells in-line skates.

· Turning right onto the trail, the bike path passes the Biltmore, a six-story former resort hotel that has been converted to condominiums.

· At 2 miles, the bike path reaches Duck's Nest, the oldest remaining house in Palm Beach. Built in 1891, the home with cedar shake siding and arched windows was assembled in New York and hauled by rail and barge to its lot on Lake Worth.

· A short distance to the east is the Bethesda by the Bay Episcopal Church, built in 1894 and accessible to its early congregation only by boat.

· As the path continues north past pastel yellow homes trimmed in white, notice the thin ribbons of asphalt that squeeze between the houses, linking the bike path with the side streets of Palm Beach. Some of the paths are marked with curbstones identifying the streets with which they connect.

· Before reaching a historical marker at 2.5 miles on the site of the town's first post office, the Palm Beach Lake Trail swerves through a shady stretch of dense, dark tropical trees.

· At 4 miles, the path takes a sharp right and detours around the long yellow clubhouse of the Sailfish Club of Florida.

· The Palm Beach Lake Trail ends with a right-hand turn that takes cyclists to North Lake Way and the middle of a Palm Beach subdivision.

At this point, you can turn around and ride the bike path back to complete an eight-mile ride. More experienced cyclists might want to weave their way east through the subdivision homes until they reach Ocean Boulevard. The two-lane road is narrow with no shoulders, but the traffic is light and the view of the Atlantic Ocean on one side is spectacular and the oceanfront homes on the other side are magnificent. Many of the oceanfront homeowners have their own private beaches and cabanas on the other side of the road.

Following Ocean Boulevard south, you can reach the other paved bike path in Palm Beach—a one-mile oceanfront multiuse trail that begins at the south end of the Palm Beach Golf and Country Club and continues to Wells Circle Road. Taking a right on Wells Circle Road will hook you back up with the Palm Beach Lake Path.

While the Palm Beach Lake Trail might not offer cyclists all the amenities of other trails, it provides some of the classiest scenery you will find anywhere in Florida.

Something you should know: The tall, graceful coconut palms that line the main boulevards of Palm Beach trace their ancestry to a shipwreck in 1878 that spilled a load of coconuts bound for Spain from the West Indies onto the shores of this barrier island. Railroad tycoon Henry Flagler changed the island forever when he started building resorts for the wealthy in the 1890s. Across the Intracoastal Waterway, Flagler created West Palm Beach for the servants, cooks, gardeners, and laborers who worked for the rich who built their homes on the island. Today, with a population of 9,800, Palm Beach remains an enclave for the affluent where house prices are high and public parking is scarce.

For more information, call Palm Beach Town Hall, (561) 838-5400, and the Palm Beach Chamber of Commerce, (561) 655-3282.

John Prince Park Paths

The Waterfront Wizard of Oz Ride

Length: 5.5 miles.
Location: Lake Worth. From Interstate 95, take exit 46. Go west on
Lantana Road. Turn north on Congress Avenue. Entrance is on the right.
From Florida's Turnpike, take exit 93. Go east on Lake Worth Road. Turn
right on Congress Avenue. Park entrance is on the left.
Amenities: parking, rest rooms, water, picnic facilities, exercise trails, ball
fields, tennis courts, playgrounds.
Surface: 6- to 8-foot-wide asphalt with mile markers on posts.

South Florida supports many exotic tropical plants, but none so fairy-tale in
appearance as the banyan tree. Sometimes called the "tourist tree" for its
curiosity appeal, the banyan tree is a stout shade tree with gargoylelike
growths on its sinewy trunk. The tree's roots drop from its branches like
escape lines for squirrels and embed themselves in the ground. Hillbilly
beards of Spanish moss complete the banyan tree's eccentric ensemble. Ban-
yans are truly the character actors of trees.

For its girth, shade, and odd appearance, the banyan is a favorite tree for
parks in South Florida. You will find these strange trees along many paved
bike trails in the parks of Palm Beach County, but the most impressive for
number and arrangement are those at John Prince Park.

The second oldest park in the state, John Prince also boasts a number of
flowering trees. Royal poincianas bloom red in the summer. Jacaranda put
forth a purplish blue flower in the late spring and early summer. In the dry
months of fall and spring, the tabedulia trees sprout yellow and pink blos-
soms.

The bike paths that wiggle and weave through John Prince Park give cyclists a waterside ride along ten miles of shoreline.

You can pick up the asphalt bike path that follows the contours of the 338-
acre Lake Osborne at several spots. But the best place to start is the Center
Drive Pavilion at the Congress Avenue entrance.

Starting from the Center Drive Pavilion and heading north, here's what to
look for on the John Prince Park bike paths:

John Prince Park

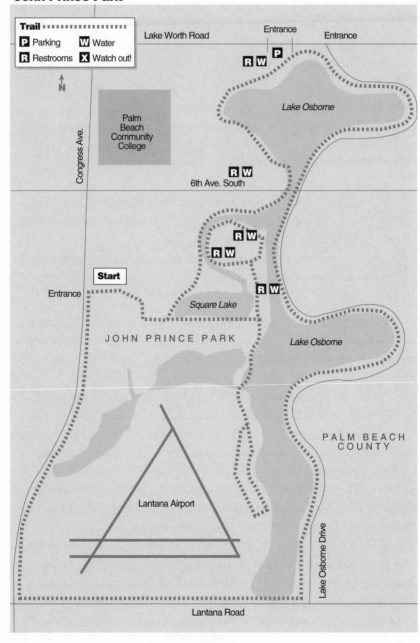

Trail ▪▪▪▪▪▪▪▪▪▪▪▪▪▪▪▪▪
P Parking **W** Water
R Restrooms **X** Watch out!

N

Lake Worth Road

Entrance Entrance

R W **P**

Palm
Beach
Community
College

Lake Osborne

Congress Ave.

R W

6th Ave. South

R W

R W

Start

Entrance

R W

Square Lake

JOHN PRINCE PARK

Lake Osborne

PALM BEACH
COUNTY

Lantana Airport

Lake Osborne Drive

Lantana Road

- The bike path passes rest rooms, a picnic pavilion, and a playground before crossing a wooden bridge. On the other side of the bridge, the path narrows to six feet or so before reaching a parade of palm trees about a half mile from the start.

- After brushing by shaggy banyan trees and slim palms, the path ducks under 6th Avenue around 1 mile.

- At 2 miles, as the path parallels the serpentine Lake Osborne Drive, a row of banyan trees suggests a chorus line of gnarly old men.

- After passing a cluster of Australian pines bent toward the water as if looking at their own reflections, the path passes under 6th Avenue again at 2.5 miles.

- Looping around an appendix of Lake Osborne, the path reaches McMillan Island with a tot-lot playground and picnic tables at 4 miles. Pond apple, red maple, and cypress trees line the shore in this area that was once swamp.

- After crossing a small bridge, the asphalt bike path ends at Lantana Road. On the right, across the lake and beyond the reeds and cattails and bull rushes, you can see the hangars and runways of Lantana Airport.

You can either return on the bike path or head west on the concrete sidewalk alongside busy Lantana Road. Except for the entrance to the airport there are no major streets to cross on your return trip to the Center Drive Pavilion. The roadside sidewalk is not as scenic as the bike path inside the park, but it's straight and wide enough to give experienced riders a chance to get up some speed and elevate the heart rate. After about a half mile on Lantana Road, the path turns right on Congress Avenue. Another half mile and you're back at the Congress Avenue entrance to John Prince Park.

Back at Center Drive Pavilion, the path squeezes between Square Lake and a canal feeding Lake Osborne for about a quarter mile. Turn left to take the half-mile loop to a peninsular complex of parking, rest rooms, picnic facilities, and playgrounds. Turn right and you pass over the canal, cross another wooden bridge and circle through a camping area with rest rooms and picnic benches. The view of the lake, airport, and streets on this half-mile loop is the flip side of the Lake Osborne Drive section of bike path.

With its weird Wizard of Oz banyan trees, the John Prince Park bike paths are a ride through a waterfront wonderland not found anywhere else in Florida.

Something you should know: John Prince Park is named for an audacious Palm Beach County commissioner who came up with the idea for a county park in 1937, then persuaded property owners and the governor of Florida to hand over the land necessary to make his idea come true. John Prince died in 1952, before the park could be completed. At the time of its inception, the park was only one of two county-owned parks in the state of Florida.

For more information, call the Palm Beach County Parks and Recreation Department, (561) 966-6600.

Okeeheelee Park Paths

The Quiet Waters Ride

Length: 8 miles.
Location: West Palm Beach. From Interstate 95, take exit 49. Take Forest Hill Boulevard west. Main park entrance is the second right.
Amenities: parking, rest rooms, water, picnic facilities, snack bar, bike and rollerblade rentals.
Surface: 8-foot-wide asphalt without mile markers.

Late in the afternoon, when the wind has surrendered and the sun is sinking, Clearwater Lake is so calm and smooth it mirrors the sky. In an open field near the lake, a batch of sweaty teenagers are finishing their last game of touch football. A father walks patiently behind his daughter riding a bike with training wheels. A pair of child's shoes and socks are left at water's edge, not far from the No Swimming–No Wading sign.

Weaving and winding through the 975-acre Okeeheelee Park, eight miles of bike paths follow the shoreline of the county park best known for the championship waterskiing that takes place on its waters. Okeeheelee is a park wrapped around water, and every mile of bike path is alongside a lakeshore. Unlike most paved bike trails, which are linear links from Point A to Point B, the Okeeheelee Park paths circle in a seemingly aimless stroll around the lakes and recreational facilities. And that's not a bad way to ride these bike paths, either. There is no single way to ride these trails. Just follow them wherever they take you.

There are points where the trails cross the roads inside the park, and you have to be alert for cars. But these self-contained, family-friendly paths are perfect for young cyclists and inexperienced riders. There are no steep hills or busy intersections and you are never far from water fountains and rest rooms.

Here's what to look for on the Okeeheelee Park bike paths:

· The northern loop, branching to the right from the main parking lot, is three miles. Following the shoreline of Clearwater Lake, the path passes the first of several picnic areas with pavilions, grills, and tables for large groups and family gatherings. It winds and curves around the edge of the

Okeeheelee Park

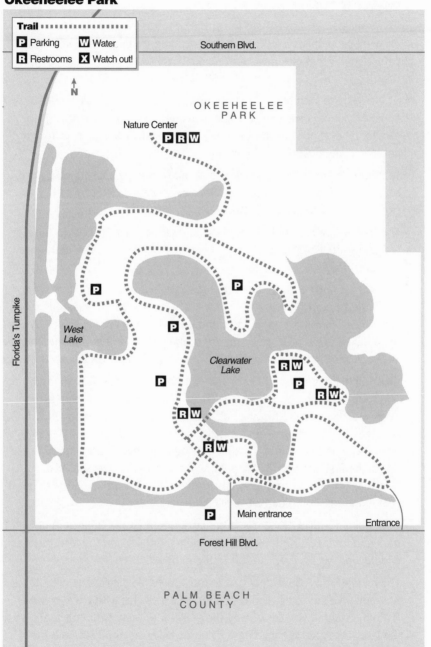

Trail ••••••••••••••••••
P Parking   W Water
R Restrooms   X Watch out!

N

Southern Blvd.

OKEEHEELEE
PARK

Nature Center
P R W

Florida's Turnpike

P

P

P

West
Lake

P

Clearwater
Lake

R W
P

R W

R W

R W

P   Main entrance

Entrance

Forest Hill Blvd.

PALM BEACH
COUNTY

lake, past ducks, small pines, oaks, and signs that warn of the possible presence of alligators.

- At 1.8 miles, the path crosses the entrance to the park's nature center. A .4-mile bike path splits off to the right, leading to the park's hundred-acre nature center that includes animal exhibits, a herd of deer, and hiking trails.

- At 2 miles, the path takes you past an area used for water ski competitions. Aluminum bleachers face the water, ski jumps, and Florida's Turnpike in the distance beyond the lake. Judges' stands, like perches for giant birds, line the edge of the water.

- At 2.5 miles, the path crosses a road at the Micanopy Pavilion ski course. After the path turns left, you can either go straight and return to the parking lot or take a right to the western loop.

- The western loop is about two miles long, encircling soccer fields, baseball and softball diamonds, and more judges' perches lined up along narrow West Lake.

- Halfway around the loop, the path meets the entrance road. Take a left if you want to return to the parking lot. Look for the Play It Again Sports bike and skate rental concession stand just inside the park entrance. A right will take you on a bike path out of the park and .3 mile along Forest Hill Boulevard where it ends at an off-road facility for BMX bikes.

- Crossing the entrance road links you with the two-mile southern loop. The southern loop also follows the shore of a long thin lake. Unlike the other loops, however, this one has a stretch that is heavily wooded with tall pines and a soft blanket of needles on the ground. About a half mile from the main entrance road, after passing the tennis courts, the path meets the first entrance to the park, which serves the park's golf course. A .2-mile trail leads out of the park at this point, linking up with a sidewalk that runs alongside Forest Hill Boulevard.

- Continuing to follow the loop around will return you to the main entrance road. Take a right to return to the parking lot and to reach the middle loop, which branches off to the right.

- The middle loop follows the road to the Tuskeegee picnic area with its Acropolis-like picnic pavilion set on top of a small hill with a playground. From the summit you can survey the park—the glassy smooth surface of the lake, the lights illuminating the courts, fields, and courses, and the serpentine bike paths that tie it all together.

Fig. 12. Judges' stands on Okee- heelee Park bike path

Something you should know: This park used to be the pits. In the 1950s and 1960s, Okeeheelee Park was a shell-pit strip mine used to extract the shell rock for roadbeds. Its genesis as a park came in 1975 when Palm Beach County began dredging the strip mine to form the lakes that would later host international waterskiing tournaments and bass fishing. The county then spent nearly ten million dollars to haul in topsoil and plant 52,000 pine seedlings and 18,000 sabal palms, cabbage palms, cypress, oak, sweet gum, and red maple trees. They even transplanted a sixty-foot-tall dead pine tree as a nesting place for osprey and eagles on a man-made hill overlooking the 119-acre man-made Lake Okeeheelee. About the only part of the park that was not re-created is the eighty acres of pinelands behind the nature center. To christen this park resurrected from strip-mine ruin, the county chose the Seminole Indian word for "quiet waters." Okeeheelee Park is, as one of its architects said, a place that can "restore your soul."

For more information, call the Palm Beach County Parks and Recreation Department, (561) 966-6600.

Dyer Park Paths

The Recycled Cycling Ride

Length: 4 miles.
Location: Palm Beach County. From Florida's Turnpike, take exit 109. Go
east on PGA Boulevard, south on Military Trail, west on Bee Line Highway,
south on Haverhill Road. Entrance to Dyer Park is on the right. From
Interstate 95, take exit 55. Go west on Blue Heron Boulevard. Turn right
on Bee Line Highway.
Amenities: parking, rest rooms, water, mountain-biking trails, picnic
facilities, playgrounds, ball fields, wheelchair access.
Surface: 10-foot-wide "glassphalt" without mile markers.

The sounds of recreation fill the air where winged scavengers once ruled.
The soft slap of a ball hitting a glove. Parents' cheers, children's shrieks as
they chase a soccer ball from one end of the field to the other. The steady
pock-pock-pock of a tennis match, the thud-thud-thud of a basketball. The
tiny buzz of radio-controlled airplanes. A cyclist's rhythmic breathing.

Dyer Park, created in 1997 from a reclaimed landfill, is a 405-acre island
of exercise and relaxation in an industrial corner of Palm Beach County.
Linking the courts, ball fields, diamonds, toy airstrips, and equestrian paths
are four miles of paved bike paths arranged in three loops.

Made with glassphalt—a mixture of asphalt and recycled glass—the bike
paths sparkle in the sun and crunch and crackle beneath the bike tires. Although the glass is too small to be a problem, it's a good idea to keep your
tires fully inflated. Hard tires are less likely to puncture.

Starting from the parking lot, here's what to look for on the Dyer Park
bike paths:

- The smallest of the loops circles the summit of a landfill mountain. Starting at the base, the path ascends for .1 mile up a heart-pumping incline.
Planted on the side of the hill are scrub oaks and spindly saplings. Thin
dirt mountain-bike trails wind back and forth between the trees along the
slope of the hillside.

  The .7-mile loop at the top gives a panoramic view of West Palm
Beach's faint gray skyline in the distance and the ball fields and courts be-

Dyer Park

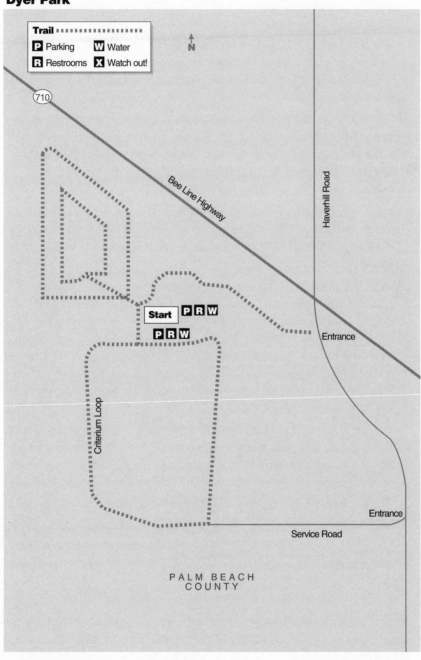

Trail ▪▪▪▪▪▪▪▪▪▪▪▪▪▪▪▪▪▪▪

P Parking **W** Water

R Restrooms **X** Watch out!

N

710

Bee Line Highway

Haverhill Road

Start P R W

P R W

Entrance

Criterium Loop

Entrance

Service Road

PALM BEACH
COUNTY

low. In the center of the top loop is an empty field with flocks of white birds who remember what's under the dirt. There are no shade trees at the top of Trash Mountain to block the sun or blunt the wind.

· A second one-mile loop circles the base of the mountain. It passes the park's man-made lake with its signs warning of alligators. White herons and other wading birds pose at the water's edge amid the bull rushes and other reed vegetation.

· Taking a left at the end of the loop, the bike path crosses a road and leads to the 1.5-mile criterium loop. There are no trees, no benches, no water stops along the way. The lack of scenery and the isolation of the loop from the rest of the park's facilities make the criterium loop an excellent opportunity for riding fast and hard.

· About a half mile into the loop, the path crosses a mountain bike trail, an equestrian trail, and the entrance to Philip Wherry Field, home to the Radio Controlled Bush Pilots. A sign warns cyclists: Caution–Low Flying Model Aircraft.

· At 1 mile, the bike path meets a service road that runs alongside the eastern edge of the loop. Turn left on the road to complete the criterium loop, or go straight on another service road that leads to the back entrance of the park. The rear entrance road is a little less than a mile long, leading to the park's 3.4 miles of equestrian trails and a parking lot for horse trailers. Although not a dedicated bike path, the two-lane road has little traffic. The road ends at Haverhill Road, facing Barney's Junkyard, which boasts We Buy Junk Cars.

· In addition to the three loop paths and the rear entrance road, there is also a .3-mile bike path that leads from the front entrance to the parking lot with rest rooms, water fountains, and a picnic pavilion. Inexperienced or young cyclists might want to skip this side trip if they feel uncomfortable riding in the road, separated from traffic only by a white line.

With plenty of rest rooms, water fountains, picnic areas, playgrounds, and recreational areas, Dyer Park is a good place for family cycling, but also offers the hard-riding serious cyclist a nice place to get dizzy riding around in circles.

Something you should know: Just about everything at Dyer Park—park benches, playground equipment, picnic tables and pavilion, trash cans, glassphalt pavement, and playground mulch—is made from recycled materials. Even the trees were recycled from somewhere else. For twenty-two years, beginning in 1968, the park was Dyer Boulevard Landfill—the county dump. In that time, 6.73 million tons of household garbage, construction and demolition debris, and trash was dumped in the landfill. Trash Mountain is actually a very large pile of construction debris. A "gas extraction system" captures and burns methane gas to remove any odor from the garbage buried in the landfill. After the landfill closed in 1990, the Solid Waste Authority of Palm Beach County spent $5.6 million to convert the landfill into a recreational park. More than twelve thousand trees were relocated to the park, many from roadway projects, to recreate the natural habitat of slash pine forests, cabbage palm hammocks, and aquatic vegetation. Future plans include a golf course over another cell of the former landfill. When it comes to Dyer Park, nothing goes to waste.

For more information, call the Palm Beach County Parks and Recreation Department, (561) 966-6600.

Key Biscayne/Old Cutler Road Trail

The Marinas, Museums, and Mangroves Ride

Length: 27 miles.
Location: Miami. From Interstate 95, take exit 1. Head east on
Rickenbacker Causeway to Key Biscayne. Crandon Park is on the left.
Amenities: parking, rest rooms, water, bike shops, ATMS, restaurants,
convenience stores.
Surface: 8-foot-wide asphalt and concrete without mile markers.

The Miami skyline, seen from the Rickenbacker Causeway on a bike, is
breathtaking. The high-rise condominiums, office towers, and bank buildings are a man-made mountain range rising dramatically over the glittering
blue water of Biscayne Bay.

But this is Miami, and with the beauty comes caution. Although the bike
path across the causeway is separated from the traffic by a concrete barrier,
signs warn cyclists to walk their bikes over the bridge, as the height of the
span, the narrowness of the lane, the wind, and oncoming joggers and walkers make the ride risky for inexperienced bikers.

The same holds true for the twenty-seven-mile bike path that stretches
from Crandon Marina on Key Biscayne to Black Point Marina in Biscayne
National Park. There are parts of the route that are as beautiful as any in the
state. And there are other parts where you are better off walking. This is the
fact of big-city bike riding—have fun, enjoy the ride, but stay alert and be
careful.

For experienced cyclists, there are alternative routes off the bike path on
side streets that lead to parks, attractions, and marinas.

The Miami bike path could be divided into three sections that minimize
the hazards for young or inexperienced cyclists. The eight-mile Key Biscayne
segment goes from Crandon Park over the causeway, past a pair of museums,
and down to Mercy Hospital. The six-mile Coconut Grove section is hazardous at points but takes cyclists past some scenic parks and through a
renowned shopping district. The thirteen-mile Old Cutler Road segment
encompasses beautiful neighborhoods, historic attractions, and parks preserving the last vestiges of Miami's hammocks and mangroves.

Key Biscayne/Old Cutler Road Trail

MIAMI

MIAMI BEACH

95

ALT 9

9

41 90

826

Rickenbacker Causeway

Virginia Key

Coconut Grove

CORAL CABLES

X

P R W

R P

Crandon Park

P R W

Start

1

P

X

Peacock Park

KEY BISCAYNE

P R W

Matheson Hammock County Park

R P W

Coral Reef Park

W

P R

874

KENDALL

Coral Reef Drive

BISCAYNE BAY

Trail ::::::::::::::::::::::::
P Parking   W Water
R Restrooms X Watch out!

821

176th St.

P R W

Bill Sadowski Park

Old Cutler Road

Black Point Marina

P R W

Finish

ATLANTIC OCEAN

N

The middle section leading to Coconut Grove is the most incomplete, with segments where the bike path disappears altogether. There are plans to eliminate this hazard, but until then novice cyclists might want to avoid this segment.

Starting on the eastern end of the trail in Crandon Park on Key Biscayne, here's what to look for on the Key Biscayne/Old Cutler Road Trail:

- There is a toll of $1 per car on the Rickenbacker Causeway and a $3.50 parking fee at Crandon Park. Free parking is available at Crandon Marina and in the waterfront parks stretched along the causeway. Crandon Park offers ample parking, rest rooms, water, concession stands, shelters, a nature center, ball fields, gardens, an amusement area, and a beachside bicycle trail that takes you past a carousel. Look for iguanas left over from when the park had a zoo.

- Watch out where the path leaving Crandon Park runs alongside the roadway a little too close for children, and be careful where it crosses Crandon Boulevard opposite Crandon Marina. The traffic is light, but there is no crosswalk light. Inexperienced cyclists and parents with young children might be better off starting at the marina, which has rest rooms, water, and a restaurant.

- At 4 miles, the bike path passes the University of Miami's Rosenstiel School of Marine and Atmospheric Science before reaching the Miami Seaquarium. The Seaquarium features performances by Lolita, the three-ton killer whale, and thirty-eight acres of marine shows and exhibits. Hours are 9:30 A.M.–6 P.M. Admission is $20.95 for those aged 9 and above, $15.95 for children aged 3–9; free under 3. Parking is $3. Phone: (305) 361-5705.

- At 4.5 miles, on the right is the Miami Marine Stadium, a landmark boat-racing facility that operated for forty years until Hurricane Andrew wrecked it in 1992. The structure remains abandoned while the city debates whether to repair it or tear it down.

- Another palm-studded waterfront parking lot with a set of rest rooms sits at the foot of the nearly one-mile-long humpbacked Rickenbacker Causeway. Cyclists should walk their bikes over the bridge, which gives more time to soak up the view of the city of Miami laid out in full panoramic glory.

- At 6 miles, on the other side of the bridge, is scenic Hobie Beach with its huge, feathery Australian pines trees providing a canopy of shade. For those who don't want to cycle across the Rickenbacker bridge, this is a good place to park and start your ride. The park includes rest rooms, parking, and picnic tables. Watch for cars entering and exiting the park.

· Around 6.5 miles, the asphalt path turns to concrete, crosses another bridge, and reaches the causeway tollbooth. For a side trip, go under the short bridge and turn right to take a sidewalk on Brickell Avenue 2.5 miles to downtown Miami.

· Following the bike path to Brickell Avenue, cyclists will take a sharp left through an infamous iron gate known locally as Stallonegate in honor of Sylvester Stallone, a former resident who led an unsuccessful effort to have the gate locked.

· On the other side of the gate is the southern end of Brickell Avenue, an oval-shaped street that passes Alice Wainright Park, a little bayside park with only ten parking spaces but a beautiful view of Biscayne Bay, as well as rest rooms, water, picnic tables, benches, and a playground. There is no bike path along Brickell, but the road is wide and traffic is rare. None-theless, remember you aren't on a bike path any longer.

· At 7 miles, Brickell meets 32nd Road. Take a right. To pick up the bike path again, turn left at Bayshore Drive, also known as South Miami 1. To reach the M-Path bike trail, cross Bayshore Drive on 32nd Road, which will take you to the pedestrian overpass that leads to the Vizcaya Metrorail Station.

· Heading south on the concrete sidewalk along Bayshore Drive, you will pass the entrance to Vizcaya Museum and Gardens, a seventy-room Ital-ian Renaissance villa built by industrialist James Deering. The thirty-four rooms open to the public are decorated with art and furnishings repre-senting Renaissance, baroque, rococo, and neoclassic periods, while the ten-acre grounds are divided by hedges and walls into gardens featuring pools, fountains, and sculptures from France and Italy. Hours are 9:30 A.M.–4:30 P.M. daily. Admission is $10 for adults, $5 for children aged 6–12. Phone: (305) 250-9133.

· Across the street is the Miami Museum of Science and Space Transit Plan-etarium, with 150 hands-on biology, natural history, space, and computer exhibits. The museum's Wildlife Center is a rehabilitation center for 150 exotic birds and reptiles. The planetarium features multimedia laser shows. Hours are 10 A.M.–6 P.M. Admission to both the Museum of Sci-ence and Space Transit Planetarium is $9 for adults, $7 for senior citizens and students with IDs, $5.50 for children aged 3–12. Phone: (305) 854-4247.

• Beyond the Vizcaya entrance, the bike path turns from concrete to asphalt. Watch out for light poles embedded in the bike path. A three-foot-high wall with Aztec-style etchings on the side runs along the perimeter of Vizcaya. Across the street, the wall of a subdivision mirrors the etchings of Vizcaya.

• At 8 miles, the path reaches the entrance of Mercy Hospital. Inexperienced cyclists or those with young children might want to turn around at this point and head back to Key Biscayne.

• Shortly after the bike path passes the hospital, it becomes a narrow strip of the road at 17th Avenue. All that separates cyclists from oncoming traffic is a painted white line and a narrow shoulder. It's about a half mile until the asphalt bike path picks up again at Kennedy Park. Even experienced cyclists should be careful along this stretch of the route. The four-foot bike lane gets squeezed down to a foot wide at points. Bayshore Drive is a heavily traveled two-lane road with cars that don't always notice, or respect, the white line separating the bike lane from the traffic—especially at corners.

• Around 8.5 miles, the trail resumes with the Siegendorf Bicycle Path at Kennedy Park. There's a .3-mile loop through the middle of the park that leads to a beautiful view of Key Biscayne and sailboats gliding across Biscayne Bay. The park has parking, rest rooms, and water for those who want to pick up the bike path here instead of driving out to Crandon Marina. For frozen lemonade, a hot dog, and local color, look for A.C.'s Ice Truck.

• At 10 miles, you can go straight on the bike path along Bayshore Drive or turn left at Pan American Drive, which takes you past Miami City Hall, a marina, and the Coconut Grove Chamber of Commerce before reaching Bayfront Park.

• Taking a right at McFarland Road, the bike path reaches Peacock Park—an oasis of shade, water, and rest rooms—and enters the Coconut Grove shopping district. There are plenty of good restaurants with sidewalk dining, fine boutiques, and bistros in the Coconut Grove business district. One of the best spots for people-watching is Cocowalk, an interesting group of shops, restaurants, and a movie theater. About three blocks west of Main Highway, on Grand Avenue, is Grove Cycle. The bike shop rents, repairs, and sells bikes.

- Turning left on Main Highway, the bike path continues south, passing the Barnacle State Historic Site, where the oldest home in Dade County has been preserved in a five-acre park. The home, with its distinct octagonal center room, was built in 1891 and named the Barnacle by Ralph Middleton Munroe, a yacht designer. Needing more room, Munroe elevated the one-story house in 1908 and built a second story below the original one. A charter member of the Key Biscayne Yacht Club, "Commodore Munroe" decorated the Barnacle with artifacts salvaged from ships that wrecked off Miami's coast. The state park includes this house, a boathouse built in 1887, and rest rooms. The park is open to the public 9 A.M.–4 P.M., Friday–Sunday. Admission is $1. Phone: (305) 448-9445.

- Around 12 miles, the path meets Douglas Road with a wall on the left and a wire fence on the right. But after you turn onto Douglas, the fence disappears and so does the bike path. There is a bike lane along Douglas, but be careful. This is a very bad intersection where cars coming toward you and turning onto Main Highway have a tendency to swerve onto the bike path.

- The Douglas bike lane goes on for .3 mile before crossing into a quiet residential neighborhood where the bike lane itself fades away and disappears altogether at Prospect Avenue. Continue south on Douglas until it meets Edgewater Drive. Take a right on Edgewater, where once again you will be riding on a residential street without a dedicated bike lane or separated bike path.

- When Edgewater meets Ingraham Highway, around 14 miles, a left turn on Ingraham takes you over a canal to Cocoplum Plaza. Check out the odd statue of a bronze shoe in the center of the plaza. Old Cutler Road shoots off the traffic circle at Cocoplum Plaza, and running right alongside the road is the first paved bike path built in Florida.

- Many Miami cyclists like to park at Cocoplum Plaza and either ride south on the thirteen-mile Old Cutler Road bike path or head four miles north to Coconut Grove. Parking is free, but limited to about a dozen spaces. There is no water at Cocoplum Plaza, no rest rooms, and no stores.

- Before heading south on the Old Cutler Road bike path, adventurous cyclists might want to take a side trip through the guard gate at Cocoplum Estates for a half-mile tour of the multi-million-dollar homes built on Biscayne Bay.

- The Old Cutler Road path itself begins by passing through an archway formed by a majestic banyan tree. There's a small stone bench set in the cool shade of the huge tree. The odd-looking banyan trees make a soothing canopy of shade over Old Cutler Road, a two-lane road that has been designated a historic site.

• Near 15.5 miles, the bike path reaches Matheson Hammock Park and Marina, where it veers away from the road through a stone wall and takes bicyclists on a short side trip through the trees. At the entrance to Matheson Park, a spur off the bike path leads into the park via a tunnel through the mangrove. One of the most magical stretches of bike path anywhere, it engulfs cyclists in the spindly mangrove trees for about a mile. The path is sometimes awash with brackish water, and should be avoided when it is submerged. The spur path ends at the marina parking lot and beach, where you will find a breathtaking view of the bay. Besides the beach, the park includes rest rooms, boat ramps, picnic areas, nature trails, and a concession stand. At the eastern tip of the park is the hundred-yard-long Atoll Pool, a bay-fed swimming pool. Next to the pool is the Red Fish Grill Restaurant, one of the most picturesque dining spots in Miami. Matheson Hammock itself is one of the most scenic and popular parks in Dade County. The hundred-acre park was built in the 1930s by the Civilian Conservation Corps from land donated by Commodore W. J. Matheson, a wealthy New York businessman. The hammocks and mangroves are remnants of an urban forest that has practically vanished beneath Dade County development. Think of Matheson Hammock Park as a museum for trees.

• Around 16 miles is Fairchild Tropical Garden. Created in 1938, the eighty-three-acre garden contains tropical and subtropical plants from around the world. Arranged in geographic and botanical groupings—fruits and vegetables from the Yucatan Peninsula, trees and shrubs from the Bahamas, twenty species of bamboo—the garden is built around eleven lakes and contemplative pathways. The Garden Shop sells hard-to-find gardening and botanical books. The Garden Cafe serves lunch. Fairchild Tropical Garden is open 9:30 A.M.–4:30 P.M. daily. Admission is $8 for adults, children under 13 free. Phone: (305) 667-1651.

• A short way beyond the gardens, the bike path ends at SW 105th Street, opposite the entrance to the Snapper Creek Lakes subdivision. Crossing Old Cutler Road at the traffic light, the bike path becomes a bike route through the subdivision. Once inside the subdivision, follow Snapper Creek Lakes Road (watching for wild peacocks as you ride) to a little bike bridge that crosses a canal at SW 104th Street.

Fig. 13. Key Biscayne/
Old Cutler Trail:
mangrove tunnel in
Matheson Hammock
Park

- Outside the subdivision, at Red Road, cyclists have a choice. They can turn right on a bike path extension that takes them a mile north to Dante Fascell Park where they will find parking, rest rooms, water, and pay phones.

- Turning left, cyclists will take the bike path .3 mile before crossing Red Road near the entrance to Parrot Jungle and Gardens at 17 miles. Opened in 1936 with an admission charge of twenty-five cents, Parrot Jungle is famous for its performing parrots and macaws and cockatoos, flocks of Caribbean flamingos, and giant tortoises. The old-style Florida tourist attraction, with its 1,200 varieties of exotic plants and 1,100 sub-tropical birds and reptiles, is scheduled to close and relocate in 2001. Hours are 9:30 A.M.–6 P.M. daily. Admission is $13.95 for adults, $8.95 for children aged 3–10, free under 3. Phone: (305) 666-7834.

- South of Parrot Jungle, the bike path rejoins Old Cutler Road. Around 18 miles, cyclists can take a left on Avenue Lugo for a side trip to view the ocean.

- Near 19 miles, at Chapman Field Park on Deering Bay Drive, water, phones, and picnic facilities are available.

- Watch out for cars at 19.5 miles when the Old Cutler Road bike path crosses the busy intersection at SW 67th Avenue, also called Ludlam Road.

- Nearing 21 miles, the bike path crosses Coral Reef Drive. Turning right off the path, cyclists can take that road a half mile to Coral Reef Park, which has a 1.5-mile bike trail loop, rest rooms, water, picnic facilities, a playground, ball fields, and tennis courts.

- At 21 miles, cyclists can turn left on 156th Street to reach 72nd Avenue and the entrance to the Charles Deering Estate Historic Site—420 acres of historical, archeological, architectural, and environmental splendor. Contained on the grounds is what remains of Cutler, an 1880s town that linked with Coconut Grove in 1882 on the historic road now paralleled by the bike path. Once owned by Chicago industrialist and International Harvester chairman Charles Deering, the park contains Deering's Mediterranean Revival–style mansion, Stone House, built in 1922 as a fortress for the preservation of his art and antiques collection. The grounds also include an 1896 inn, 115 acres of coastal hardwood hammock, 150 acres of pinelands, a meandering nature trail, and the burial mound of Indian chieftains interred face down like spokes of a wheel. Hours are 10 A.M.– 5 P.M. daily. Admission is $9 for adults, $5 for children aged 4–17, free under 4. Phone: (305) 235-1668.

- Just beyond the 22-mile mark, the bike path passes the high-water mark of Hurricane Andrew in 1992 and then crosses over Cutler Canal. The canal marks the northern tip of Biscayne National Park to the left. The national park is an undeveloped stretch of coastal mangroves and tropical park that hugs the shoreline south of Miami. Accessible only by boat, most of the park's 175,000 acres are under water, including the coral reef popular with divers.

- Around 22.5 miles, cyclists can take a right on 176th Street for a half mile to Bill Sadowski Park, a 26-acre facility with nature trails, water, rest rooms, 6.5 acres of critically imperiled pine rockland habitat, and 14 acres of a tropical hardwood hammock with trees found nowhere else in the United States.

- At 25 miles, cyclists again have a choice. They can continue on Old Cutler Road for the last two miles until the bike path ends suddenly near Florida's Turnpike at 224th Street. There are plenty of fast-food restaurants, gas stations, convenience stores, and ice cream shops, but little else of interest at this tail end of the Old Cutler bike path.

- Most cyclists choose at 25 miles to take a left on the three-mile bike path that follows SW 87th Avenue to Black Point Park Marina—the closest you can get to Biscayne National Park without a boat. The park has water, rest rooms, a dockside restaurant and bar, picnic pavilion, bikeways, jogging trails, and live entertainment on weekends. Watch for alligators in the canal to the right and a resident crocodile who lives in a lake to the right around 2.5 miles.

From Key Biscayne to Biscayne National Park, from Crandon Marina to Black Point Marina, the Miami bike path offers plenty to see and do along the way—especially if you are up to the challenges of riding a bike in the big city.

Something you should know: Miami was the first city in Florida to construct bike paths, some sections of the path along Old Cutler Road dating back to the 1970s. But the city's population growth and financial problems (Miami nearly went bankrupt in 1995) have left it trailing much of the rest of the state in the construction and maintenance of multiuse paved trails. The stretch of missing bike path after 17th Street, for example, is a case where road widening erased an existing section of bike path. Bicycle advocates hope Miami's lag-behind legacy is ended with the city's financial rebound and new transportation funding dedicated to improving and expanding the Miami bike path network.

For more information, call Metroplan, (305) 375-1735.

M-Path Bike Trail
The Urban Challenge Ride

Length: 9 miles.
Location: Miami. From Interstate 95, take exit 2. Go east on 8th Street for two blocks. Turn right on SW 1st Avenue to the Metrorail's Brickell Station parking lot.
Amenities: parking and rest rooms at Metrorail stations, convenience stores, restaurants, bike shops.
Surface: 8-foot-wide asphalt without mile markers.

For cyclists who like their wild life in the ride instead of the scenery, there is nothing in Florida like Miami's M-Path. There are no languid alligators warming their reptilian bellies on the asphalt, no cows, and no rare wading birds, but plenty of adventure and obstacles to overcome on this bike path.

This is Miami, and the M-Path is as big-city as a bike path can get. Weaving beneath the concrete supports of the elevated Metrorail mass transit system, the M-Path takes cyclists from downtown Miami to the city's southern suburbs. Along the way, it passes the Vizcaya Museum and Gardens, the Museum of Science, the University of Miami campus, and the city's antiques district.

If you're up to a challenge and an up-close look at the streets of Miami, this is the bike path for you. But be warned: They don't make it easy. This is urban riding. It is made less hazardous by having a dedicated bike path, but it's a bike path with intersections that lack traffic lights or crosswalks or curb cuts, with confusing forks and sections that seem to disappear altogether, and with signs that only add to the confusion.

Nothing about the path makes it a family-friendly ride for parents with young children. And with twenty cross streets in nine miles, the M-Path is not a test track for pace lines or experienced cyclists who like to put their heads down and crank it up to twenty miles an hour.

Although the M-Path does not pass through bad neighborhoods, it could use some of the signs posted on the St. Mark's Trail that advise cyclists not to ride alone. And like the Van Fleet Trail that closes at sunset, this path lacks lighting, so you don't want to be riding after dark.

M-Path Bike Trail

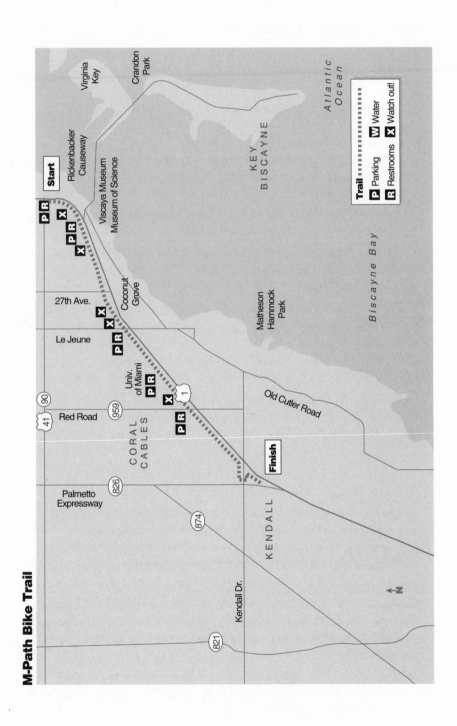

If all this doesn't scare you away from the M-Path, you were born to bike in Miami.

Starting from the north end, here's what to look for on the M-Path Bike Trail:

· Right from the start at the corner of SW 1st Avenue and SW 12th Street, the M-Path identifies itself as the path of multiple transportation modes. Trains, cars, and bicycles converge at Brickell Station where the M-Path shares its northern terminus with the city's elevated Metrorail and Metromover. Interstate 95 is a couple of blocks to the west; U.S. 1 is a couple of blocks to the east.

· Within the first half mile, watch out while crossing SW 25th Street, which lacks a crosswalk, and SW 26th Road, where cars are exiting I-95.

· Cyclists can hook up with the Key Biscayne Bike Path at this point by heading east on the sidewalk along SW 26th Road a half mile to the Rickenbacker Causeway.

· Just beyond the 1-mile mark, the path reaches the Vizcaya Metrorail Station. There is a bike ramp and pedestrian bridge at the station that crosses Dixie Highway and takes you to both the Vizcaya Museum and the Museum of Science (see previous chapter). It also links cyclists with the Key Biscayne Bike Path.

· Near the 2-mile point, watch out and be patient when navigating the intersection of SW 16th Street, SW 3rd Avenue, and SW 1st Avenue. There is no traffic light. Fortunately, there is a food store and deli on the right, if you need food or drink . . . or aspirin.

· Same advice applies at 2.5 miles when the path reaches SW 22nd Avenue. The intersection is five lanes wide with no crosswalk.

· At 3 miles, turn right on SW 28th Avenue to reach an antiques district with rows of shops. Cross at SW 27 Avenue to pick up the M-Path at the Coconut Grove Metrorail Station. The path seems to disappear, but you will find it wedged between U.S. 1 and the metro station.

· Watch out again when the path reaches the Douglas Road Metrorail Station around 4.5 miles. Douglas is another difficult intersection to cross. The best way is to cut left through the Walgreen's parking lot to the path next to U.S. 1, cross Douglas, and pick up the path alongside the highway again.

· Another difficult intersection arrives at 5 miles when the M-Path trail crosses Grand Avenue, Ponce De Leon Boulevard, and Le Jeune Road— yet another three-way intersection lacking a crosswalk. Look to the left for the Japanese Village—one of several themed subdivisions built by a Miami developer.

- At 5.5 miles, you are officially out of Miami and inside the city limits of Coral Gables, home of the University of Miami. The little canal you cross is the Coral Gables Canal. To the right, as you cross the bridge, you can see the painted spires of the historic Biltmore Hotel, anchoring the Biltmore Country Club and Biltmore Golf Course.

- At 6 miles, the path crosses Stanford Drive, the main entrance to the college campus. Stanford Drive leads to the Lowe Art Museum with its ten-thousand-piece collection of Renaissance, baroque, Native American, pre-Columbian, Asian, and nineteenth- and twentieth-century American art. Opened in 1952, the Lowe Museum was the first art museum in South Florida. Hours are 10 A.M.–5 P.M. on Tuesday, Wednesday, Friday, and Saturday; noon–7 P.M. on Thursday; noon–5 P.M. on Sunday; closed Monday. Admission is $5 for adults, $3 for students and senior citizens, free under 12. Phone: (305) 284-3535.

- It's been a rough ride so far on the M-Path Obstacle Course Bike Path, but to the left on the other side of U.S. 1 is an oasis—the Shoppes of Sunset Place. Like something leaping out of a cartoon, the large, bright shopping complex features a Virgin Megastore, FAO Schwartz, Nike Town, a soaring atrium, air conditioning, food, and fun. But before you indulge, be sure to lock up your bike.

- At Red Road and Dixie Highway is another tricky intersection. Once on the other side, you have crossed the city limits into South Miami. Once again, you need to weave around and find your way through the South Miami Metrorail Station. After you master that, there's SW 72nd Street, another of those intersections without a crosswalk where you have to find your own way across.

- At 7.5 miles, you'll find Mack Cycle and Fitness bike shop, offering sales, repairs, and maps, a half block to the right at 5995 Sunset Drive.

- The path crosses one more street, SW 80th, and passes the Bikes To Go bicycle shop before it makes an abrupt and unannounced end at Ludlam Road. Just a few blocks beyond the reach of the M-Path is the Dadeland Mall, one of the largest and oldest malls in Miami.

As frustrating as it can be riding the M-Path with its challenging cross streets and Houdini stretches of disappearing bike path, the path still proves the point that a day riding a bike is better than a hour stuck in traffic. As you are riding the M-Path, what you will hear is the screech of tires, blare of horns, and shouts of profanity from motorists in a hurry to get somewhere but going nowhere fast. Cars cutting off other motorists. Cars slamming on brakes just inches from somebody else's rear bumper. Look at their faces and you will see people feeling frustrated, getting angry, acting rude, isolated from each other in their coffins of metal and glass and gasoline.

Think about the irony of the term "rush hour" as you glide on your bicycle past all those drivers stopped and stuck in traffic, and an eighteen-mile round-trip ride on the M-Path doesn't seem so bad after all.

Something you should know: You can carry your bike on the Metrorail with a free permit obtained from the city. For more information about the passes, contact the Bicycle/Pedestrian office. Being able to hop on and off the train with your bike makes the M-Path Bike Trail more accommodating and much of Miami accessible by bike. About a mile separates the M-Path Bike Path from the South Dade Bus-Way Bike Trail. The shortest route along U.S. 1 is hazardous—lots of traffic, no bike lane, no road shoulder, hostile motorists. The best way is to take a series of sidewalks that lead to the start of the South Dade Bike Trail.

At Ludlam Road, turn right at SW 80th Street on a sidewalk that goes for four blocks to SW 70th Avenue. Cross SW 70th Avenue at the crosswalk and take the sidewalk on the left-hand side of the street. Follow the sidewalk through the Dadeland Station shopping complex to the Dadeland Metrorail Station. Cross 85th Street and follow the sidewalk right for one block. Turn left on the sidewalk that goes around the Dadeland Mall. At the intersection of U.S. 1 and Kendall Drive, cross Kendall to pick up the South Dade Bus-Way Bike Trail. Follow the bike trail through the Metrorail parking lot, cross Dadeland Boulevard under the Dadeland Station, and continue on Datran Boulevard to the southern terminus of the Metrorail.

Many Miami cyclists are not thrilled with the M-Path, just as Miamians put down the Metrorail as a mass-transit system that goes nowhere. The path was originally intended as a service road for the Metrorail and was turned into a bike trail only as an afterthought, which explains why it seems so bicycle-unfriendly. Long-awaited funding for improvements to the M-Path should smooth some of the worst spots on the bike path with crosswalks and curb cuts.

For more information, call the Miami-Dade Bicycle/Pedestrian Coordinator, (305) 375-4507.

South Dade Bus-Way Bike Trail

The Mass Transit Mall Ride

Length: 8 miles.
Location: Miami. From Florida's Turnpike, take exit 20. Go east on SW 88th Street (North Kendall Drive) to Dadeland Mall. Bike path begins at the Dadeland Station of the Metrorail.
Amenities: parking, bike shop, convenience stores, restaurants, wheelchair access.
Surface: 10-foot-wide asphalt without mile markers.

The South Dade Bike Trail follows a dedicated bus-way that links three Miami malls—the old Dadeland Mall, the upscale Falls shopping center, and the seen-better-days Cutler Ridge Mall. Along the way, it parallels Dixie Highway (U.S. 1), separated from the highway by about fifty feet. One of the pleasures of the bike trail is passing all those cars stalled in traffic on busy Dixie Highway.

The South Dade bike path picks up where the Metrorail and the M-Path Bike Trail leave off. Not nearly as scenic as the Key Biscayne/Old Cutler bike path, South Dade is also not as frustrating for cyclists as the M-Path. While the bike path crosses sixteen streets, the cross streets include functioning crosswalk signals. Just watch out for traffic turning off and onto Dixie Highway.

Heading south from the SW 88 Street intersection, here's what to look for on the South Dade Bus-Way Bike Trail:

· Around 1 mile, experienced cyclists can take a detour to the Matheson Hammock Park and the Fairchild Tropical Gardens by following SW 104th Street about 2.5 miles to the left. But this requires riding in the road with traffic. There is no connecting bike path to get there.

· At 3 miles, the bike path reaches The Falls with its Bloomingdale's and Macy's and other upscale stores built around waterfalls and rock gardens. The bicycle racks at main entrances invite cyclists inside. The Cycle Mart bicycle shop, which sells and repairs bikes, is across Dixie Highway in a strip mall on the southeast corner.

South Dade Bus-Way Bike Trail

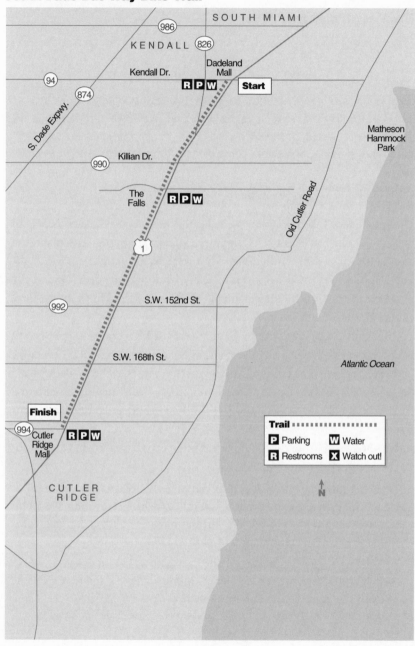

- At 4.5 miles, the bike path veers away from U.S. 1 as it crosses SW 160th Street and passes behind a row of commercial businesses. At SW 168th Street cyclists enter an industrial neighborhood. The Charles Deering Estate is 2.5 miles to the left, but again there is no bike path leading to the attraction.

- At 6 miles, when the path reaches SW 184th Street, the Larry & Penny Thompson Park, with campgrounds and water slides, is 2.5 miles to the right. Again, there is no bike path connecting the park to the South Dade Trail.

- After passing under Florida's Turnpike at 7.5 miles, the path comes to an end at SW 112th Avenue, across U.S. 1 from the Cutler Ridge Mall. Signs point to the Old Cutler Trail, two miles to the left, and this time there is a connecting trail/sidewalk that takes you to the bike path. Be warned, though, that it's not a smooth ride or the finest neighborhood.

- To reach the Old Cutler Trail, cross U.S. 1 onto the right sidewalk. At .8 mile, turn left at SW 216th Street and onto a nice wide sidewalk. The sidewalk takes you under the turnpike and over a canal, and becomes a bike path again at 1.7 miles. At 2 miles, the bike path joins the Old Cutler Trail at the entrance to the Lakes by the Bay subdivision. Cyclists can either turn left on the Old Cutler Trail or continue straight through the subdivision and take the connector to SW 87th Avenue, where they can turn right to Black Point Marina.

If you enjoy mall-hopping by bicycle, the South Dade Bus-Way Bike Trail was meant for you. For other cyclists in a big city with few bike paths, the South Dade beats having nothing at all.

Something you should know: Despite South Dade's shortcomings, plans are in the works to make it longer. Eventually the bike path, which follows an old Florida East Coast Railroad bed, will extend another eleven miles to Florida City.

Sometimes longer is better.

There are also ambitious plans to take the Dadeland Mall and convert it into an urban center that will become a sort of artificial heart for the communities that surround the mall. Heading the effort to revamp the old mall is Elizabeth Plater-Zybert, who runs the University of Miami's architecture department and was one of the designers behind the popular Seaside resort in the Florida Panhandle.

For more information, call the Miami-Dade Bicycle/Pedestrian Coordinator, (305) 375-4507.

Shark Valley Loop
The Roadside Gator Ride

Length: 15 miles.
Location: Dade County. From Interstate 95, take exit 2. Head west on U.S Highway 41 (Tamiami Trail) for 35 miles. Entrance to Shark Valley Visitor Center is on the left. Park admission is $8 per vehicle.
Amenities: parking, rest rooms, water, maps, vending machines, bike rentals, gift shop, wheelchair access.
Surface: 20-foot-wide asphalt with mile markers on the pavement.

At the start of the fifteen-mile Shark Valley Loop a small information marker advises cyclists to be alert to the subtleties of the Everglades: "Stop for a minute. Listen quietly. Look carefully. Life is abundant, but not always obvious. There is more here than meets the eye."

One-tenth of a mile down the path there is nothing the least bit subtle about the five-foot alligator sunning itself on the side of the asphalt road. Pedal a little farther and there's another . . . and another . . . and another. Especially in the winter when the asphalt is like an electric blanket for an alligator, gators line the bike-and-tram roadway like charms on a child's bracelet. Park rangers advise visitors not to provoke the alligators—especially the little black-and-yellow-striped gator hatchlings whose mother is usually not far away and extremely protective. But if all you do is look as you ride past, there is nothing to fear from the docile reptiles.

The Shark Valley Loop is shaped like a bobby pin—long and straight on the west side, curvy on the east. Rollerbladers and motor vehicles are prohibited on the loop, so the only traffic cyclists contend with are the tourist trams.

The only water available on the loop is at the trailhead and at the sixty-five-foot observation tower seven miles down the trail. So be sure to bring along your own water bottles. And since this is the Everglades, it's wise to apply mosquito repellent and sunscreen before setting off on the bike path. Except for the Observation Tower halfway around the loop, there is no shade on the ride.

Shark Valley Loop

Trail ■■■■■■■■■■■■■■■■
P Parking   **W** Water
R Restrooms   **X** Watch out!

COLLIER
COUNTY

DADE
COUNTY

N

MONROE
COUNTY

41
90

94

41 90

Miccosukee Indian Reservation

Start

P
W
R

Finish

Shark Valley Loop Road

THE EVERGLADES

W
R

Heading south, here's what to look for on the Shark Valley Loop:

· Take some time along the first mile of the Shark Valley Loop to read the information boards that will give you a clue on the wildlife you will see along the way. More than just alligators, the loop abounds in wood storks, roseate spoonbills, great blue herons, tricolor herons, pelicans, anhingas, and ibises.

· The first wildlife observation op comes when the path passes Bobcat Boardwalk, an unpaved trail to the left that takes you into one of the islands of trees that you will pass. Tropical hardwood hammocks and smaller bayheads provide habitats for bobcats, panthers, owls, deer, and snakes. The Bobcat Boardwalk and Otter Cave Trail, both within the first mile, are the only opportunities on the trail to get off the bike and walk among the trees.

· The hammocks and bayheads appear like islands in the sea of grass that stretches on both sides like a prairie. The "river of grass" is a shallow, slow-moving sheet of water covered by saw grass as brown as wheat in the winter. Running alongside the bike path to the right is a canal with tea-colored water that flows beneath the bike path through culverts. Where the water flows beneath the asphalt, the thick weeds and hyacinths part to give cyclists a chance to see turtles, bass, bluegills, and Florida gar.

· Look for "gator holes" in the saw grass where alligators nest by clearing mud holes in the vegetation, especially in the hot, dry months. Gator holes are like La-Z-Boys for alligators. Cyclists are their cable TV.

· At 7 miles, the path reaches the Observation Tower where there are rest rooms, picnic tables, shade, water, and clever crows capable of unzipping and looting bicycle bags while riders are tower-gazing. From the tower, visitors get the vulture's view of the Everglades—the wide, flat expanse of grass freckled with spots of open water and clumps of trees and shrubs.

· Around 7.5 miles, the bike path starts to meander through the bayhead and hammock islands. Without entering the islands, the path nudges up close enough that you can start to image what animals—maybe even the elusive Florida panther—live inside those trees, shrubs, and vines.

· At 8 miles, off to the right, is the first of four borrow pits excavated for the limestone that forms the roadbed of the Shark Valley Loop. The borrow pits have become watering holes for alligators, turtles, wading birds, and ducks.

Fig. 14. Gator encounter on Shark Valley Loop

- For the next three miles, geography plays tricks on the eye. The large hardwood hammocks up ahead look like high ridges—the Everglades Mountains?—but when you reach them, they shrink down to stands of tall trees and dense foliage.

- Birds with stiletto beaks and pencil-thin legs are plentiful along the eastern side of the loop. White egrets, with their S-shaped necks, look awkward standing around—geeks of the bird world—but so graceful when they take flight.

- At 12 miles, the path passes the third borrow pit pond on the right, then straightens out before reaching the last borrow pit on the left at 14 miles.

- Just before the path concludes at 15 miles, it passes the east end of Bobcat Boardwalk. Small lizards skitter across the path, hoping to make it to the other side before meeting bike tire or bird's claw.

An ideal ride for young and inexperienced cyclists who don't want to worry about hills, cross streets, and cars, the Shark Valley Loop with its broad, flat surface and wide open spaces is also built for speed. Experienced cyclists will like the length of the loop and the fact it's not clogged with rollerbladers. But the faster you ride, the more you miss—from the obvious to the sublime.

Something you should know: The shallow water six inches to three feet deep that covers the Everglades originates around Orlando, 240 miles to the north. Rainwater from the Kissimmee Valley flows into Lake Okeechobee and then seeps southward through the Everglades. Since the 1920s, canals and dikes and valves and gates have controlled the flow of water into the Everglades, affecting the natural cycle of flooding and replenishing necessary for the swamp's wildlife. Since the 1930s, the number of nesting wading birds in the Everglades has declined from 265,000 to 18,500.

Created in 1947, the Everglades National Park covers 1.5 million acres—about 20 percent of its original size. In 1989 Congress added the 107,000 acres of the Shark Valley Slough to the park. The fifty-mile-wide natural channel funnels water toward the mangrove estuaries along the Gulf of Mexico. The ecological health of the Everglades is measured by the count of wood storks, which feed by touch rather than sight. Swinging their beaks back and forth beneath the water, the storks snap up fish, frogs, snakes, and baby alligators with a lightning-fast touch reflex. Placed on the endangered list in 1984, wood storks are disappearing from the Everglades as they die out or seek out habitats that provide a consistent source of food.

For more information, call Everglades National Park, (305) 242-7700, and Shark Valley Tram Tours, (305) 221-8455.

Florida Keys Bike Paths

The Ghost of Henry Flagler Ride

Length: 45 miles.
Key Largo: 18 miles.
Islamorada/Lower Matecumbe Key: 9.5 miles.
Marathon: 9 miles.
Key West: 8.5 miles.
Location: Monroe County. From Miami, take U.S. 1 south 40 miles.
Amenities: parking, convenience stores, restaurants, city and county and national parks, motels and campgrounds, ATMs, bike shops.
Surface: 5- to 6-foot-wide asphalt without mile markers.

The Overseas Heritage Trail is a bicyclist's dream: 110 miles of bike paths linking Key Largo to Key West. Unfortunately, that's all it is: a dream. Cycle enthusiasts, sympathetic transportation planners, and bike-path advocates have proposed a plan for a paved bike path that parallels the Overseas Highway—old U.S. 1—from one end of Monroe County to the other. The highway occupies the original railroad bed of Henry Flagler's Overseas Railroad, which linked Key West to the Florida mainland in 1912. A 1935 hurricane wiped out Flagler's Florida Keys railroad, ending the era of trains as transportation through the Keys. The Overseas Highway ushered in the era of the automobile in the Florida Keys. Cars, trucks, and buses have ruled ever since.

Yet the Florida Keys provide one of the best places for paved bike paths. The land is flat, the weather is tropical year-round, and the scenery—Gulf on one side, ocean on the other—is spectacular. And as U.S. 1 is the Keys' only major thoroughfare, there exists a need for paths that offer bicyclists a safe alternative to the highway's heavy traffic.

The concept of the Overseas Heritage Trail is to supply that alternative, with an asphalt bike path that runs alongside the Overseas Highway from one end of the Florida Keys to the other. Monroe County and the Department of Transportation are working to fill in the gaps between existing bike paths. That could be completed as soon as 2005, but may take until 2010. The county is also working on a master plan that would add trailheads along the way.

What exists today is a series of paved bike paths throughout the thirty-two islands strung like pearls on a necklace of two-lane asphalt. The downside for cyclists is that the paths are either too short or disconnected from each other by the numerous bridges that tie the islands together.

The bridges pose a big problem. Some are wide enough to accommodate bicyclists, and some are not. None have dedicated bike lanes for cyclists. Even on the shortest of the bridges, riding a bicycle can be a scary experience when large trucks brush by within inches of the cyclist. The Seven-Mile Bridge, intimidating to motorists, is a barrier for even the most experienced cyclists.

While the bike paths offer an alternative to the traffic on U.S. 1, cyclists must ride alert to numerous cross streets, intersections, driveways, and cars crossing the path to reach business parking. Bike advocates also warn that tourists visiting the Keys are more likely to be looking at the scenery than keeping an eye out for bicyclists.

Key Largo–Plantation Key: The Ride to Eat and Eat to Ride Ride

The eighteen-mile path is the longest of the paved bike trails on the Florida Keys. If eating and exercise go together for you, this is your bike path. Along the way, you will pass a smorgasbord of restaurants offering everything from Florida Key staples like conch fritters and Key Lime pie to barbecue, Mexican, and steaks. No problem finding fresh seafood in Key Largo.

Starting on the eastern end of the island, here's what to look for on the Key Largo bike path:

- The path begins at Abaco Road, near Captain Slade's Atlantis Dive Shop. Across the street is the Shell Man, one of those roadside attractions left over from the days of ice cream shops shaped like giant ice cream cones and barbecue joints that look like big pigs.

- There is no designated parking for cyclists using the path, but you can find places to park at this end on side streets, at defunct stores, or by patronizing businesses catering to tourists. The Florida Keys Welcome Center is about three miles from the eastern end of the bike path.

- The best place to start, however, may be John Pennekamp Coral Reef State Park, about 3.5 miles from the eastern end. One of the most popular places in Florida for divers, John Pennekamp has a beautiful beach, plenty of parking, rest rooms, pay phones, and water fountains. The park offers camping, swimming, glass-bottom boat tours, snorkeling tours,

Key Largo/Plantation Key Bike Path

Trail ▪▪▪▪▪▪
P Parking **W** Water
R Restrooms **X** Watch out!

N→

905

1 5

Start

R
W
P

John Pennekamp
Coral Reef
State Park

R **W** **P**
Key Largo
P

1
P

X

R **W** **P**
Tavernier

P

Finish

P

Plantation Key

Plantation

Florida Bay

MONROE
COUNTY

Atlantic Ocean

boat rentals, paddleboats, canoes, kayaks, and scuba lessons. There is a dive shop, a concession stand, and picnic facilities. The park is open from 8 A.M. to sundown. Admission is $1.50 for bicyclists, $4 per car, and 50¢ per person. Phone: (305) 451-1202.

• Beyond John Pennekamp is the Maritime Museum of the Florida Keys, containing treasure recovered from shipwrecks and archeological exhibits. The museum is open 10 A.M.–5 P.M., Friday–Wednesday. Admission is $5 for adults, $3 for children aged 6–12. Phone: (305) 451-6444.

• Approaching 5 miles, the bike path reaches a Publix and Kmart shopping center that includes the Equipment Locker bicycle shop, which rents, repairs, and sells bikes. At 5 miles is Friendship County Park with parking and picnic tables.

• Near 7 miles there is a four-story undersea memorial painted on the side of a building and welcoming everyone to the Florida Keys. Beyond this point, the commercial businesses thin out and the path passes long patches of undeveloped land with walls of vegetation alongside the bike path.

• On the right, around 8 miles, is a place where the key juts into the Gulf forming a protective harbor that, until Bogie and Bacall made Key Largo famous in film, was called Rock Harbor. After the movie's release in 1948, locals changed the name of the harbor to Key Largo.

• At 9 miles you reach a straight, shady stretch of bike path bracketed by a dense stand of trees and shrubs. At the end of the stretch, around 9.5 miles, the bike path crosses U.S. 1 to the ocean side of the median.

• Around 11 miles, the path enters Tavernier, a town that sprang up along with Henry Flagler's railroad, supplanting an earlier settlement wiped off the map by four hurricanes. The oldest of the town's buildings is a house built in the 1920s and relocated—but left standing—by the 1935 hurricane. Also still standing is the Old Tavernier Post Office built in 1926, the Tavernier Hotel, which once housed a movie theater, and the Tavern Store, which began its life as a drugstore.

• At 13 miles, the path reaches Harry Harris County Park, named for a flamboyant Tavernier mayor who once held court at an establishment called Harry's Tea Room. The park has water, rest rooms, picnic facilities, a playground, and a boat ramp.

• Though Harris Park may seem like paradise to some, a true bicyclist oasis is another half mile down the road where the path passes a Dairy Queen.

Fig. 15. Marine mural on Key Largo bike path

- At 14 miles, on the Gulf side of U.S. 1, Tavernier Bicycles and Hobbies offers bicycle sales, rental, and repairs.
- A half mile beyond the bike shop, if you are lucky, you will encounter one of those unexpected joys of cycling through the Keys. Set up beneath a shade tree, Eugenio García, an aged Cuban fisherman, sells colorful hand-painted strings of fishing buoys, and old wooden lobster traps. He has occupied this spot, off and on, since the early 1990s, after giving up a life lived on the sea. He now sells the tools of his old trade to people as poolside decorations and restaurant ornamentation. As you travel down U.S. 1, you will see García's bright fishing buoys trimming fences and dangling from front porches.
- Around 15 miles, the bike path temporarily disappears, taking cyclists on a frontage road paralleling U.S. 1. Cross over the highway at the traffic signal at Tavernier Creek Bridge to pick up the bike path on the Gulf side.
- The path passes Plantation Elementary School before ending at the parking lot of Plantation Key's public works government center at 18 miles.

Of all the Florida Keys paved bike paths, the one that runs the length of Key Largo to Plantation Key offers the widest cross-section of life in the Keys. Some parts are as uninspiring as any city street stocked with franchise stores.

But sprinkled throughout are enough sights and scents unique to the islands to make this ride worthwhile for anyone visiting the Florida Keys on a bicycle.

Something you should know: The John Pennekamp Coral Reef State Park is the jewel on the Key Largo bike path. Named for a crusading journalist dedicated to preserving Florida's endangered coral reefs, the park opened in 1963 as the nation's first underwater park. Divers and snorkelers swim among the fish, shipwrecks dating back to the 1600s, and the nine-foot Christ of the Deep statue.

For more information, call the Key Largo Chamber of Commerce, (305) 451-1414, and the Monroe County Bike/Pedestrian Coordinator, Planning Department, (305) 289-2500.

Islamorada/Lower Matecumbe Key: The Scenic Seashore Ride

No other bike path in the Florida Keys will offer you as much of the Atlantic Ocean and the Gulf of Mexico as the three miles between Whale Harbor Channel and Tea Table Relief Channel.

Four bridges separate the Islamorada bike path on Upper Matecumbe Key from another 3.5-mile bike path on Lower Matecumbe Key. Together, the paths create a 9.5-mile ride. However, the bridges are narrow and the traffic is heavy. Children and novice riders should avoid riding across the bridges. Only experienced cyclists should attempt it.

Starting from the east end of the island, here's what to look for on the Islamorada bike path:

- The Islamorada bike path starts just outside the Island Christian School. The path runs on both sides of U.S. 1. If you ride on the north side, beware of cars pulling into and out of the parking lots and businesses that line the road.

- At the 1-mile mark, inside a little red caboose with a parking lot, is the Islamorada Chamber of Commerce.

- Nearing 2 miles, in the road median, is the island's hurricane monument dedicated to the 1935 hurricane that devastated the Keys and destroyed Henry Flagler's Florida East Coast Railroad. The cremated remains of about three hundred people who died in the storm are interred in a crypt

Islamorada/Lower Matecumbe Key Bike Path

Trail ▪▪▪▪▪▪ **W** Water

P Parking **X** Watch out!

R Restrooms

Plantation Key

Start

W

P

P

Upper Matecumbe Key

①

X

P

Shell Key

X

Florida Bay

MONROE
COUNTY

P

Indian
Key

Atlantic Ocean

X

Lignumvitae Key

X

Lower Matecumbe Key

Finish

N→

in front of the keystone monument showing coconut palms bending in the wind as an angry sea laps at their trunks.

- At the 2-mile mark, the bike path reaches the Green Turtle Inn, a local landmark restaurant that has been around since 1947. Until the 1970s, when the green turtle became a protected species, the restaurant's specialty was green turtle steaks. You can still order a slab of green turtle, but the meat comes from farm-raised turtles.

- At 3 miles, watch out as the bike path on the south side ends, forcing cyclists to cross U.S. 1 without a crosswalk. On the other side, the path jogs a little as it passes a row of gumbo-limbo trees with their slick brown bark trunks. There's a little picnic area among the trees with a couple of concrete benches.

- At 4 miles, cyclists get their first full view of the Atlantic and Gulf while crossing a bridge at Tea Table Relief Channel. The bike lane here is separated from the road only by a white line, but the bridge is short and easy to cross. Another bridge a half mile farther down the path will also force cyclists to merge with the traffic. Inexperienced cyclists and children might want to just savor the view and turn around for the return ride.

- Before the bridges, there's a seaside parking lot that affords a spectacular view of the water. It sparkles like a sea of sequins, stretching in ripples to the horizon. Three notable islands are visible—Shell Key and Lignumvitae Key to the north, Indian Key to the south.

- Beyond the two bridges, at 5 miles, another parking lot, this one anchored by old cannons, is stocked with brochures on the area's animals and plants and past. The triangle formed by the three nearby islands contains some of the Keys' most fascinating history.

- On Lignumvitae Key in the 1500s a shipwrecked Spaniard was captured and held prisoner by Indians for seventeen years; his diary became the first detailed description of Florida. At sixteen feet above sea level, Lignumvitae Key is the highest ground in the Florida Keys. Spared from development, the island contains the last native tropical forest in Florida. The 280-acre island was home to William J. Matheson, who built a grand house with electricity provided by a windmill. Today the key is a state botanical site, preserved for visitors who can reach it only by boat and can tour Matheson's home and grounds only with a guide. Boats leave Robbie's Marina in Islamorada at 10 A.M. and 2 P.M., Thursday through Monday. Phone (305) 664-9814 for reservations, and arrive a half hour early.

Fig. 16. Sea and asphalt on Lower Matecumbe Key

- Indian Key was a Spanish trading post purchased in 1831 as headquarters for the wrecking industry that salvaged ships that had run aground on the coral reefs. In the 1830s it had homes, a hotel, bowling alley, post office, wharves, and warehouses. The island was burned by Indians in 1840 in a major battle of the Second Seminole War. Accessible only by boat, Indian Key is open to the public. For information call Long Key State Recreation Area, (305) 664-4815.

- Not far from Indian Key the sunken remains of a Spanish ship, run aground by a hurricane in 1733, have been preserved as a living museum by the state since 1989. The cannons at the parking lot came from that shipwreck.

- A half-mile bridge spans the Indian Key Channel, followed by a shorter bridge crossing the Lignumvitae Channel. The first bridge is narrow and hazardous, a challenge only experienced riders should attempt. The shoulder is just six feet wide, and the trucks that rush by come harrowingly close to cyclists. And that's too bad, because on the other side of those two bridges the three-mile Lower Matecumbe bike trail picks up and takes cyclists on an up-close tour of the Keys' lobster and fishing industry. If the bridges were wider or bicyclists separated from the traffic by concrete barriers, the bike paths from Islamorada through Lower Matecumbe Key would be one great scenic ride.

- Cyclists coming off the bridge will stay on the road as it descends to a short frontage road paralleling U.S. 1 for less than half a mile. The Lower Matecumbe Key trail picks up around the 6.5-mile mark.

- After the Tropic Air Motel, look for a house sitting on the edge of the Gulf at the end of a long driveway. The owner has dubbed this domain Best of Both Worlds—the sign of a lucky soul who knows it. A short way down the trail, a neighbor has posted another anthem to life in the Keys, calling that place Almost Heaven.

- Around 8 miles, you are entering one of the prettiest stretches of bike path in the Keys. A row of houses built on stilts let the Atlantic Ocean shine through their legs. There are palm trees and light green passion plum bushes, sidewalk coconuts for sale for a quarter, and whimsical manatee mailboxes.

- Near 9 miles, when the arrow-straight asphalt path dances a little jig, wooden lobster traps are stacked like a child's blocks and the ground is strewn with long strings of multicolored fishing buoys. A fishing marina, the Lobster Walk Fish Market, sells fresh lobsters and stone crabs for $4.49 a pound. Across the road, the ocean is a big wide open expanse, glittering and gleaming in the sun.

- In front of signs advertising crabs, fish, shrimp, beer, bait, and ice, the path joins the frontage road, separated from cars by a white stripe. Passing the Sally Rogers Campground, the bike path ends short of Anne's Beach county park and the Channel Two bridge as it nears 9.5 miles. Tollgate Boulevard, where the path ends, is the entrance to the Seabase Nautical Boy Scout Facility.

With the smell of the ocean in your nostrils and a strange yearning for fresh seafood, you turn the bike around and head back.

Something you should know: Dade County was born in 1836 when Jacob Housman, who ran the salvage operation on Indian Key, petitioned for the creation of a new county independent of Key West. Later eclipsed by Miami, Indian Key was Dade County's first county seat. Monroe County, which today encompasses all the Florida Keys and part of the Everglades, was created as Florida's sixth county in 1823 and named after President James "Era of Good Feeling" Monroe, who obtained Florida from Spain.

Islamorada is Spanish for "purple island"—a reference to its mauve appearance from a distance at sea. In the 1950s Islamorada's most famous winter resident was Red Sox slugger Ted Williams, who spent the off-season in pursuit of tarpon and bonefish.

Tollgate Boulevard, where the path ends on Lower Matecumbe Key, takes it name from the days when the southern end of the island served as a ferry terminal. Anyone wanting to proceed westward had to pay a toll to ride the ferry.

For more information, call the Islamorada Chamber of Commerce, (305) 664-4503, and the Monroe County Planning Department, (305) 289-2500.

Marathon: The Bridge over Beautiful Waters Ride

The reward of the nine-mile Marathon bike path is the last two miles, when you are riding above the water over the remnants of the Overseas Highway's original Seven-Mile Bridge. Below you, in more colors of green than you can count, the Gulf of Mexico and the Atlantic Ocean merge. The outlines beneath the shallow, crystal-clear water look like an underwater world, continents marked by the map pins of orange channel buoys.

At the end of the bridge, you have indeed reached another world. Below are yellow houses with white trim and tin roofs, the remains of a settlement called Pigeon Key. A trolley hauling visitors from a parking lot at the other end of the bridge passes as you coast down a curling ramp to the island of restored houses.

But to reach this reward, the journey starts to the east at Coco Plum Drive where the Marathon bike path begins. You'll know when you hit Marathon—it's where U.S. 1 widens from two lanes to four. If you have run low on money, Marathon is the place. There are five banks and a dozen convenience stores in the first six miles. Most have cash machines.

Starting on the east end, here's what to look for on the Marathon bike path:

• The best place to start is the Greater Marathon Chamber of Commerce Visitors Center a quarter mile from the eastern end of the bike path. You'll find parking, rest rooms, water, and everything you need to know about the Middle Keys.

Marathon Bike Path

Start

Finish

Gulf of Mexico

PIGEON KEY

Seven-Mile Bridge

MARATHON

Sunset Point

BOOT KEY

VACA KEY

Sombrero Beach Rd.

Aviation Blvd.

Marathon Airport

KEY COLONY

FAT DEER KEY

Coco Plum Dr.

GRASSY KEY

Hawk Channel

Straits of Florida

Trail ■ ■ ■ ■
P Parking **W** Water
R Restrooms **X** Watch out!

N

- At .5 mile, cyclists will pass the Equipment Locker and Sports—Marathon's only true bike shop.

- At 1 mile, the bike path crosses two busy intersections, at 107th and 109th Streets. Be aware of impatient motorists trying to pry their way into the flow of traffic on U.S. 1.

- For the next mile, the bike path runs alongside Marathon Airport, which caters mostly to private aircraft. The airport terminal has rest rooms, water, and a snack bar. The main runway was built in the late 1930s by the federal government as a landing spot for the B-17 Flying Fortresses that would use Marathon as a stopover during World War II for missions to Africa and Europe.

- Watch out at 3 miles when the bike path reaches Aviation Boulevard. There is no traffic light at the intersection, which is notorious for fender benders. Be careful for the next mile as the bike path disappears at spots, melting into the parking lot pavement of the businesses along this stretch.

- For those who want to add a little distance to their ride, there is a 5.5-foot-wide bike path that goes around the back side of the airport for about two miles at Aviation Boulevard.

- Around 3.5 miles, you'll find a Marathon institution—Herbie's, a rickety old restaurant with waiting lines for the best fish sandwiches on the island.

- At 4 miles, the bike path reaches a traffic light for Sombrero Road on the left. A two-mile bike path spur runs alongside Sombrero Road past Marathon High School to Sombrero Beach County Park. It's a nice side trip to add some extra miles to the ride, but you'll find no shade along the bike path and no amenities except for picnic tables and a water fountain, spewing warm water, at the park.

- Also at the intersection, you will find the museums of Crane Point Hammock. These include the historic home of George Adderley, built around 1906; remnants of an African American village once occupied by Bahamian farmers, boatmen, and railroad workers; and the Museum of Natural History of the Florida Keys and the Children's Museum. For more information, call (305) 743-9100.

- At 4.5 miles, the bike path crosses over U.S. 1 to the ocean side of the key, and then crosses back over to the Gulf side a quarter mile later. Watch out crossing the highway when the bike path does this zigzag.

You might be better off staying on the Gulf side where there is a sidewalk. Watch out when the path passes the Stuffed Pig restaurant; its parking lot merges with the highway.

· Around 5.5 miles, the bike path reaches the Marathon library, where cyclists can take a breather with air conditioning, water fountain, and rest rooms. The Sheriff's Office next door also has a cold-water drinking fountain. The government offices are on Vaca Key, which takes its name from the Spanish word for "cow"—a reference to the sea cows (manatees) found in the area.

· Around 6.5 miles is Shucker's, an oceanside restaurant that has outdoor dining and the best sunset view in Marathon in the winter months.

· At 7 miles, the bike path reaches the bridge. Before riding across, take a path down to the water's edge and the chance to see tarpon or rays swimming by.

Pigeon Key is now a historic village and museum, accessible by bike, on foot, or via a tram that leaves from the Pigeon Key Visitors Center. At the time of the 1935 hurricane, Pigeon Key was the camp for construction workers building the Overseas Highway. Other work camps vanished, but Pigeon Key remained as Toll District headquarters. The structures on the island date from 1912 to 1938. Hours are 10 A.M.–5 P.M. daily. Admission is $7.50 for adults, $5 for children aged 5–12; free under 5. Phone: (305) 289-0025.

Although not as scenic as some of the other Florida Keys bike paths, the Marathon path offers plenty to see, lots to eat, and no shortage of convenience stores and cash machines. And, of course, the spectacular view from the bridge.

Something you should know: Marathon was named by railroad workers who, when they reached the seven-mile stretch of open water, feared their work on the Overseas Railroad would never end. Vaca Key became the supply depot for three to four thousand men working on the railroad construction. A wooden bridge was built from Knight's Key at the tip of Marathon to Pigeon Key where construction of the original Seven-Mile railroad bridge commenced. Begun in 1908, the bridge took four years to build—and one hurricane in 1935 to destroy.

The western tip of Marathon is Knight's Key, which served as the southern terminus of Flagler's railroad until 1912 when the railroad reached Key West.

While using Knight's Key as the terminus for his railroad, Flagler also built a port for his Occidental & Pacific steamship line. He used the port for passenger business to Cuba and to import special saltwater-resistant concrete from Germany for the Seven-Mile Bridge. When the bridge was completed, workers dismantled Flagler's Port of Marathon. Not a trace of the once-bustling port remains.

For more information, call the Marathon Chamber of Commerce, (305) 743-5417, and the Monroe County Planning Department, (305) 289-2500.

Key West: The City of Bikes Ride

Key West, the Capital of the Conch Republic, is a city built for bikes. The narrow streets—seasonally clogged with tourists—are easier to navigate by bicycle than by car. Parking is also a problem if you have a car. If you're on a bike, all you need is a short length of chain and a strong lock.

This is a city best savored at street level, at the pace of a stroll or a gliding bike. There is so much to see and it is so easy to get there on a bike. There are the 2,500 historic buildings including the homes of writers and the gingerbread houses crafted by sea captains. There's the carnival of people at Mallory Square to witness the sun setting and on Duval Street with its boutiques, bars, and T-shirt shops. There are the beautiful beaches that don't back up to hotels.

But Key West is street riding, so you have to be alert for cross streets and driveways.

Bicycle paths cup Key West like a cowboy's spur. The shank, extending west from the Florida Keys Community College, branches at Roosevelt Boulevard, curving north toward Key West's business district and its historic downtown, and south toward the beaches and Key West International Airport. Jet-set cyclists could fly into Key West, unpack their bikes, and see the whole city without ever trying to parallel park. (It's an idea.)

For the rest of us, parking is available at the Florida Keys Community College, next door to a hospital and elementary school. The path from the parking lot is a six-foot-wide concrete sidewalk that runs alongside a canal and the Key West Golf Course for a half mile.

Heading west from the community college, here's what to look for on the Key West bike paths:

Key West Bike Path

Trail ▪▪▪▪▪▪▪▪▪▪
P Parking **W** Water
R Restrooms **X** Watch out!

N

Gulf of Mexico

MONROE COUNTY

Saddlebunch Keys

El Chico

Naval Air Station

Straits of Florida

Artesia St.

Fleming Key

Start

Roosevelt Blvd.

International Airport

Finish

Key West

1
5
1
941

- Turning right on U.S. 1, the bike path becomes an irregular strip of asphalt that wiggles alongside the highway. The one-mile stretch runs by liquor stores, motorcycle shops, mobile-home parks, a tattoo parlor, and the Coral Isle Bar with its marquee offering Free Beer Tomorrow.

- The path gets a little bumpy before it crosses over Cow Key Channel at 1.5 miles and narrows to four feet approaching Roosevelt Boulevard. Just before the canal bridge, which separates cyclists from traffic with a concrete barrier, there is a park-and-ride lot.

- At 2 miles, the bike path runs into Roosevelt Boulevard, with its signs pointing left to the beaches and right to the business district.

- Heading right, the path is a wide concrete checkerboard-slab sidewalk with palms planted in weedy squares along the curb. On the right is the shimmering emerald water of the bay, with gently rocking kayaks, canoes, charter boats, and yachts. On the left, the ride becomes a Tour de Franchises: Holiday Inn, Travelodge, Ramada Inn, Hampton Inn, McDonald's, Checkers, Friday's, Taco Bell, Pizza Hut, Radio Shack, Sears Town, Big Kmart, Blockbuster, Amoco, Circle K. It's like you never left home!

- Those needing cash, look for First State Bank at 2.5 miles and First Union Bank at 3 miles.

- Along this stretch, watch for the light blue Holy Trinity Lutheran Church with its white steeple pinned between two hotels, and the Tunnel drive-through convenience store where you can buy propane without leaving your car.

- At 4 miles, watch out when the bike path crosses busy 1st Street. To the left, fishing and party boats rock in their stalls on Charter Boat Row.

- The path ends a half mile down the street at Bayview Park on Eisenhower Drive and Truman Avenue. Free maps of the city are available at an information center on the corner. Bayview Park—its land donated to the city by a man who made his fortune making cigars before they became chic—features a statue of José Martí, the Cuban writer and revolutionary, and monuments to dead Confederates.

From here, you can continue down Truman to Duval Street, where you will find the restaurants, bars, art galleries, and gift shops, then to Whitehead Street, which takes you right to Mallory Square or left to the Southernmost Point Monument. Or choose a less direct route and weave your way through the residential streets of Key West, none of which is without some point of interest. At the corner of Olivia and Frances Streets you will find the Key West Cemetery where Ernest Hemingway is happy not to be buried. "I'd rather eat monkey manure than die in Key West," said Papa, who elected to die in Idaho.

For a less commercial, more scenic ride in from the community college to Old Town Key West, take the southern route. Here's what you'll see:

- At 2 miles, when the path runs into Roosevelt Boulevard, cross the boulevard and take a left at the Quality Inn. After passing the VA clinic, the bike path crosses back over Roosevelt at Flagler Avenue.

- Running alongside the water, the Key West bike path takes you past the remains of Houseboat Row, where squatters have lived on boats with flower boxes and second stories since the 1940s. Key West and the State of Florida have been trying to evict the squatters—without much luck. Courts ruled the houseboats must leave, voter referendums said they can stay. In 1998, Hurricane George trashed Houseboat Row, sinking all but about sixteen of the residences. Beaten up by the weather and beaten down by the government, Houseboat Row is finally being dismantled and the floating homes moved to a city marina.

- At 3 miles, the bike path rounds a corner and gives cyclists an unobstructed panoramic view of where ocean and sky meet, one a darker shade of the other. The beaches of Key West are festooned with coconut palms, a sandy front porch to the waves rolling in from the Atlantic.

- The ten- to twenty-foot-wide bike path along the beaches undulates like a concrete rollercoaster of ramps that rise, plateau, and descend. The ramps are actually storm water culverts draining street runoff into the ocean. Watch out along this stretch for loose sand that can make concrete as slippery as ice.

- At 3.5 miles, you will pass the entrance to the airport before the bike path reaches the brick, mortar, and iron bars of East Martello Tower Museum. The never-used Civil War–era munitions fortification has been restored by the Key West Art and Historical Society to house island memorabilia, the junk art of Stanley Papio of Key Largo, and wood carvings of folk artist Mario Sánchez. A welder and junk dealer, Papio turned his junkyard into an art museum after being arrested six times for violating Key Largo's zoning restrictions for neatness. His witty sculptures of car bumpers, ceramic toilets, and other discardables were moved to the East Martello Museum after his death in 1982.

- There is metered parking along Roosevelt Boulevard as the bike path rolls alongside the seashore to Smathers Beach at 5 miles. The beach includes parking, bike racks, water, rest rooms, picnic tables, and shelter from the sun.

- From Smathers Beach the path winds along Atlantic Boulevard and Higgins Beach anchored by another munitions facility, the West Martello Tower, now home to the Key West Garden Club. The path through Higgins Beach concludes, around 6 miles, at the White Street pier—a future trailhead for the Overseas Heritage Trail.

You can also reach the Southernmost Point from Higgins Beach. At the corner of Whitehead and South Streets—just ninety miles from Cuba—the Southernmost Point in the (continental) United States is anchored by a huge concrete buoy for picture taking. From the Southernmost Point, you can find Hemingway's old house by heading north on Whitehead. Duval Street is just one block to the east.

Wherever you ride in Key West, there's something to see. Just make sure, when you share the streets with cars, that motorists see you first.

Something you should know: Plans are under way to extend the Key West bike path eighteen miles east to Sugarloaf Key, although there's no time frame for its completion.

The original Spanish name for the place now occupied by Key West was Cayo Hueso—Bone Island. The Spanish may have been referring to its use as an Indian graveyard, or foretelling a future when Key West would be given up for dead only to resurrect itself over and over again.

The town has been wiped out by hurricanes, gutted by fires, and declared bankrupt in 1934; it has provided sanctuary to pirates and drug runners, and generally fulfilled its geographic destiny by being the end of the road for lost souls, outcasts, and wanderers. Among the island's heroes is Henry Mulrennon, who blew up his own home to stop a fire spreading across the city, and Julius Stone, who saved the city from financial ruin by remodeling it as a tourist attraction. Stone was also credited with introducing Bermuda shorts to Key West, although some Conchs claim he was just walking around in his boxer shorts.

Closer to Havana than to Miami, Key West has always maintained an eccentric sense of independence. It celebrates its own mock attempt at secession each April with Conch Republic Days. Another excuse to party, the festivities commemorate Key West's declaration of independence to protest the traffic jams caused by Border Patrol roadblocks looking for drug smugglers. Somebody invented a flag, somebody else made Conch Republic T-shirts, and other entrepreneurs printed up border passes and passports. A secession ceremony was held on Mallory Square dock where indignant speeches were delivered, a loaf of Cuban bread tossed into the air, and a symbolic shot aimed at the United States government. The revolution lasted one hour until the Conch Republic surrendered to become eligible for foreign aid, but the party went on for a week.

For more information, call the Key West Chamber of Commerce, (305) 294-2587, and the Key West Bike/Pedestrian Coordinator, (305) 293-6495.

On the Way

Future Bike Paths

Bike Path	Location	Length
Fort Pickens Trail	Santa Rosa County	5 miles
Navarre Beach Trail	Santa Rosa County	7 miles
Gopher-Frog-Alligator Trail	Tallahassee-Carrabelle	53 miles
Goose Pond Trail	Tallahassee	4 miles
Dixie-Levy-Gilchrist Greenway	Dixie, Levy, Gilchrist Counties	31 miles
Jacksonville S-Line	Jacksonville	4 miles
Lake Butler–Palatka Trail	Union, Clay, Putnam Counties	45 miles
Lehigh Greenway Rail Trail	Flagler County	7 miles
Suncoast Trail	Hillsborough, Pasco, Hernando Counties	41 miles
Upper Tampa Bay Trail	Hillsborough County	15 miles
Tav-Lee Trail	Lake County	4 miles
Shingle Creek Trail	Orange County	6 miles
Seminole-Wekiva Trail	Seminole County	14 miles
Lake Mary Trail	Seminole County	6 miles
Lake Monroe Loop	Seminole, Volusia Counties	20 miles
Springs-to-Springs Trail	Volusia County	15 miles
Lake Helen Greenway Trail	Volusia County	4 miles
Lake Okeechobee Scenic Trail	Belle Glade	120 miles
New River Trail	Broward County	3 miles
Biscayne Trail	Dade County	33 miles

Source: Florida Office of Greenways and Trails, Rails-to-Trails Conservancy, Florida DOT Bicycle/Pedestrian Program, county recreation and public works departments.

Contacts

Florida Department of Environmental Protection
Office of Greenways and Trails
3900 Commonwealth Boulevard
Mail Station 795
Tallahassee, FL 32399-3000
(850) 487-4784
website: www.dep.state.fl.us/gwt

Rails-to-Trails Conservancy, Florida Chapter
2545 Blairstone Pines Drive
Tallahassee, FL 32301
(850) 942-2379
website: www.railtrails.org

Florida Department of Transportation
State Bicycle/Pedestrian Program
605 Suwannee Street
Mail Station 82
Tallahassee, FL 32399-0450
(850) 487-1200
website: www.dot.state.fl.us/safety

Index of Place Names

Academy of the Holy Name, 122
Abercrombie City Park, 107
Alachua Lake, 36
Alice Wainright Park, 169
American Folk Art Museum and Gallery, 18
Anclote River, 112
Anne's Beach County Park, 198
Apalachicola National Forest, 18
Apopka, 68, 69
Archie Carr Wildlife Refuge, 101
Atlantic Ocean, 152, 199, 206

Bagdad, 4
Bailey-Matthews Shell Museum, 140
Baldwin, 25, 28, 105
Ballast Point Park, 120
Barnacle State Historical Site, 171
Barrier Islands Ecosystems Center, 102
Battle of Natural Bridge Historic Memorial, 19
Bayfront Park, 170
Bayshore Trail, 120, 123
Bayview Park, 205
Beach and Trail Bike Shop, 107
Bear Creek, 107
Belle Glade, 209
Beverly Beach, 96
Big Lake Henderson, 50
Big Red Fish Lake, 13
Bike Route, 140
Bikes Are Us Rentals, 10
Bikes, Boats, and Beach Stuff, 139
Bikes to Go, 179
Bill Sandowki Park, 174
Bings Landing Park, 94, 95
Biscayne National Park, 166, 174, 175

Biscayne Trail, 209
Blackcreek Trail, 30
Black Point Marina, 166, 175, 183
Blackwater Heritage State Trail, 1, 3
Blackwater River State Forest, 4
Boca Ciega Bay, 107
Boca Grande Chamber of Commerce, 136
Boca Grande/Gasparilla Island Rail Trail, 131, 133, 135
Boca Grande Lighthouse, 131; Museum, 131
Boulware Spring City Park, 34
Branford, 21, 105
Brevard/A1A Bike Trail, 98, 100
Brevard County, 98, 100, 102, 103, 104
Brinson Park, 85
Brooksville, 48
Broward County, 146, 147, 209
Bunnell, 97
Butterfly Bike and Beach Rentals, 10

Cady Way Trail, 70, 73, 77, 82, 83
Captiva Island, 141
Carrabelle, 209
Cary State Park, 28
Cecil Field, 28
Cedar Key, 41, 112
Central Winds Park, 77
Chapman Field Park, 174
Charles Deering Estate Historical Site, 174, 183
Chimp Farm Inc., 111
Chisholm Park, 87
Citrus County, 44, 48, 49, 51, 52
Citrus Springs, 46, 51
Citrus Tower, 62

Clarcona Horseman's Park, 68
Clay County, 33, 39, 209
Clearwater, 109, 113
Clearwater Lake, 158
Clermont, 59, 62
Coconut Grove, 168, 170, 174
Coconut Point Park, 101
Cocoplum Plaza, 171
Cole Key, 135
Cooter Pond, 50
Coral Gables, 179
Coral Reef Park, 174
Crandon: Marina, 166, 175; Park, 166, 168, 170
Croom, 48; Wildlife Management Area, 46, 47
Cross Creek, 37
Cross Seminole Trail, 72, 74, 76, 77, 83

Dade City, 46
Dade County, 172, 184, 209
Damp Creek Lake, 14
D&S Bikes, 108
Dante Fascell Park, 173
Daytona Beach, 97
Deer Lake State Park, 13
Depot Avenue/Waldo Road Greenway, 38, 39
Destin, 5
Dixie County, 209
Dixie-Levy-Gilchrist Greenway, 209
Doctors Lake, 30, 32
Douglas Park, 104
Dry Creek, 37
Duck's Nest, 152
Dunedin, 110; Beach, 113
Duval County, 25
Dyer Park, 162, 164, 165; Paths, 162

East Coast Surf Legends Hall of Fame, 102, 103
East Lake Tohopekaliga, 86, 87

East Martello Tower Museum, 206
Edgewater Park, 110
Energy Conservatory bike shop, 110
Equipment Locker and Sports, 201
Equipment Locker Bike Shop, 192
Everglades National Park, 184, 186, 188

Fairchild Tropical Gardens, 171, 181
Fantasy of Flight aviation museum, 58
Fernandina Beach, 41
Finnimores Cycle Shop, 140
Flagler Beach, 96, 97
Flagler County, 209; Trail, 92, 95, 97
Flatwoods Loop, 124, 126
Flatwoods Park, 124, 127
Floral City, 44, 49, 51, 105
Floral Park, 48
Florida A&M University, 16, 18
Florida DOT Bicycle/Pedestrian Program, 209
Florida Keys, 192, 194; Bike Paths, 189, 193, 202
Floridana Beach, 101
Florida Office of Greenways and Trails, 209
Florida State University, 20, 66
Fort Brooke, 122
Fort Cooper State Park, 49
Fort De Soto County Park, 114, 116
Fort De Soto Park Trail, 114, 116
Fort Lauderdale, 56
Fort Pickins National Park, 8, 9
Fort Pickins Trail, 209
Four Arts Plaza, 148
Fred Ball Park, 122
Freedom Park, 109
Friendship County Park, 192
Friendship TrailBridge, 113, 117, 119

Gainesville, 34, 36, 38, 39, 43
Gainesville-Hawthorne State Trail, 34, 38, 43
Gamble Rogers Memorial State Park, 96

Gandy Bridge, 117, 119
Gasparilla Island, 131, 135, 136
Gasparilla Island State Recreation Area, 131
Gen. James A. Van Fleet State Trail in the Green Swamp, 53, 55, 56, 57, 62, 124, 176
Gilchrist County, 209
Goose Pond Trail, 209
Gopher-Frog-Alligator Trail, 209
Grayton Beach, 12, 13; State Recreation Area, 12
Green Cove Springs, 33
Green Swamp, 53, 56, 57
Grove Cycle, 170
Groveland, 62
Grove Park, 37
Gulf Islands National Seashore, 7
Gulf of Mexico, 111, 114, 135, 194, 199
Gulfport, 113; Beach, 107

Hammock, 94
Hammock Park, 110
Hampton's Edge Trailside Bikes, 48
Harry Harris County Park, 192
Hawthorne, 34, 38
Henry Morrison Flagler Museum, 148, 150
Heritage Village and Historical Museum, 108
Hernando, 50; County, 44, 51, 209
Hibernia, 33
High Springs, 27
Highway 30A Parallel Bike Path, 10
Hillsborough County, 124, 209
Hillsborough River, 56
Hobie Beach, 168
Holder, 50, 51
Hyde Park, 122

Ichetucknee Springs State Park, 21
Indian Key, 196, 197, 198
Indian River, 104; County, 103

Inverness, 49, 51
Iron Bridge Day Use Area, 47
Islamorada, 194, 196, 198, 199; Chamber of Commerce, 194, 199
Islamorada/Lower Matecumbe Key Bike Path, 189, 194
Island Bike and Beach shop, 134
Istachatta, 48
Ivey Memorial Park, 21

Jacksonville, 27, 56, 69, 97, 209
Jacksonville-Baldwin State Trail, 25
Jacksonville S-Line, 209
Jay Blanchard Park, 79, 82
Jay B. Starkey Wilderness Trail, 128, 130
J. N. "Ding" Darling Wildlife Refuge, 137, 141
John Pennekamp Coral Reef State Park, 190, 192, 194
John Prince Park, 157; Paths, 154, 156

Kelly Park, 69
Kennedy Park, 170
Key Biscayne, 166, 168, 170
Key Biscayne/Old Cutler Road Paths, 166, 168, 171, 178, 181, 183
Key Largo, 189, 190, 192, 193, 194, 206
Key Largo-Plantation Key Bike Path, 190
Key West, 33, 189, 198, 202, 203, 206; Bike Path, 189, 198, 202, 203, 206; Cemetery, 206
Kissimmee, 83, 86, 87; River, 56
Kissimmee/Neptune Road Bike Path, 83, 85, 88
Knight's Key, 202, 203

Lake Apopka, 65, 69
Lake Butler-Palatka Trail, 209
Lake County, 53, 56, 59, 62, 63, 209
Lake Gear, 72
Lake Helen Greenway Trail, 209
Lake Holathlikaha, 49

Lake Mary Trail, 77, 209
Lake Minneola, 59; Scenic Trail, 55, 61, 62
Lake Monroe Loop, 209
Lake Okeechobee Scenic Trail, 209
Lake Osborne, 154, 156
Lake Tohopekaliga, 83, 85
Lake Worth, 154
Largo, 108, 113
Larry and Penny Thompson Park, 183
Lee County, 131, 137
Lehigh Greenway Rail Trail, 97, 209
Leon County, 19
Levy County, 209
Lighthouse Beach, 137
Lignumvitae Key, 196
Little Big Econ State Forest, 77
Little Econ Greenway Trail, 72, 79, 81
Little Econlockhatchee River, 79
Little Lochloosa Creek, 37
Little Red Fish Lake, 13
Little River Springs Park, 21, 23
Lochloosa Wildlife Management Area,
    34, 37
Long Key State Recreation Area, 197
Louis Von Steel III Memorial Park, 102
Lou the Bike Guru bike shop, 109
Lowe Art Musuem, 179
Lower Matecumbe Key, 198

Mabel, 55, 57
Mack Cycle and Fitness, 179
Mallory Square, 203, 205, 208
Marathon Key, 189, 199, 202; Bike Path,
    199
Marineland, 92
Maritime Museum of the Florida Keys, 192
Mascotte, 62
Matheson Hammock Park and Marina,
    172, 181
McLarty Treasure Museum, 103
McMillian Island, 156
Meade Gardens Park, 72

Melbourne Beach, 98, 104
Melbourne Shores, 101
Miami, 166, 171, 172, 175, 178, 181, 198;
    Museum of Science and Space Transit
    Planetarium, 169, 176; Seaquarium,
    168
Micanopy, 37
Mickie's Bike Shop, 108
Mike's Bike City, 109
Milton, 1, 4
Minneola, 62
M-Path Trail, 169, 176, 178, 181
Monroe County, 189
Museum of Natural History of the Florida
    Keys, 201
Museums of Crane Point Hammock, 201

National Railway Historical Society
    Museum, 66
Navarre Beach, 9; Trail, 209
Neptune Cyclery, 112
New Port Richey, 128
New River Trail, 209
Nobleton, 48

Oakland, 62, 63, 65
Ocala, 38
Ocklawaha River, 56
Ocoee, 63
Okeeheelee Park, 158, 161; Paths, 158
Orange County, 62, 63, 65, 72, 79, 82, 209
Orange Park, 30, 32
Orlando, 44, 51, 58, 63, 70, 83, 92, 183,
    188; Naval Training Center, 70,
    72, 73
Osceola County, 83, 86, 87, 88, 91, 105
Overseas Heritage Trail, 189
Oviedo, 74, 77, 83
Ozona, 110

Pasco County, 44, 46, 51, 128, 209
Painter's Hill, 96

Palatka, 39
Palm Beach, 111; County, 162; Lake Trail, 148, 150, 151, 152, 153
Palm Beach Bicycle Trail Shop, 151
Palm Coast, 95, 97
Palm Harbor, 111
Panama City, 10
Parrot Jungle, 173, 174
Paynes Prairie State Preserve, 34, 36, 43
Peace River, 56
Peacock Park, 170
Pensacola, 4; Beach Trail, 5, 8, 9
Pensacola Bay, 4
Picnic Island Park, 119
Pigeon Key, 199, 202
Pinellas County, 105, 108, 113, 114, 119
Pinellas Trail, 105, 107, 108, 109, 110, 112, 113
Pioneer Park, 110
Plantation Key, 193
Pleasant Hill Road Recreational Pathway, 88
Polk City, 51, 53, 55, 56, 58
Polk County, 51, 53, 55, 58, 91
Pompano Beach: Air Park Bike Path, 144, 146; Sand and Spurs Equestrian Park, 146, 147
Pope Duval Park, 27, 28
Prairie Creek, 34
Putnam County, 209

Ridgecrest Park, 108
Ridge Manor, 44
Rochelle, 37
Rosemary Beach, 14
Rychman Park, 104

St. Augustine, 4, 9
St. Cloud, 86
St. Johns River, 33
St. Marks Lighthouse, 20
St. Marks National Wildlife Refuge, 20

St. Marks River, 16
St. Petersburg, 62, 69, 109, 113, 117, 119, 122
Sandestin, 10
Sanford, 62
Sanibel Island, 137, 140, 141, 142, 143; Bike Paths, 137, 141
Sanibel Lighthouse, 137
San Marcos de Apalache State Historic Site, 19
Santa Rosa County, 3, 4, 209
Seacrest, 14
Seagrove Beach, 10, 12, 13
Seagull Cottage, 148, 150
Seahaven, 10
Seaside, 5, 10, 12, 14, 15, 183
Seaside Swim and Tennis Club bike rentals, 10
Sebastian Inlet State Recreational Area, 98, 103
Seminole City Hall Park, 108
Seminole County, 72, 74, 209
Seminole-Wekiva Trail, 77, 209
Shark Valley: Loop, 184, 186, 187; Tram Tours, 188
Shell Key, 196
Shingle Creek Trail, 209
Siegendorf Bike Path, 170
Smathers Beach, 207
Soldiers Creek Park, 77
Sombrero Beach County Park, 201
South Dade Bus-Way Bike Path, 180, 181
Southernmost Point Monument, 205
South Lake Bikes, 61
Spessard Holland Park, 98, 100
Spring Hammock Preserve, 77
Springs-to-Springs Trail, 209
Square Lake, 156
Stallonegate, 169
Starkey, 124
Steamboat Dive Shop and bike shop, 21

Stone House, 174
Sumter County, 53
Sun Coast Bicycles, 50
Suncoast Trail, 209
Sunnyland Beach, 102
Suwannee River Greenway at Branford, 21

Tacachale, 42
Tallahassee, 16, 209
Tallhassee-St. Marks Historic Railroad State Trail, 16, 18, 19, 20
Tampa, 51, 58, 117, 119, 120, 126; Bay History Center, 122; Parks Department, 123, 133
Tarpon Springs, 105, 112, 113
Tavernier, 192
Tavernier Bicycles and Hobbies, 193
Tav-lee Trail, 209
Taylor: Park, 108, 109; Reservoir, 108
Teriscope Garden Park, 151
The Cycle Mart, 181
Tony Jannus Park, 122
Townsen Lake Regional Park, 48
Trail Sports, 107
Trilby, 46, 62
Trout Creek Parks, 127
Turner Beach, 137, 141

Union County, 209
University of Central Florida, 74, 82
University of Florida, 39, 58
University of Miami, 179
Upper Tampa Bay Trail, 209

Vaca Key, 202
Varn Park, 95
Vizcaya Museum and Gardens, 169, 176, 178
Volusia County, 92, 97, 209

Wakulla County, 19
Wallace Brooks Park, 50
Walsingham County Park, 108
Walt Disney World, 83, 87
Walton County, 10, 13, 15
War Veterans' County Park, 107
Washington Oaks State Park, 94
Ward Park, 70
Weedon Island, 119
Wekiva Springs State Park, 69
West Florida Railroad Museum, 4
West Lake, 160
West Orange Bike Shop, 66
West Orange Trail, 62, 63, 67, 68, 69
West Orange Trail Bikes and Blades, 63
West Palm Beach, 158
Wilderness Park, 127
Whitehall, 148, 150
Whiting Field Naval Air Station, 3
Winter Garden, 63, 69, 105; Heritage Museum, 66
Winter Park, 70, 77
Winter Springs, 74, 77
Withlacoochee: River, 56; State Forest, 46; State Trail, 44, 46, 49, 50, 51, 62
Woodville County Complex, 18

Yellow Water Weapons Depot, 28

Jeff and Gretchen Kunerth live in Altamonte Springs, Florida. They have two sons, Chad and Jesse. Jeff is a reporter with the *Orlando Sentinel*. Gretchen works for a printing company. Jeff and Gretchen have been cycling together for more than twenty years.